The five great problems
of salesmen
and how to solve them

The five great problems
of salesmen
and how to solve them

by *Percy H. Whiting*

The Five Great Rules of Selling
How to Speak and Write with Humor
Former Vice President of
Dale Carnegie & Associates and Former Managing
Director of the Dale Carnegie Sales Course

McGraw-Hill Book Company   *New York   Toronto   London*

This book,
and my life,
are dedicated to Gene,
my wife

Acknowledgments

I am much obliged to a number of people for advice, criticisms and corrections.

I am especially grateful to the following people for their help:

To my wife, Gene, and our friend, Mrs. Ethel Knight (Polly) Pollard—both of whom, when in business, were successful as salesmen and later as sales managers—for reading copy and proof of this book and for helpful advice and a multitude of valuable suggestions.

When I needed immediate help on the final revision, Polly gave it to me unstintingly. In all my life I never before saw work on an editorial job so unremitting and so efficient.

My gratitude also to:

My secretary, Mrs. Jane B. Filippini, who uncomplainingly plowed through a mess of hashed-up copy and transformed it into readable manuscript; and to my former secretary, Mrs. Isabel H. Fidler (a marvelous copyreader), who gave the manuscript a final reading—which it needed!

Those authors and publishers who have given me permission to use material from books, magazine articles and speeches.

George Mather for his help and advice, especially when I was struggling with the section on standardized sales talks.

My friend Ed Michel, for his many useful contributions.

A quick glance at the contents of this book

	Acknowledgments	*vi*

PART ONE

	The Five Great Problems	1
	Introduction	2
1	A salesman transformed himself from a bleak failure into a blazing success by solving one sales problem	3
2	Some salesmen can double their income. Many can increase it 25 to 50 per cent if they will organize their selling	7
3	The average salesman manages to spend only about 15 per cent of his working hours on the one job that counts—selling	10
4	Do you realize how little time you spend in the presence of your prospect, and how much goes into unproductive acts?	12
5	If you have a goal in life, it will help motivate you to stick to your time schedule	15
6	Now let's begin to think what we must do to get going on the job of organizing ourselves and our work	17
7	You need a schedule for each week and a schedule for each day—and that takes time, care, and thought	19
8	You need to keep records (no matter how you hate them!), prospect lists, and a "tickler" or similar device	24
9	You can now solve the toughest of the Five Great Problems of Salesmen—use these rules, sell more, earn more	26
10	If you have not organized your work you ought to start to do it this very day—*now!*	30
11	For every salesman who uses not only legs but brains in selling, there are hundreds who depend solely on legs	32

12   Any salesman can develop ideas that will help him sell if he will take just five relatively simple steps   36

13   This great truth is so simple that it sounds silly, but here it is anyway—"First find out what your problem is"   39

14   The last step in getting ideas is to select the "likeliest" idea of the lot—this may not be as easy as it sounds   42

15   Another way to develop sales ideas is to use the brainstorming method in which you work with fellow salesmen   44

16   If you have a sense of humor and don't mind laughing at yourself, you may get some fun out of these maxims   48

17   If you are one of the many salesmen who find it hard to answer objections, you can get help from this section   51

18   You may have heard of every rule in this chapter, but are you using them in your day-to-day selling?   55

19   Choice bits of sales wisdom about how to answer prospects' objections—culled from books by selling experts   62

20   No wonder salesmen fail in self-motivation—it is one of the world's hardest jobs!   67

21   To force ourselves to do the things we know we ought to do is hard—we'll never score 100, but we can improve   71

22   Next some minor rules and some "don'ts" to help you to motivate yourself to be a better salesman   75

23   Since salesmen communicate so much, it will pay them to learn to do it effectively   77

24   Eloquence can do more for many salesmen than a rich grandmother or an oil well, and is much easier to acquire   82

25   If you can't speak in public you may miss the chance to make money and gain advancement to a sales executive job   88

26 Until you know how your product will both benefit
    and serve your listeners, you can't make an effective
    group talk   91

27 To make an effective talk to a group follow many
    of the rules you use when you are making a talk
    to one person   94

28 Now that you know what to do to make an effective
    talk to a group, I shall tell you a lot of things *not
    to do*   100

PART TWO

29 All salesmen—from "near failures" to natural-born
    successes—can learn in this section how to sell
    more   109

30 Every salesman knows *where* to look for product
    knowledge—the trouble is, most of them don't
    bother to look   115

31 If you are honestly convinced that you have a
    product that will really benefit the prospect, you are
    a hard man to stop   121

32 If you are naïve enough to believe prospects mean
    it when they say "No," you will lose sales that
    belong to you   124

33 You can develop a sales talk so worded as to give
    you the best possible chance to get a favorable
    decision every time   132

34 Any sales talk you write for yourself is flexible—you
    can change it as you go along   135

35 Don't get the standardized talk which you write for
    your own use confused with the "canned talk"   137

36 The best reason why you should standardize your
    sales talk is—you will sell more and earn more   141

37 Are the objections you raise against standardized
    sales talks *real* reasons or *plausible* reasons?   144

38 How to whip your standardized sales talk into such
    shape that it will increase your sales   148

39 Ask yourself the questions presented in this chapter
    —they have helped many salesmen to improve their
    talks   *150*

40 Questions asked in this chapter will help you make
    your sales talk interesting, convincing, and
    productive   *154*

41 When you "work over" your talk, you not only
    improve it, but also you fix it forever in your memory   *157*

42 After you finish writing your talk, "work it over"
    again to make certain the bugs are out and the juice
    is in   *160*

43 You'll find it a bit of a problem to ask helpful
    questions   *162*

44 Sage thoughts by the sages on an unpopular
    subject: hard work!   *164*

45 This one section may help you more than all the
    rest of the book   *166*

46 If you are now in a selling slump, cheer up—
    "slumpitis" can be cured and I tell you here how to
    cure it   *167*

47 If you are the victim of a slump, your first step
    toward a cure is to find out what causes the slump   *170*

48 Here we face the critical questions—"Why do I get
    into slumps, and what can I do to get out and stay
    out?"   *172*

49 No matter how well you are selling—or how badly
    —you will profit if you answer the questions in this
    chapter   *173*

50 Don't hesitate to change your talk so long as the
    change improves it, but don't drop successful
    techniques   *176*

51 It will cheer you up to consider your good points as
    a salesman and why you *should* be successful—*even
    if you aren't!*   *177*

52 Let's resume our study of what's wrong with your
    sales efforts   *179*

53 In this chapter we take up more of the possible
    causes of your slump—wife trouble, loquacity,
    insincerity   *183*

54 I wasted nine years of business life because I worked at a job I didn't like—so read this and avoid the mistake I made   186
55 Luckily, the rules for curing slumps work also to increase the production of those who are doing a good job now   191
56 If you are in a slump, it isn't enough just to improve your sales pitch—you must also learn to think and act positively   194
57 If you feel inferior when you aren't, you'd better do something about it now—it may be the cause of your low morale   201
58 If you are in a selling slump, try to get help from your wife, your boss, your customers, and fellow salesmen   205
59 If your morale is low because you are deep in debt, you should get advice from some expert on budgets and economy   211
60 Many salesmen will read, a few will study, but it is almost impossible to get one of them to *think*   218
61 Now you know how to cure your slump the question arises, "What will you do to get back into production?"   222
62 You will have to read this chapter to find out what it's about—and why the subject is so secret   224
63 If you are now ready to admit that you are not completely devoid of fear, let's consider how you can develop more courage   230
64 A few salesmen know how to cure fear, but don't be sure you are one of them until you have studied this section   231
65 I know why salesmen fear to admit that they are cowards, but do *you* know why?   234
66 The more you know about your fears the less horrible they seem—so analyze them   236
67 To get your fears out in the open where they belong, talk them over with one you trust—your wife, I hope   240

68 It takes guts to put this rule to use, but if you will observe it, you can forget the rest 241

69 The next rule, "act brave," is easy to say, but hard to observe 242

70 Affirmation will cure cowardice—if you don't use faith talks now, you ought to start to do it today 246

71 I've told you what to do to cure fear—now I tell you a few things you shouldn't do 250

72 What some great men, from Confucius to Norman Vincent Peale, have said in aphorisms about fear and courage 252

PART THREE

73 If you work for a company that has adopted the "marketing" concept, you may find yourself in a more responsible job 259

74 Buying in the billions is done yearly by committees, so it behooves salesmen to learn to sell to committees 262

75 A single twenty-two-word sentence converted an apparently hopeless failure into a sparkling success 271

76 "Tell cowards they are brave and you induce them to become brave," said Napoleon, who was an authority 272

77 If you don't know all you should about how to use these "talks," this chapter will be of real help 274

78 You are not ready to make your pitch until you know what your prospect wants and why he wants it 277

79 "Dominant buying motives" and "primary interests" are worthy of attention 279

80 You can get some real sales help from these magic formulas for sales success by best American writers on salesmanship 283

Index 290

PART ONE

The five great problems of salesmen and how to solve them

Great Problem 1 Salesmen fail to organize their selling.

Great Problem 2 Salesmen do not think creatively.

Great Problem 3 Many salesmen do not know how to answer objections effectively.

Great Problem 4 Salesmen do not know how to motivate themselves to do their best work.

Great Problem 5 Salesmen rarely communicate efficiently.

Introduction

Salesmen: Solve your problems—
Thus increase your sales and income.

If you are a salesman you must at times ask yourself, "Why don't I sell more—what are my selling problems?"

This question was considered so important by the New York Sales Executives Club, the largest sales executives club in the world (I am a charter member) that they made a survey to get the answers. The Club sent out two questionnaires to their 3,000 members to find out not only (a) what are the greatest problems of salesmen, but also (b) what are the top problems of management in dealing with salesmen?

This research was done under the direction of Al N. Seares, retired Vice President of Remington Rand and past President of Sales and Marketing Executives, International.

When I consolidated the findings of these two questionnaires, I concluded that the five great problems of salesmen (in the order of importance) are that:

I.   They fail to organize their day's work.
II. They don't think creatively to solve their own or their customers' problems.
III. They don't know how to answer objections.
IV. They can't motivate themselves.
V.   They lack the ability to communicate effectively.

You will find, in this book, formulas for solving these five great problems of salesmen. Surely this knowledge will be worth more money to you than the cost of a shelf of books.

This book also gives you the answers to many other problems —less "great" but serious enough to cost you sales, prestige and money—unless you know how to solve them. The salesman who learns the answers to the great problems of his profession—and then acts—can make more sales and more money.

2

CHAPTER 1

A salesman transformed himself from a bleak failure into a blazing success by solving one sales problem

This flabbergasting story of how a salesman changed himself from a pitiful failure to a sensational success by solving one of the problems of salesmanship was written for me by my friend Kenneth D. Harrison, of Columbus, Ohio. Kenny wrote:

On February 26, 1958, when Johnny Post rode to work with me, he had hit bottom as a salesman—yes, the underside of bottom!

The day before, Johnny had told me of his background, and I was amazed. He said that, at the age of nineteen, he had inherited $90,000 from his father. By the time he was twenty-one, he had married and had built a new restaurant on the west side of Columbus. Two years later he had a son. In another two years, he had lost the restaurant and the remainder of the $90,000 through mismanagement, and his wife and little boy through the divorce court.

At that time, Johnny felt he had hit the depths, but that was hardly the beginning of his slide.

Next, Johnny tended bar in Columbus at the Fourth and Long Grill, then at Chez Paree, then at the Aquamarine Club. He finally gave up bartending in disgust and went into direct selling. He started to work for Spitzer Motors of Columbus, Inc., and was fired after three months because he couldn't meet his quota. From

3

Spitzer's he went to Brown Brothers, Inc., and tried to sell storm windows, storm doors, and aluminum siding. Johnny worked there four weeks, at a peak income of $15.34 a week. Then he quit and got a job through a friend with the Jan Ross Foreign Automobile Company. Because of Johnny's appearance, he wasn't allowed to have floor time in the showroom. His job was to drive an Isetta through the streets with the phrase "65 miles per gallon" printed on the side. If he could sell a car as he drove around, he was permitted to keep the commission. In January and February of 1958, he managed to sell two Isettas.

I remember shivering as I looked at Johnny as he sat beside me on that day in February 1958. He was wearing a suit purchased for $5 in a pawnshop. It was too small, and was fastened in front with a paper clip.

How the solving of one problem saved a salesman

Johnny had on a short-sleeved white summer shirt, a coffee-stained tie, a pair of Keds and no underclothes.

I recalled how a pep talk had stimulated my enthusiasm and given me self-confidence. I felt it might help Johnny, so I told him to look in the rear-view mirror of my car and repeat the following sentence aloud: "I am the best salesman in the City of Columbus, and I will sell more cars today than I have ever sold."

Johnny said, "Kenny, you're as crazy as hell."

I sold hard, and kept at it until finally he tried it in a haphazard sort of way. I coached him as he tried again, again, and again to say the magic words. Finally, I could actually see a change in his expression—he had literally caught fire!

When we arrived at the dealership, Johnny didn't ask for floor time—he grabbed it! From nine in the morning until ten at night, Johnny sold three automobiles. But he didn't stop there! From that day until November 1958, Johnny sold 125 foreign cars, and was the leading salesman of foreign cars in Columbus.

Today, three and a half years later, Johnny dresses as a successful sales manager, because he is one. Johnny is now sales manager of Spitzer Motors of Columbus, Inc., the company that had fired him three and a half years before.

Later: Johnny has taken up his family name again (Apostolou), is with the Olds agency in Columbus, has acquired a wife, and lost 45 pounds. He says he made well over $10,000 last year, which is considerably more than he made in any year before he solved his great problem of selling.

How did Johnny do it?

Why was Johnny Post, who was a miserable failure the morning of February 26, 1958, a successful salesman before sunset that night? The answer is, that day he solved one of the tough problems of salesmen: "How can I get myself into the right mental attitude to sell?"

The moment Johnny solved that problem he became successful. He still is.

Johnny's problem may not be yours. It is not even one of the Five Great Problems of Salesmen; it is one of the lesser ones.

But doesn't Johnny's experience give you an idea of what you may be able to do to make your own selling more successful?

When you master the simple but vital principles in this book, you will have mastered the Five Great Problems and many of the lesser ones.

In Part I of this book we shall take up the solutions of the Five Great Problems. In later sections we shall consider some of the lesser but still vitally important ones.

Solve problems—increase sales

You must at times ask yourself, "Why don't I sell more? What are my gravest selling problems?"

This question was considered so important by the New York Sales Executives Club, the largest sales executives' club in the world (I am a charter member) that they made a survey to get the answers. The club sent out two questionnaires to their 3,000 members to find out not only (1) what are the greatest problems of salesmen, but also (2) what are the top problems of management in dealing with salesmen.

When I consolidated the findings of these two questionnaires, I concluded that the five great problems of salesmen, in the order of their importance, are these:

1. They will not organize their selling.
2. They don't think creatively to solve their own or their customers' problems.
3. Objections floor them.
4. They can't motivate themselves.
5. They can't communicate effectively.

You will find in this book formulas for solving these Five Great Problems of Salesmen. This knowledge will be worth more money to you than the cost of a whole shelf of books.

This book also gives you the answers to many other problems—problems less than "great," but serious enough to cost you sales, prestige, and money, unless you know how to solve them. Surely the salesman who learns the answers to the great problems of his profession, then acts on those answers, can make more sales and more money.

GREAT PROBLEM 1

Salesmen fail to organize
their selling

"Get organized or get out!" say sales managers

The survey conducted by the New York Sales Executives Club showed that the worst fault of present-day salesmen is: *They do not organize their selling.*

Most sales managers report that they release more salesmen because the salesmen fail to organize their selling than for any other reason.

Is failure to "get organized" one of your problems? If so, you need what you can learn from this section. Even if you are fairly well organized, you will get ideas from this section that will help you to organize your selling so it is more efficient— and you will earn more money and more recognition as a result.

CHAPTER 2

Some salesmen can double their income.
Many can increase it 25 to 50 per cent if
they will organize their selling

Unlike men in other vocations, a salesman does not sit at a desk and find work accumulating before him. He must make his own work.
—BERTRAND R. CANFIELD IN his book, *Salesmanship*

Salesmen and sales managers agree—something they don't often do—that more salesmen fail because they do not observe a one-word rule than for any other reason. The rule is: *Organize!*

The New York Sales Executive Club survey, which emphasized the need for this book, gave evidence that the top weakness of salesmen is: (1) they don't make the best use of their selling time; and (2) they have poor work habits.

This finding is nothing new. Several years ago 3,000 salesmen (not sales executives) were asked, "What is the most important requirement for selling?" Three qualities tied for first place: ambition, enthusiasm, and self-organization. A more recent survey put self-organization *first*.

Let's be fair—not all salesmen are guilty of bad organization.

In my four decades of managing salesmen I have known a few who had organized their selling efficiently. I would estimate that maybe one salesman of twenty-five does at least a half-way good job of organizing his work; maybe one of a hundred does a thoroughly good job—but I doubt it.

Hard work is not enough— you must also "sell smart"

If you think like other salesmen think, you recognize that the salesman who makes the big money is the salesman who "sells smart."

The first step for the man who wants to qualify as a salesman who "sells smart" is, of course, to organize his day's work.

Three salesmen who were interviewed in the sales training film "Salesmanship, a Rewarding Career" (produced for the Marketing Institute of the Ford Motor Company, F. E. Zimmerman, Director) had some interesting things to say on the subject of "smart selling versus wheel-spinning." Here is part of what one salesman said in that film:

To be successful, *organize* yourself . . .

You have to set a goal and just work toward it good and hard. . . .
I believe for certain that we have to work like hell, because we've only got so much time to sell.

Selling can mean an awful lot of income, but you don't have time for coffee breaks . . .

You have to work hard, but more important, you have to "work smart!" You have only so many hours in a selling day, and if you are working hard and *not* smart, you spin your wheels forever (and get nowhere).

If you have not yet learned to "sell smart," if you have not organized yourself, you may ask, "How do I go about organizing my day's work?" Maybe you add, "Just what do you mean by 'get organized'?"

Well, when you organize anything, according to the *Thorndike-Barnhart Dictionary*, you "put it in working order."

You wouldn't take an important trip in your automobile unless you had the car in working order, would you? Your motor, your spark plugs, your timer, as well as your tires, must be in working order.

Maybe you just don't want to get organized

Why *don't* you get *yourself* organized for *daily* sales success? Is it because (1) you lack the skill to organize your time? The formulas in this book have helped thousands of salesmen to organize. Is it because (2) you have poor work habits? Follow the formulas in this book and improve them. Or is it that (3) you just don't give a hoot whether or not you are organized? Do you run your selling business with "great cry and little wool, as the devil said when he sheared the hogs"?

Do you sometimes get in the "sales doldrums" because you have not organized yourself and your selling? A *cure can be quickly accomplished, provided you will co-operate!* Are you ready?

I shall give you some general rules for self-organization. Organization methods are fundamentally the same, though details differ from one line of selling to another. The methods of an insurance salesman, for instance, will be different from those of a jobber's salesman.

Firmly establish in your selling the fundamentals I give you in this book. Then look to your boss, your fellow salesmen, your trade or professional magazines for specific details. Even inside a particular field of selling, organization plans differ. They differ even from salesman to salesman in the same company.

However, organization simmers down to one simple fact on which all salesmen agree: *Every salesman's plan of organization must aim in one direction—and that direction is to provide the salesman with the most time in the presence of prospects.*

And remember this—to get more time face to face with

your prospects than you now get, you must: (1) want to get it; (2) plan for it; (3) work at it; and (4) keep working at it! Items 1, 3, and 4 you must do for yourself. As for Item 2, "plan for it," the "how-to" is waiting for you when you turn these pages.

CHAPTER 3

The average salesman manages to spend only about 15 per cent of his working hours on the one job that counts—selling

> *He who gains time gains everything.*
> —BENJAMIN DISRAELI, FORMER PRIME MINISTER
> OF GREAT BRITAIN

> *Time is a fixed income and, as with any income, the real problem facing most of us is how to live successfully within our daily allotment.*
> —MARGARET B. JOHNSTONE

"Why bother to organize my time—I've got all there is!" Salesmen who take this attitude don't seem to realize that they seldom sell a prospect until they are actually face to face with him. Practically the only productive time you have is the time you spend in the presence of your prospect—the time when you actually *sell*. Obviously, the more time you have in the presence of prospects, the more of your product you will sell and the more money you will make. If you increase your productive time 25 per cent, probably you will increase your sales 25 per cent. It's the simplest sort of arithmetic!

Forget the exceptions. I know about them too, but they aren't important here.

So now let's consider this amazing stuff—time.

> *Time is the inexplicable raw material of everything
> ... The supply of time is truly a daily miracle ... You
> wake up in the morning, and lo! your purse is magically
> filled with the unmanufactured tissue of the universe of
> your life ... No one can take it from you ... It is un-
> stealable. And no one receives more or less than you
> receive ...*
>
> *You cannot draw on the future. Impossible to go into
> debt ... you cannot waste tomorrow; it is kept for you.*
> —ARNOLD BENNETT IN
> *How to Live on 24 Hours a Day*

Don't waste time. That's a giant rule of selling—and of life.
If you throw away love, money, health, you always have a
chance to get them back. *Time* once gone you can never
get back—it is gone into the past, gone forever.

If you waste time, you waste life.

Have you ever asked yourself these questions: (1) What is
time? and (2) What can time mean to me?

If you want to know what a deep mystery time is, just try
to define it. Go ahead, try it. Start with, "Time is ..." then
go on from there.

Some salesmen don't sense the fact that time is their most
valued possession—at least, not until "Old Father Time" takes
a swipe at them with his scythe and says, "Boy, your time
is up."

When time is gone, everything is gone.

Don't be like the office girl to whom her boss said, "Miss
Jones, how do you do it? You've been here two weeks, and
you're already a month behind."

The time you waste you never get back

As Arnold Bennett pointed out in *How to Live on 24 Hours
a Day,** "Time is worth more than money. (Efficiently used,

_____
* Published by George H. Doran Co.

time can give us not only money but also the fulfillment of
our dreams and the achievement of our goals).''

If you have time, you can get money. If you have no time,
you can get no money—or anything else.

You can't buy time—you have to earn it. You can't waste
more than the passing moment. You can't waste next week—
it's right there for you when you arrive.

As Bennett puts it, "We shall never have any more time.
We have all the time there is from birth to death."

Our problem is to use time to attain our goal in life. Earle E.
Richardson summed it up well in *Sales Management
Magazine:*

Realize you have at the most about fifteen years from the time
you are thirty-five until you are fifty to make whatever progress you
will probably ever make. That's about 180 months, or 5,400 days,
or 129,000 hours and your success clock will be either run down or
wound up. You will do one of two things . . . you will either master
time, or you will be mastered by time. While the clock is running,
listen carefully. Those ticks you hear could easily be your own
heartbeats registering your rapid progress to the inevitable end of
your selling days.

─── **CHAPTER 4**

Do you realize how little time you spend
in the presence of your prospect, and how
much goes into unproductive acts?

> *By the time folks realize that time is golden, they're
> too old to open a savings account.*
> —*Grit* MAGAZINE

I doubt if you realize how little time you spend each day face
to face with your prospects.

Bertrand Canfield, in his book *Salesmanship*, makes the startling statement that a salesman's "actual selling time is short—*only about an hour and a half a day.*" Here are the figures:

A salesman's working time in a year	2,336 hours
Waiting for prospects to see him	467 hours
Traveling	935 hours
Record keeping and planning	584 hours
Face to face with prospects, actually selling	350 hours

Thus, about 15 per cent of his working time is spent in contact with prospects. (These figures are based on a compilation by The Life Insurance Sales Research Bureau.)

Have you ever counted up how many days in a year you can't or don't sell? J. C. Aspley did in his book *Strategy in Selling*. He said:

On every salesman's calendar there are some "red days." There are Sundays—fifty-two of them. There are holidays—twelve of them. There are twelve vacation days. To which might be added "pink Saturdays," the week between Christmas and New Year's, the day before and the day after most holidays. . . .

This means that out of 365 days in a year, there are 76 days when some salesmen don't work at all, and 71 more days when salesmen usually feel that they can make only a few calls—if any. Thus, considerably more than one-third of each year (147 days) is lost.

You know your problem—now act!

If, as I hope, I have convinced you that you must do something to increase the amount of time you spend face to face with the prospect, you naturally want to know what to do about it.

Your first job is to keep for a month a record of the time you spend actually making your sales talk. Don't bother to tell me that you hate to keep records—that records are something for bookkeepers! I've known that all along. I hate to keep records myself. However, if I can materially increase my income by keeping records, I keep records!

This record of time spent in the presence of the prospect is easy to keep: (1) note the time when you start each interview and don't be afraid to consult your watch, because your prospect will probably regard that as a favorable sign, (2) then note the time the interview ends; jot down the figures; at night, total them.

If you divide the number of hours you faced prospects in a day into the amount of money you earned that day, you arrive at the amount you earned in an hour. For example, if you had two hours in the presence of your prospects and if you earned $20 that day, you earned $10 per hour.

Nothing quite equals this earning-per-hour figure to motivate a man to find ways to spend more time face to face with his prospect.

Thomas J. Watson, one of the world's truly great sales executives, said in substance:

You will find that such a record will reveal much that you do not realize in the way of inefficiencies and time unnecessarily lost.

Such records are of no value, of course, unless you analyze them, think about them, and finally do something right now—today—to improve the utilization of your time.

CHAPTER 5

If you have a goal in life, it will help motivate you to stick to your time schedule

When a man does not know what harbor
he is making for, no wind is
the right wind.

—SENECA

How you are thinking today determines what you will
be and where you will be tomorrow.

—FROM *The Power within You*
BY CLAUDE M. BRISTOL AND
HAROLD SHERMAN

Here is one of the vital rules for organizing your time: Set a goal—then never take your eyes off it.

Perhaps you will ask, "What's the connection between a goal in life and a plan of organization?"

Motivation!

Realize this right now: It is hard to organize yourself and plan your work, and it's a hundred times harder to follow your plan. Unless you strongly motivate yourself, you will not succeed.

A stirring example of what a man can do who has a goal in life and can use that goal as a "motivator" was given me by my friend Harry B. Brock of Birmingham, Alabama.

Harry said that when he took the Dale Carnegie Sales Course in 1959 each member of his class was asked to write on a card his goal in life and to state the amount of time he would allow himself to reach that objective.

Harry said that he wrote on his card, "My goal in life is

to become president of a bank in a city of 25,000 or over by the time I am forty years old."

He kept that objective secret except for one person. He did tell it to a close friend—the man who had been best man at his wedding.

This friend came back at Harry with a challenge: "To make it more interesting, I'll just bet you $50 that you don't make it."

Harry said, "I am a banker, not a gambler, but that challenge was so great I had to take him up."

"Exactly two years and one month ahead of schedule I cashed the check for $50. I will admit we had to organize a new bank (Central Bank and Trust Company of Birmingham) in order to make that goal and I'm happy to report we are not the smallest bank in Birmingham. We have deposits in excess of $7,000,000 and resources in excess of $8,000,000, and we are fourth from the top and still growing!"

The salesman who has no goal is a tragic figure

I've known salesmen with no more stimulating, morale-building objective than merely to stay alive!

Salesmen without goals seem to feel that it doesn't matter where they are going, so long as they keep moving. They think that the best way to prepare for old age is to ignore it. They never ask themselves, "What would happen to my wife if I died before she did?" Or "Who will support my children and pay for their education if I die before they are out of college?"

Other questions most salesmen ignore are: "What about my own later years?" "Will I have income enough to do some of the things I have always wanted to do—travel, fish, hunt, play golf, or just plain rest?" "Will I even have enough so that I don't have to live on the generosity of my children?"

A lot of salesmen have $1,000 in insurance, a couple of hundred in the bank, a wife, three children, and a spirit of optimism. These men were practically penniless when they started selling, and they have just about held their own!

To give yourself a strong motive to organize your day's work and to keep it organized, get a goal in life—or maybe several goals. I leave you to decide about your religious, recreational, and social goals. As to your financial goal, talk it over first with your wife, assuming you have a wife. Then get in touch with a reliable life insurance agent. Of course, he will try to sell you insurance—and I hope he succeeds.

In addition, he can help you to decide: (1) how much you must have in your educational fund to provide a college education for your children; and (2) how much you must have in investments so that the income from them will (a) support your wife and family in case you die before they do, and/or (b) support you and your wife in comfort after you retire.

Brace yourself when you face these figures—they probably will appall you. I hope, also, they will give you a hint of how much you must earn, save, and invest in insurance, stocks, bonds, and real estate in order to look out for all your responsibilities.

Get your wife to help you establish a suitable plan—and help you live up to it.

CHAPTER **6**

Now let's begin to think what we must do to get going on the job of organizing ourselves and our work

Efficiency . . . depends more than has been supposed upon the willingness of men to do their best.
—SUMNER H. SLICHTEN, IN *Modern Economic Society*

I hope that by now you are ready to agree with me that:

1. Bad work habits are costly to a salesman.

2. The purpose of organizing your work is to get more selling time in the presence of your prospects—and, therefore, to sell more.
3. At best, about 85 per cent of your time is "unproductive" —that is, not spent face to face with your prospects. Probably 50 per cent of it is actually wasted.
4. Time is your most valued possession, and should not be wasted.
5. You need a goal in life to motivate you to organize your life and then to stick to your plan.

Here's what we can do about it

Now, let's start organizing.

To start, secure a full description of your job. Here's how: Ask your boss if he or the company can supply you with a job description. If you can't get one ready made, make one yourself. Fortunately, it is easy. You list every job you do in a regular working day, such as: get up, bathe, dress, shave, eat breakfast, lay out your route for the day, go to the office (if you must), go to the place where you will make your first call, make calls, lunch, brief rest after lunch, calls, quit for the day, return to the office (if necessary), go home, eat supper, participate in recreation or study, go to bed.

Next, briefly describe each job on your list—what you do, how you do it. Record the most effective way you have found to handle every task.

Now you have a job description and you are ready to begin to lay out a "time schedule," that is, you are ready to decide at exactly what time you should perform each act listed in your job description.

CHAPTER 7

You need a schedule for each week and a schedule for each day—and that takes time, care, and thought

> *He who works with his hands is a laborer. He who works with his hands and his head is a craftsman. He who works with his hands, head and heart is an artist. He who works with his hands and his head and his heart and his feet is a salesman.*
>
> *—Management Review*

"Just how do I make out my schedule?" you ask.

The answer: you follow the general rules and basic principles we give you in this section and you fit them into your personal schedule.

The first principle which we give you here applies to every salesman. It is: as you prepare your schedule, keep in mind your main objective—*to get the greatest possible amount of selling time face to face with your prospects.*

I don't have to tell you that the most important factor in your drive to get more time face to face with your prospects is *calls.* The more calls you make—other things being equal—the more time you will have with prospects and, therefore, the more sales you will make.

I know I have talked of this before, and I don't guarantee I shall not do it again.

How many times have you sat down to your evening meal with the feeling that you had not made as many calls that day or yesterday or the day before as you should have?

Tomorrow night you will probably have the same feeling.

Selling is not exactly a "restful occupation"

"Philosophers long ago gave up seeking for the principle of perpetual motion," said an unknown author, "but there are a lot of salesmen who are still hoping to discover the principle of perpetual rest!"

A good rule for the man who doesn't make enough calls is: When you think you are through for the day, make one more call.

James J. Corbett, once heavyweight boxing champion, said it well: "Fight one more round. . . . When your nose is bleeding and your eyes are black and you are so tired you wish your opponent would crack you one on the jaw and put you to sleep, fight one more round. . . . The man who always fights one more round is never whipped."

Another rule for doing a full day's work that applies to most salesmen is: Prepare two sets of schedules—one a general schedule for the week, the other a specific schedule for each day.

The general schedule (or guide) should tell you where you will be each day and what you will be doing there. It includes items such as the date of your weekly sales meeting, club meetings, mortgage payments (God forbid!), and birthdays of customers.

You need an itemized schedule for each day

Next, of course, you must have a schedule for each working day.

Make out your schedule for the week on Saturday or Sunday. When you have finished your schedule for the week, make out your itemized schedule for Monday. If you can avoid it, do not put off this job until Monday morning. If you can't do it Saturday or Sunday, get up at 5:00 A.M. on Monday!

Make out the Tuesday schedule Monday night—and so on through the week.

Ask yourself some questions

In order to make out an efficient schedule for a day, first ask yourself such questions as these:

1. On whom am I going to call tomorrow?
2. Why? (An honest answer to this question may cause you to refrain from making calls that are not worth making.)

Then ask yourself questions 3 to 8 inclusive as to each prospect you plan to call on tomorrow:

3. From whom is this prospect now buying the product I sell?
4. Why? And why not from me?
5. Do I have adequate pre-approach information about my prospects and, if not, how will I get it?
6. Do I know—and if not, how can I find out—this prospect's:

    A. *Primary objective.* (That is, if he buys your product, what will be his most important gain, how will he most benefit? If you don't know, how can you find out?)

    B. *Dominant Buying Motive.* (Is his DBM fear, greed, ambition, love of family, desire to be important, or what? If you don't know, how can you find out?)

7. What will I say in my "interest step" to show him how my goods or service will benefit him?
8. What objections am I likely to meet and how will I answer them? (You will rarely have to ask yourself all these questions about each prospect. However, they give you an idea of the information you need to make an intelligent presentation.)
9. What is the shortest route?

Now make out your schedule for the day

With these facts at hand, make out your schedule for the day.

Don't give yourself an impossible schedule. Don't set up a schedule of fifteen presentations in a day when you know that twelve is about the limit of human endurance. Go the limit, of course, but stop there.

When you make out your schedule, note the following points:

Start early before your competitors are "up and about"

1. Schedule an early start.

The *Chicago Tribune* sagely remarked: "Scientists have invented an earthquake detector that goes off like an alarm clock. What is really needed is an alarm clock that goes off like an earthquake."

One of the greatest business builders a salesman can find is presented in this one sentence: *Get up an hour earlier.*

Dr. George W. Crane, in his newspaper column, quoted a shrewd business executive as saying: "It is surprising how many executives and proprietors get to their plants or offices from 6 to 7 A.M. every day. I had formerly made my first call at about 8 A.M., until one day I met one of my minor-league competitors just leaving a large industrial plant at 8 o'clock with the business buttoned up for the next six months."

So get up an hour earlier every day. This extra hour you gain will give you time for a leisurely breakfast, time to give yourself a faith talk (see page 246 for directions for faith talks), time to read, study, and think. This extra hour will enable you to start making calls perhaps half an hour earlier than usual.

Don't tell me you can't find prospects that early in the morning. Salesmen in most lines who really want to locate prospects at 8:30 A.M. will find them.

"I wouldn't get up an hour earlier to please any sales manager," you say.

Friend, no matter whose payroll you are on, you are not working for your sales manager—you are working for yourself. So don't get up early to please the boss (though it will), but get up early to make money for yourself and your family.

There's more to selling, of course, than exposing yourself to a lot of prospects. On the other hand, no salesman has ever regularly converted a pint of calls into a gallon of sales.

Calls take work—but work makes sales, and success. Historian Douglas Southall Freeman said, "The difference between a career and a job is the difference between sixty and seventy hours a week."

Relaxation is beneficial—in moderation

2. Allow yourself time for relaxation, but don't overdo it and get all tired out looking for leisure.

3. Allow enough time for your meals. Don't skimp here. The time a salesman saves when he bolts his meals is "fool's time."

4. Discard time-wasting habits.

5. Establish a "daily objective."

Dave Osborne suggests that a salesman should have a daily objective which should provide three minimums: (a) hours of work; (b) number of demonstrations or presentations; and (c) number of sales (or dollar volume of sales).

With minimums like those, your day's work is not finished until you have accomplished *all three*. For example, if you have reached your quota of demonstrations and sales, but have not worked the required number of hours, you have not met your day's total quota. So keep going!

If you observe these three minimums, your nose and the proverbial grindstone will never be far apart—and you will soon be paying off the mortgage.

> If I ignored my schedule
> I'd soon be in a jam;

Without it I would never know
How far behind I am.

—Slightly changed from a jingle in my notes.
The author's last name is illegible.

_____ CHAPTER 8

You need to keep records (no matter how you hate them!), prospect lists, and a "tickler" or similar device

Everybody ought to do at least two things each day he hates to do—just for practice.
                                            —WILLIAM JAMES

To keep your work organized, after you once get it organized, you need, if you are like most salesmen:

1. A prospect list.
2. A customer list.
3. A daily record of calls made, presentations made, and sales made. This you should summarize at the end of each week, each month, and each year.
4. A record of your expenses to go to the company, if it pays them; for yourself, if you pay them. (As you know, your income tax man may need them—to save you money.)
5. A "tickler" or follow-up file.
6. Some way to keep track of advance engagements— unless you use your "tickler" for this purpose.

On your prospect list and your customer list you will want such information as:

1. Name and address of prospect.
2. His business.

3. What he bought, or may buy—what he is interested in. That is, what is he a prospect for?
4. Name of company or individual from whom he now buys (in addition to your own, perhaps).
5. His primary interest in what you are trying to sell him, if you know it—and you *should* know it!
6. Financial standing based on Dun and Bradstreet reports, or some similar service, or based on what you have learned from others and by observation.

(*Note:* Naturally, the nature of the information you want will depend on your business.)

As to the equipment you need:

Lists of prospects and customers. Most salesmen use a 3-by-5-inch card for recording the names of prospects. This is a handy pocket size, but you may need a slightly larger card.

You need something to nudge your memory

"Tickler" or *follow-up file.* When I was actively a sales manager, I maintained two "ticklers"—one on 8½-by-11-inch cards and one on 3-by-5-inch cards. In the larger file I had a set of guides numbered 1 through 31 and a set of January-to-December guides. Anything I wanted brought to my attention within the month, I filed behind the appropriate 1-to-31 guide. Anything to come up in a subsequent month I filed behind the appropriate month guide. Then, on the first day of each month, I took everything that was behind the month guide and sorted it behind the appropriate 1-to-31 guides.

Such a "tickler" will probably not be needed by a salesman unless he has other salesmen or "bird dogs" under him.

A smaller "tickler" file can be kept on the 3-by-5-inch cards with guides for the 365 days of the year. To use it, you make reminder cards and put them where they belong in the file. For example, if you felt that John Smith should be called on January 25, you would write yourself this message: "Call John Smith Jan. 25th." Tuck that away behind the January

25 guide and forget it. The "tickler" will do the remembering for you.

Each morning look in your "tickler" to see what you have scheduled for the day.

A "tickler" is simple, efficient, and for most salesmen almost indispensable. Get one now—and immediately put it into service. I put behind appropriate guides such items as birthdays of prospects, customers, friends, and relatives; dates payments are due, if any; time when books I have lent should be returned to me; reminders that stores in Fairhope (our shopping town) close Thursday afternoons, the Fairhope Bank closes all day Thursday, and so on and on.

A "tickler" will help you to remember many things both important and trivial. You will bless it all the days of your business life.

_____ CHAPTER 9

You can now solve the toughest of the Five
Great Problems of Salesmen—use these rules,
sell more, earn more

Heaven ne'er helps the man who will not act.
—SOPHOCLES, IN *Fragments*

You may complain, "You've given us a lot of fine generalities, but how should I schedule *my* job?"

As I have pointed out, it isn't practical for me to give specific directions on how to organize the day's work of thousands of salesmen in hundreds of different lines of selling. So I will merely make some general suggestions. Then it is your responsibility to make the directions specific for your particular job.

Get help from your boss all through this campaign to organize your day's work.

The don'ts are as important as the dos

Let's consider now a few don'ts that will help you get more selling time face to face with your prospect.

1. Don't waste time between calls. Walk fast, drive fast. Stay within the law, of course, but don't dawdle along in your car as though you were going nowhere and didn't care if you ever got there!

2. Don't make your pitch too long. The section on standardized sales talks tells you how to make your talk short and effective.

3. Don't lunch heavily or eat fast. Instead, eat a light, leisurely meal, and thus stave off nervous indigestion and ulcers. Don't try to do any selling at lunch time—that is, while you eat. What good are sales made at the cost of your health?

4. Don't start your calls late—and don't stop early. Suppose that, by doing this, you increase the average number of presentations you make in a day from six to seven. You should (assuming you are on a commission basis) increase your earnings by 16⅔ per cent. (If you had been making $100.00 a week you would increase your weekly earnings to $116.67.)

If you save the minutes, the dollars will save themselves

5. Look for prospects you can interview before 9:00 A.M. and after 5:00 P.M. They will then rarely be surrounded by a mob of clamoring salesmen.

6. Don't waste time on coffee breaks, and don't go into bars.

7. Don't talk baseball—talk business. If the talk strays away from your product, you can say something like, "I

mustn't take too much of your time. What I wanted to tell you was . . ."

8. Don't leave home with a car that needs repairs. Have your breakdowns on your own time.

9. Don't leave the office until you are sure you have all the necessary supplies: order blanks, pen, a notebook, portfolio, and the like.

10. Don't take this bit of Mark Twain's advice too seriously: "Never put off until tomorrow what you can do the day after just as well." (That's good as a gag, but poor as advice.)

11. Don't fail to ask yourself, at the end of each day's selling: (A) "Could I have made more calls today?" (B) "Why didn't I?"

12. Don't fail to (A) review each day's work before you go to bed, or (B) to schedule the next day's calls.

13. Don't waste too much time on prospects just because they are friendly. To chat with friendly non-buyers may be good for morale, but it's bad for production.

14. Don't fail, when practicable, to make appointments with prospects. If it requires you to make a time-consuming trip to get to a prospect's place of business, be sure to phone for an appointment.

15. Don't wait till Monday *afternoon* to make the first sale of the week. Start Monday *morning*.

16. Don't spend much time reading newspapers. They aren't made to be *read*—they are made to be *skimmed*. Save the time you now waste on newspapers and invest it in reading business magazines, books, and company bulletins.

17. Don't waste your waiting time. Use it to go over in your mind the sales talk you plan to use on the prospect. Or review any notes you made after previous calls on him. Or read trade magazines, which are usually found in waiting rooms.

18. Don't make out reports in the office on your good selling time. Since you don't get paid for report writing, do it on non-productive time.

Don't just sit—circulate!

19. Don't spend a second longer than you must in the office. It's so easy to sit in a comfortable chair, fiddle with papers, and chat with secretaries—but it doesn't produce sales! A friend told me of a salesman he knew who always kept his hat on while in the office. "To remind me," he said, "that I have no business being there."

20. Don't stop making calls just because it's Saturday or a holiday. If you can't make sales calls, make good-will or courtesy calls.

21. Don't contract that dread disease, "storm-itis." Don't be one of those salesmen who dens up when it rains or snows. A little snow or rain never hurt any salesman. The postman doesn't stop because it is raining or snowing—neither does the policeman or the milkman. (And they aren't on straight commission, either.) They keep going because it is their job to keep going. It's yours, too. Remember, raincoats and rubbers are relatively cheap, and will keep you dry enough to operate and help you make stormy days produce sales and commissions.

I've had my salesmen come to me on a rainy day and say, with sobs in their voices, "Boss, prospects don't like us to come in all sopping wet and drip water on their floors."

Who says they don't?

That alibi will never fool any sales manager—not as long as rubbers, raincoats, umbrellas, and galoshes can be bought at any department store.

One thing you gain when you make sales calls on stormy days—you don't have much competition.

_____ CHAPTER 10

If you have not organized your work you ought to start to do it this very day—now!

You can't get orders in the past or in the future. You must get them today.
Energy is wasted without organization.
                                    —GEORGE WESLEY BLOUNT

Now, just before the benediction, let's list what you are going to do about this greatest of all the Great Problems of Salesmen. I suggest that you say to yourself:

—I admit that organizing my day's work is a pressing problem with me.

—I am determined to solve it.

—I shall take up the problem with my boss and get his advice.

—I shall follow, to the best of my ability, the rules and suggestions I have read in this section.

—I shall persist—I shall keep on fighting this great weakness of mine until I have it licked.

—I am confident that by organizing my day's work I shall increase my sales, my earnings, my chances for advancement.

—I promise not to quit this undertaking until I have organized my job. I promise also that for the rest of my selling life I shall keep my work organized.

Time is the essence of life. Tomorrow is now. Begin today.
                                    —GEORGE WESLEY BLOUNT
                    *   *   *

No one can expand by standing still. We must walk around, look around—and think far!
                                    —GEORGE MATTHEW ADAMS

GREAT PROBLEM 2

Salesmen don't think creatively to solve their customers' problems or their own

You can create ideas—solve selling problems

If you think creatively, you can solve your customers' problems and your own. If you gain the ability to create sales ideas, you will fast rise out of mediocrity (if that's where you are) and into the ranks of the real sales professionals.

Few salesmen ever heard of "creative selling" until recently. Now the demand for it is both loud and strong. In the New York Sales Executives Club's questionnaire, the need for creative thinking was placed second in the list of salesmen's needs by sales managers, third by salesmen.

When salesmen think creatively, they tend to do it largely to solve problems—the prospect's and their own.

Sol Broad says, "If salesmen thought more, they would walk less, talk less and sell more."

"How to solve sales problems by creative thinking" is the subject of this section.

CHAPTER 11

For every salesman who uses not only legs but brains in selling, there are hundreds who depend solely on legs

> *Creativity can be likened to an imaginative leap into the unknown.*
> —DAVID MAXWELL IN *Sales Management*

Maybe you are *calling* as hard as you can, but certainly you are not *thinking* as hard as you can. No salesman I ever knew did.

Thomas A. Edison, America's greatest inventor, said: "Why do so many men never amount to anything? Because they don't think."

For every salesman who fails because he doesn't use his legs, a hundred fail because they don't use their brains.

What I shall do in this section is:

1. Show you how to solve a problem that keeps you from earning as much as you would like.
2. Tell you how you can create ideas that will help you make more sales.

Of course you have imagination

> *Imagination is more important than knowledge, for knowledge is limited, whereas imagination embraces the entire world.*
> —*Personnel Journal*

The kind of creative thinking which produces sales ideas and solves sales problems calls for creative imagination.

"That lets me out," you say with emphasis. "I have no creative imagination, and very little of any other kind."

"You undoubtedly do have creative imagination," is my reply, "and you can develop more." You use imagination every day. It takes imagination to remember names by the use of mind pictures. Every time you remember anything by this method, you get practice in the use of your imagination. You need imagination also in the "desire" step of the selling process—because you must tell your prospect how he will look, act, and feel when he uses your product.

An example of the use of creative selling was given me by our friend, Mrs. Ethel Knight ("Polly") Pollard. Here is the story as Polly told it.

When I was in the real estate and subdivision business in Washington, D.C., one of our subdivisions in nearby Virginia had one lot we knew would be hard to move. It was treeless and in a marshy ravine. Every one of our fifty salesmen avoided showing it.

In an attempt to get the salesmen interested in that lot we offered a bonus of $100 to any man who would, within ten days, bring in a signed contract for that lot with a binder.

On the third day one of our salesmen, Fred Herron, rushed in and threw the signed contract for $3,100 on my desk, along with a check for $500.

"How did you do it?" I gasped.

"Why, I just tried to help Mrs. Brandon see herself enjoy living on that lot," Fred said. "I pointed to the tree-lined hillside lots of such well-known people as Donald C. Peattie [the naturalist and writer] and Willard Kiplinger [whose *Kiplinger Letters* were gaining national renown] and I said, 'Mrs. Brandon, when you build your house on this lot, you can save money on excavating—it's all excavated for you now. And anyway wouldn't you rather sit here on your porch and look up at those lovely hillside homes than to sit up there and look down into this valley?' "

Every salesman who heard him gasped—then laughed. I call that an example of imaginative, creative selling!

Creative imagination is just what its name implies—imagination which creates something, or enables you to do it.

"Creativity can't be created," says Robert Zinn, vice-president of marketing for the Standard Register Company, in an interview in *Sales Management Magazine,* "but it can be developed. Given some small degree of imagination and initiative in a man, it is possible to develop these characteristics into a surprisingly high degree of creativity."

Alex Osborn, in his booklet, *Creative Thinking,* says: "You were born with creative imagination. The chances are you possess much more of this talent than you realize."

Even if you have little imagination now, you can, with practice, sprout a lot of it.

It's easy—all you have to do is *think*

Actually, "creative selling" is merely the application of "creative thinking" to selling problems, and "creative thinking," according to a *Reader's Digest* article by Blake Clark, is "the ability to produce fresh and useful ideas."

An example of how creative thinking was used to solve a problem was given by Joe McCarthy in *American Weekly.* He wrote:

"Sal Mineo says he knows a N.J. farmer who was much annoyed by fast drivers who speeded by his place, so he put up a large sign that slowed them down to a crawl. It said, 'Nudist Camp Crossing.' That's creativity!"

You need to do creative thinking to solve your problems. "What kind of problems?" you ask. Problems such as the eleven that follow:

Problem 1. How can I sell my product when it is little or no better than that offered by our competitors?

Problem 2. How can I sell the big account that has never bought anything from us?

Problem 3. How can we get back the business of the XYZ Company that our chief competitor took away from us?

Problem 4. How can I get in to see the president of the AB Company?

Problem 5. How can I sell these "sticky" bonds or this "white elephant" house, or some other slow-but-good item?

Problem 6. What is the "big sales idea" for my product?

Problem 7. How can I keep up my morale when selling gets tough?

Problem 8. How can I get along with this cantankerous sales manager of mine?

Problem 9. How can I become a creative salesman? (A creative salesman, according to the magazine *Printers Ink*, is "Someone who does not like the way things are and has enough courage and desire to try to make something new.")

Problem 10. How can I find out how the retailers to whom I sell are reselling our product? How can I help them to do it better?

Problem 11. How can I show my customer how he can make more money? This question applies primarily to salesmen who sell equipment or some product that is resold to consumers. An article in a recent issue of *Nation's Business* said:

"No longer are persuasion, personality and product emphasis the only keys to [a salesman's] success. The salesman not only serves as a marketing counselor ... but advises his customers on new products, production costs, distribution problems and engineering. He becomes a business counselor."

Any salesman who has any regard for the truth will admit that his brain is actually crowded with unsolved problems and that he could make a lot more money if he could solve them.

Now we shall tell you not only how to solve problems, but also how to develop sales ideas.

And please remember this maxim: "Brains never go out of style."

CHAPTER 12

Any salesman can develop ideas that will help him sell if he will take just five relatively simple steps

> *Planning for creativity is like standing on a mountaintop during a rainstorm and trying to provoke lightning to strike your trial balloon. It's a hell of an inefficient way to charge your car battery—but zowie, what a thrill when it works!*
>
> —QUOTED BY DAVID MAXWELL IN
> *Sales Management Magazine*

We salesmen have problems. All of us. All the time.

One of our great problems is how to develop ideas that will help us sell.

Alex Osborn, in his booklet *Creative Selling,* says:

Often the factor that decides whether A or B gets the business is the power of ingratiation (To "ingratiate" is to bring oneself into another's favor). If Salesman A can think up more things than Salesman B to please and help the buyer, Mr. A will probably get the breaks. The right kind of ingratiation is, therefore, a vital key to successful selling. And the key to successful ingratiation is imagination—the generation of ideas that will please and help the buyer.

To solve our sales problems and to increase our sales we need sales ideas and problem-solving ideas.

How do we get them?

Here is a plan. It is based on recent books (notably *Idea Tracking*), magazine articles, and on my own experience in chasing down ideas and on the experiences of salesmen I have known. Any salesman who wants to think creatively should read Frank Alexander Armstrong's book *Idea Tracking*. It is published by Criterion Books of New York and sells for $4.95.

It's easy enough—when you know how

Here are the steps to take that will enable you to solve your problems:

Step One—First assemble all relevant facts. You must know how the problem arose, what has been done about it, why previous efforts failed. You should learn all you can about the people and organizations involved.

For example, suppose your company has lost a big account because the shipping department made a series of mistakes in handling orders. Your problem is how to get this account back.

To solve this problem, you need to know why the account was lost, exactly what mistakes the shipping department made, what efforts have been made to pacify and placate the offended customer, and why these efforts failed. In addition, it will help to know all about the offended company—history, past dealings, officers, financial standing. Almost any piece of information about the company, its personnel, and its business can help.

1. Look for facts first—opinions come later.

You will gather opinions later, but for now gather only facts.

For example, take the prospect who is a big user of the kind of goods you sell, but who has never bought a dime's worth from your company. Nobody knows why—and the prospect will not tell. Some of the questions you will ask (of anybody who seems likely to know the answers) as you gather facts, might be:

A. Who organized the company?
B. Why has it been successful—facts, please, not opinions!
C. Which of your competitors does it buy from?
D. Do you know why? (Again, insist on facts, not opinions.)
E. What reasons do they give for not buying from your company? And so on and on. Questions, facts, more questions, more facts. Put each fact on a 3-by-5-inch

card. These can be shuffled around and later worked into
their proper order.

2. Go back over your facts and check them to find out if
they are really facts—or mere guesses.

For example, your boss thinks that the reason your competitor is getting the business is that he is splitting his commission with the buyer or otherwise giving handouts.

That's what your boss thinks—but is it true?

Remember, the more a suggested solution is taken for
granted, the more likely it is that nobody knows the real facts.

3. Look for the "key fact." For example, in our imaginary
case it may be that the real reason this company doesn't buy
from you is that the buyer feels he was once slighted, and he
still resents it. So he is prejudiced against your company. In
that case the key fact is: "The buyer is prejudiced because he
feels he was once slighted by the company."

4. "Apply the time check," says Armstrong. That is, find out
if facts that were true yesterday are true today.

Let's take this imaginary case: The reason this company will
not buy from you is that sometime long ago the president of
your company and the president of your prospect's company
ran for the same office in a national organization—and your
company's boss won. After that the word went to your prospect's purchasing department not to buy from your company.
Gradually a precedent was established. Years have passed, both
presidents are dead—yet nobody tries to upset this old order.

When you apply the time check to this problem, you see
how absurd it is that your company is kept out of this business
for no other reason than that two men, long dead, had a fight!
A reason that seemed valid years ago is invalid today. Once you
have used the time check you can solve this problem, and are
in a position to get the business back.

Don't accept opinions until you know all the facts

5. Now begin to gather opinions. As you do, check each one
by asking: "Where did this opinion come from? When? Why?

Are conditions the same now as they were when the opinion was formed?"

For example, your sales manager might have heard that the XYZ Company doubted if the goods you sell are equal in intrinsic worth to your competitors'. So you ask: "Where did you hear it? From whom? Why do you think he told you that? How long ago was it? At that time, were our goods really as good as those our competitors offered?"

6. As you put these opinions on cards, strain out adjectives, over-statements, and half-truths.

In the following chapter we consider the next three steps for discovering ideas.

CHAPTER 13

This great truth is so simple that it sounds silly, but here it is anyway—"First find out what your problem is"

It is better to stir up a question without deciding it than to decide it without stirring it up.
—J. JOUBERT, *Education Digest*

Step Two—Decide exactly what your problem is.

Obviously you can't solve a problem until you know what it is—though I have seen it tried many thousand times.

An interesting example of this appeared in the Report of Proceedings of the Sixth Annual Creative Problem-Solving Institute. It was given by Dr. Sidney J. Parnes, Director. He said:

Upon arrival at a meeting room about fifteen minutes before presenting a discussion about creative thinking, I found that no lectern had been provided.

I wondered where I could get one in a hurry.

Suddenly I asked myself: "Why do I need a lectern? What really *is* my problem?"

I decided that the basic problem was to find a suitable way to place my notes. Having re-defined the problem, I looked around the room and spotted a rectangular wastebasket.

By visualizing this basket on its side, I immediately saw it as an adequate lectern ...

In our thinking we too often seek to improve mousetraps instead of finding better ways to get rid of mice.

Another good example of problem-defining came in an article in *The Reader's Digest* for October 1960, "You Can Learn to Think Creatively," by Blake Clark.

It told of some young mothers who were discussing the trying problem of how to get their children to eat eggs.

Someone asked the question, "Why do you want your children to eat eggs?"

"They need the protein" was the substance of the reply.

So the problem really was "How can I get enough protein into my child?"

It's worth while to define your problem carefully

To decide what your problem is, take these steps:

1. Make a quick offhand guess as to what your problem is. Write it down.

2. Look through your assembled facts for those which will be important when you work out a final definition of your problem.

3. Then write a more careful definition. Now check it by asking:

A. Is the definition clear?
B. Have you left out any necessary facts?
C. Is it accurate?
D. Can you eliminate any unnecessary adjectives? (Most adjectives are unnecessary.)

E. Hand the definition to others to find out if it means to them what it means to you.

Step Three—Set your subconscious mind to work on the problem.

1. Before you go to bed, state the problem to your subconscious mind. To do it, run through the important facts thoughtfully and read your definition of the problem. You may wake up in the morning with the answer to the problem —supplied by your subconscious.

2. If you don't get the answer at once, state the problem to yourself again and again throughout the day so that it may be "stewing."

3. Read the statement of the problem from time to time to give your subconscious a chance to come up with the solution.

4. Don't try too hard.

Leonard E. Read put that "take it easy" idea well in *Science of Mind* when he said, "You cannot force yourself to have an idea. Feed yourself the problem to which you want answers, and then *relax and wait*."

Finally you turn on the "idea machine"

Step Four—Now grind out ideas.

> *Remember, the best selling is helpful selling, which calls for creative ideas. Use more imagination than selling. Keep sprouting idea after idea.*
> —VINCENT F. SULLIVAN, *How to Sell Your Way into the Big Money*

You can't depend on your subconscious mind to solve all your problems—you must use your conscious mind, too. Here are suggestions for doing it.

1. Select a time and place that will guarantee you against interruptions, at least most of them.

2. Sit down comfortably and ask your mind to come up with some ideas.

3. Write down every idea that comes—good or bad.

4. Check each worthwhile idea against your definition of the problem. This will tend to keep you on the track.

CHAPTER 14

The last step in getting ideas is to select the "likeliest" idea of the lot—this may not be as easy as it sounds

One idea may spark a thousand sales.

—W. J. NEWHOUSE

Get others to help you select the best idea

Step Five—Now select the *best* idea.

1. Ask outsiders and insiders to pass on the promising ideas.

John Liesveld, a Kansas City florist, has, I am told, introduced more new ideas into the business of selling flowers than any other five florists put together. At the Mobile Sales Executives Club's annual sales clinic in 1961 he told us how he got a good idea from an unexpected source. He said:

About ten years ago when my eleven-year-old son, Jack, caught a ride home with one of our flower-delivery men on a cold, snowy day Jack did some observing. The book I had written, *The Retail Florist*, had just been published by the Macmillan Company. In one chapter I had recommended the procedure of securing signed receipts for every package delivered.

That evening my son asked: "Daddy, why do you have people sign for their flowers? It takes so long—especially in this weather."

"Son, we do it that way so that we know who received the flowers. Then if there should be a question about our having delivered them, we look it up and tell the customer who received them."

"What if they still say that they didn't receive the flowers?"

"Jack, of course we'd send them another arrangement of flowers."

"Well, then why get the receipt in the first place?"

From that day on, we have not asked for delivery receipts on flowers. I estimated that from that date, by eliminating the receipts, our men have saved a total of at least 5,200 hours.

A child's observations saved me over $7,500.

Thus, an eleven-year-old boy showed an expert that one of his pet ideas was wrong.

The moral is: Let outsiders help you select the best idea.

2. Drop the idea-chasing for a day or two—and let your ideas ripen for awhile.

3. Give the ideas a final check. Compare them with your statement of the problem and ask, "Will this idea solve this problem? Will it do what I want it to do?"

4. If you narrow the search down to two ideas and are having trouble deciding between them, use the Ben Franklin technique. That is, write in one column all the points in favor of one of the ideas, and in another column all the points in favor of the other idea. Then weigh one against the other and see which one weighs most.

5. Now see if the idea you have selected works in actual practice. If it does, stick to it.

Dun's Review, in an article entitled, "Are You Creative?" said: "All the creativeness in the world adds up to little if another quality is lacking, perseverance. Good ideas, spewed forth in abundance, and responsive to the most critical problems, are of no value until they are carried out."

CHAPTER 15

*Another way to develop sales ideas is to use
the brainstorming method in which you work
with fellow salesmen*

> *Maybe there's new business in a customer's plant,
> store, factory, or home. It's the job of the salesman to
> find it.*

Many of the sales problems which you face are faced also by
other members of your sales force. Perhaps the smart way to
solve some of them would be to bring a half dozen of your
fellow salesmen together to brainstorm the problems.

What is "brainstorming" and how do you do it?

A booklet titled *Brainstorming*, put out by General Foods,
defines it as: "A method whereby the ideas, the life blood of
any business, are created and nurtured." Perhaps a better definition, for our purpose, would be: "Brainstorming is a method
by which groups produce ideas."

Here are a few situations or problems that might be worthy
of a brainstorming session:

1. Suppose you and some of your fellow salesmen have gone
into a slump. What should be done?

2. Suppose a competitor is gaining on you—taking business away from you. Why? And what's to be done about it?

3. You have a new product that should be moving fast—
and isn't. What can be done to get it rolling?

4. Retailers say your product is not moving. What can be
done to promote more active retail distribution?

5. Should your company produce a new product or improve an old one?

This gives you an idea of the kind of problems you and your
fellow salesmen might profitably brainstorm.

Now let's see how we tackle such problems:

The preliminary steps for getting ideas from groups are similar to those taken by an individual in his efforts to produce ideas. Here are suggestions for brainstorming:

1. Define your problem.

2. Gather facts which bear on the problem and its possible solution.

3. Select your prospective brainstormers—preferably not fewer than six, not more than twelve.

"Have only one level of personnel present" says the magazine *American Salesman. The boss should not be allowed to come.* 'If you have one piece of brass,' says expert brainstormer Willard Pleuthner, 'you are likely to have eleven polishers!' "

4. Supply each prospective brainstormer with the facts and with the problem. Ask them to study these facts and to analyze them as they apply to this problem. This should be done three or four days before the brainstorming session.

5. Suggest to each brainstormer that he state the problem to himself just before he goes to bed each night—to give his subconscious mind a chance to work on it while he sleeps. (This ought to appeal to salesmen—they sleep while their brains work!)

6. Select a man to serve as leader—preferably a member of the group *with no title.* Your sales manager or field manager may feel that he ought to have that job. Try to talk him out of it. If you can't, then make the best of it.

Much of the effectiveness of a brainstorming session depends on the leader. It is his job to move the meeting fast, to stir up enthusiasm for the job at hand, to keep the discussion on the subject. If ideas come too slowly, the leader should ask questions or make suggestions that will get the ideas to pop again.

7. Now hold your brainstorming meeting. Bring your group members together in some room where they will be reasonably free from interruptions. State the problem, then ask group members to suggest solutions. From this point on, discourage

explanations, justifications, and long-winded statements. Urge
the brainstormers to submit their ideas in a few words. For
instance: "Make it heavier," "Try another source," "Have a
committee study the problem," "Make deliveries faster,"
"Switch to testimonial advertising."

How to go about solving a problem

Suppose you were at work on the problem, "How can we
get some business from the Jones Manufacturing Company?"
You might get from the brainstormers some ideas like:

—Improve our product.
—Ask the Jones purchasing agent what's keeping us out.
—Have our president get in touch with their president.
—Try the old reciprocity gag.
—See if the members of our board have any contacts—any
    "in's"—with the Jones Company.
—Quit fooling with the Jones Company and devote our time
    to more promising prospects.

Your common sense tells you that some of the suggestions
are idiotic, some are dishonest, and some are impractical. Don't
worry about that. What you want now is a lot of ideas—you
will criticize, analyze, evaluate, and eliminate later.

Every idea should be recorded, no matter how absurd. You
will need two stenographers or a tape recorder.

Note these rules about this idea-generating period:

—Keep the suggestions brief—only a few words. Accept no
    explanations at this point. Pound on the fact that you
    want *ideas*, briefly and clearly stated.
—Accept no criticisms. Let nobody say, "Shucks, that won't
    work." Insist that, at this point, the brainstormers present
    ideas, not *judgments*. C. R. Duncan wrote, "Too many
    ideas are killed off with deadly phrases such as: 'The boss
    will scream—we tried that before . . . that'll never work.'
    If we can eliminate negative thinking in our desire to

think creatively, we have in 'brainstorming' a dramatic, exciting and valuable technique."

—Keep the ideas coming fast. Don't let the meeting drag. "We must treat ideas," said Anne Heywood in *Forbes Magazine*, "somewhat as though they were baby fish. Throw thousands out into the water. Only a handful will survive—but that is plenty." If your group starts too slowly, prod their thinking by asking questions. Try the questions used by the U.S. Army in World War II: Why is it necessary? Where should it be done? When? Who should do it? What should be done? How should it be done? Alex Osborne suggests such questions as: "What about? What if? What else? What other uses? What is there like this from which I might get an idea? Is there something similar I could modify?" Obviously these questions of Mr. Osborne's apply largely to the improvement of products. However, they may give you an idea.

—Encourage wild ideas as well as sensible ones. As John Arnold said (quoted by Joseph N. Bell in *You Can Think Better Than You Think*), "It's easier to tone down a wild idea than to tone up a dull one." If a panel member has an idea related to a suggestion just voiced, he snaps his fingers. The moderator calls on him next. Thus the free flow of improvement on ideas can be maintained. These related ideas or improvements on ideas are called "hitchhikes."

When the salesmen run out of ideas—*quit!*

When the flow of ideas stops, stop the meeting. Before you dismiss the group, ask each one to continue to think about the problem and to send you the next day any additional ideas.

"Only about six per cent of the ideas from any one session," says *The Wall Street Journal*, "are expected to be practical. 'After all, new ideas are hard to come by,' says one business man who has used the technique. 'But just as important as the ideas,' he adds, 'is the stimulation the experience gives the participants to use their imagination.' "

8. Next, evaluate the ideas.

On this subject of evaluating ideas, the booklet on brainstorming published by General Foods says:

> After the conference is over the real work begins. What to do with a batch of ideas scattered all the way from sound and sensible to wild and weird? . . .
> People most familiar with the brainstormed questions are the most competent judges but they must be thoroughly acquainted with all that has happened, and be in tune with the proceedings. Also, they should realize that most new ideas are greeted with skepticism; usually the greater the idea—the greater the skepticism. Many examples can be given of this including the Wright brother's airplane, which some people thought would never fly.

9. Put the useful ideas into use.

If you act on these suggestions, you will have more sales ideas, will sell more, and will earn more.

Note. The standard book on brainstorming is *Applied Imagination*, by Alex Osborne, published by Charles Scribner's Sons ($4.50).

_____ CHAPTER 16

If you have a sense of humor and don't mind laughing at yourself, you may get some fun out of these maxims

If you lack a sense of humor, just skip this chapter. You would neither understand it nor enjoy it.

I laughed over all the maxims presented here—and loudest over some that hit me hardest. Maybe you will, too.

*   *   *

If a salesman gets lost in thought, it's usually because he hasn't been there before!

*   *   *

If salesmen thought more, they would walk less, talk less and sell more.

*   *   *

Despite inflation, a penny for salesmen's thoughts is still a fair price.

—WITH APOLOGIES TO SOL BROAD

*   *   *

The salesman's dream:
"For what can pow'r give more than food and drink,
To live at ease and not be bound to think."

—DRYDEN, SLIGHTLY MODERNIZED

*   *   *

This example of creative selling was written by Neal O'Hara of the *Memphis Commercial Appeal:*

The telephone rang in the real estate office and a soft feminine voice asked, "Do you sell maternity clothes?"

Without pause the salesman replied: "No madam, but could we interest you in a larger house?"

*   *   *

And now for a couple of serious maxims:

*   *   *

To face tomorrow with the methods of yesterday is to encourage stagnations.

—Grit

*   *   *

There is no upper limit to human ability, and much of what people are capable of doing with their minds is probably unknown today.

—Curtis Courier

GREAT PROBLEM 3

Salesmen don't know how to answer objections effectively

You can't exterminate objections, but you can learn to live with them

No sane salesman ever claimed it was easy to answer all objections. Objections are part of the business of selling—a hard part. You must learn how to take them casually and answer them effectively.

An objection in a sales talk is like a small piece of eggshell in an order of soft-boiled eggs. When you run onto the shell, you remove it—and go on with the business at hand. You don't get much annoyed or disturbed. You should treat objections the same way.

"When you get your first objection," says *Nylic Review*, "don't pick up your hat and leave. The prospect has not *closed* the interview. He has finally *opened* it."

CHAPTER 17

If you are one of the many salesmen who find it hard to answer objections, you can get help from this section

Behind every objection is somebody's ignorance.

* * *

The world is full of cactus but we don't have to sit on it.

—WILL FOLEY, *Good Business*

I was astonished to learn, from the New York Sales Executives Club survey, that salesmen rated as their third toughest problem: "Objections."

Most sales trainers regard objection-answering as—well, not exactly a kindergarten subject for salesmen, but at least a primary subject.

A complete set of rules to tell you how to answer objections does not belong in this volume—this book is not primarily for beginners. It is for men who know how to sell, but who want to know how to sell better.

You can learn how to answer objections—if you don't know already—from any fairly complete book on salesmanship.

In my book *The 5 Great Rules of Selling,** I devote thirty-one pages to objection-answering. J. C. Aspley in *Strategy in Selling* uses sixty-two pages, and Ivey and Horvath in *Successful Salesmanship* twenty-nine pages.

If you want to go the limit—to find out all you really ought to know about objections—you should read *How to Overcome Objections in Selling*, by Walter Horvath. (Try a library or a second-hand book store because the book is out of print—but still good!)

* Published by McGraw-Hill Book Company, Inc., New York, New York.

Now let's have a go at solving Great Problem 3

Let's start with perhaps the most important rule of answering objections, which is: *Cushion the answer to every objection your prospect raises.*

This is perhaps the most frequently disregarded rule in the whole Great Book of Selling.

What this rule means is that a smart salesman, when confronted with an objection, always states some point of agreement with his prospect before he begins to answer the objection.

We know salesmen often violate this rule—we've caught them doing it!

So many times when I have sent field men to work with a fading salesman, the field manager has reported that the salesman lost business and friends because he slammed into the answers to objections without "cushions," that is, without "softening the answer" by first *agreeing* with the prospect about something.

"Quick talkers" often give too-quick answers

It is the alert, aggressive salesman who often fails to cushion his objections. He knows his product, he knows the prospect needs it, he knows the recommended rules for answering objections, he knows the answers. And that's what traps him! When the prospect comes up with an objection, the salesman is ready with an answer—all too ready, unfortunately. He jumps at the prospect the way a prize fighter lunges when his opponent drops his defenses and leaves an opening for a knockout blow.

Alas, the prospect is not knocked out by this quick blow. He is merely annoyed, irritated, irked. He feels that his stout objection has been brushed off, stamped on, annihilated by this smart-aleck salesman.

The prospect may know that the salesman is right—that the objection had no merit. But does he admit it to the salesman? I should say not!

The prospect is ready for an argument—in fact, he usually insists on an argument.

If a salesman gets into an argument, you know where his chances of making a sale have gone! Argument-ville is a place from which sales seldom return!

What should that all-too-eager salesman have done? He should have *cushioned* his answer to that objection. He should have softened his reply.

You can cushion your answers in many different ways, but the best cushion usually is to agree with the prospect about something—anything except that his objection is valid!

To be agreeable, agree!

Most experts agree that a salesman should learn a half-dozen or more "cushions" or "answer softeners."

In using a "cushion," you first agree with the prospect about something, as for example:

1. "I'm sure I know exactly how you feel about that..."
2. "You may be interested to know that I once thought exactly that same thing."
3. "Yes, lots of people feel exactly as you do."
4. "That's a reasonable position to take, Mr. Blank."
5. "Surely you don't want to waste your money—no argument about that." Then you swing into the answer to his objection with such words as these:

A. "Of course, there are always two sides to every question. Let's think for a minute about the other side."
B. "I changed my views on this point when I learned more about it. I..."
C. "In fairness now, let's look at the other side."
D. "Have you ever thought of this?"

I certainly do not present these as model cushions. For one thing, I think perhaps they are too brief. All I try to do here is give you the idea.

Here is one cushion we used when Dale and I sold the Dale Carnegie course in effective speaking—in fact, I learned it from Dale. If a prospect said, "Your price is too high," Dale would say something like this: "Yes, Mr. Blank, the price of our course is high. We believe ours is the highest-priced public-speaking course in the world. But a man like yourself is not so much interested in how many dollars a thing costs as he is in what he gets for each dollar he spends." Then Dale would tell the prospect what the course would do for him. The result? Almost always an enrollment, because Dale was a great salesman.

Invent your own cushions—tailored to fit your proposition, your personality, and your prospects. Then memorize them.

Of course there are other ways to cushion objections besides the "agreement method."

If you don't *cushion*—evade

Walter Horvath, in his book *How to Overcome Obstacles in Selling*, goes at cushioning in a different way. His rule is: "Evade it." He says, "Avoid a discussion of the obstacle [objection] on its merits. Instead, reply in such a way that you swing the conversation to a different point."

Mr. Horvath gives an example, of which this is the summary:
Prospect: "We're all bought up on handbags."
Salesman: "Granted that you're all bought up ... (pause) ... won't you take two or three minutes to look at a few novelty numbers that a buyer like you should know about?"

Mr. Horvath admits that this evading technique works in only about one of three trials, but points out that if it fails, you are no worse off than you were before.

Don't be sure you are not guilty

Maybe you say, "You don't mean *me!* Pshaw, I always agree with the prospect before I answer an objection."

That's what you *say*, brother, but what do you *do?* Are you absolutely sure you never fail to "agree before you disagree?" Can you prove that you never lose sales because you don't bother to get in step with your prospect when he has raised an objection?

I wouldn't suspect you if our field men hadn't found so many cases where even top-flight salesmen were losing sales and money because they didn't observe that rule.

For a few weeks, check up after every one of your sales failures to see whether or not you used a cushion every time you answered an objection.

If the failure to use cushions is costing you sales and income, and if I have talked you into using them every time you answer an objection, this book will return to you many times what you paid for it.

CHAPTER 18

You may have heard of every rule in this chapter, but are you using them in your day-to-day selling?

If you are now completely sold on the rule "Use cushions," let's run quickly over some of the other mistakes that salesmen commonly make when they answer objections—then consider what to do about them. Let's put our suggestions in the form of don'ts.

1. *Don't argue—ever.*

Don't discuss the merits of the objection with the prospect. Many sales experts toss off that rule as though it were easy to follow.

Unfortunately it isn't—always. You say, "Our machine is the most efficient one built."

The prospect says, "Oh no, it isn't. The XYZ machine is 10 per cent more efficient."

Wow! What a set-up for an argument!

How do you keep out of it?

First you *cushion* it—you agree with the prospect about something. You might say, for instance, "Yes, I know that the XYZ is a first-class machine. Lots of users speak well of it."

Next you *evade it.* You might say, for example, "Let me point out some exclusive features of our machine that I think make it fit into your situation." Then go back into your "conviction" step, that is, state facts, and follow each fact with its related benefit.

If the prospect is still eager to argue, he may say, "Oh, yes, but I still think the XYZ is better."

Again you cushion it: "I admire a man who believes in what he believes in, and I like a man who says what he thinks. Have you noticed that our machine has . . ." Then give more facts and benefits. Bring out your testimonials, your examples, your charts, your photographs, your whole portfolio of material. And keep on talking about what *your* machine will do to solve the prospect's problems.

Hidden objections are the "booby traps" of selling

2. *Don't let your prospect hide an objection from you.*

If you have proved the prospect's need for your article, if you have convinced him that it is a good product, if you have answered every objection he has raised, and still he will not give you the order, you'd better look for the "hidden objection." Remember the saying, "Prospects raise two kinds of objections—the real ones and those that sound good."

I remember once, when I was trying to sell the Dale Carnegie course in effective speaking to a man in an advertising agency, I seemed to be making progress—backwards!

This man admitted he needed the course and that ours was the best. I answered several half-hearted objections. But he kept on shaking his head.

Finally I said, "Come on now, and help a poor salesman in distress. What's the *real* reason you won't enroll?"

His answer was: "As you know, I am a partner in an advertising agency. We top agency men can't admit that there is anything we don't know or anything we can't do. If I should admit that I can't make an acceptable speech—that I am taking a course to learn something—I would risk losing clients and money."

"So you see," he added, "why I just can't take your course." And he didn't!

If that man hadn't told me his real reason, I would have gone to my grave wondering why in thunder I couldn't sell him.

When it's easy to get, nobody wants it!

A good example of how people will try to fool you with objections that "sound good" was given to me by my friend Alton Littlefield of Augusta, Maine.

I hired Alton about 40 years ago to work for Central Maine Power Company. He was employed as: (1) a glorified office boy; (2) a member of the scrub team of advertising writers; and (3) a second-string salesman. He has done all right. He is now executive vice-president of the company!

Alton recently reminisced:

One day I shall never forget you sent me to call on three electric customers who had bought our preferred stock—and now wanted their money back.

You told me you wanted me to persuade these customers to hold their stock. You suggested a sales talk for me to use to persuade them to hold their stock and, in addition, gave me this good advice, "Always be ready to answer the customer's needs."

My first call was on a dear old lady. She told me a pitiful story about how badly she needed the money, a real tear-jerker of a yarn —so, instead of my selling her, she sold me.

I didn't even finish my sales talk. I felt it would be brutal to keep the money away from someone who needed it so much. I told her: "If you really need your money, as you say you do, we have customers waiting to buy this stock. You can get your money back immediately." The old lady paused, then said, "Well, if I can get my money back as easily as that, and if other people want these shares, I guess I will keep them myself."

Her real reason was not the one she gave—that she "needed the money." Her real reason was that she feared she could not get it!

In this case, I stumbled on the real objection. However, I learned from that experience a great rule—"Always look for the real reason" —a rule that has been valuable to me all through my business life.

So if you suspect that a hidden objection is keeping you out of a signed order, try to smoke out the objection. Ask questions. Encourage the prospect to talk.

Questions that may help you to get the prospect to give you his real objection are: "Have I made this clear?" or "So, doesn't it seem logical that this would give you the benefits I mentioned?"

When all other tactics fail to dig out the real objection, tell your prospect you are sure he has another objection. Ask him in the plainest possible language what it is. If he tells you, you have gained a lot; if he doesn't, you have lost nothing.

3. *Don't wait for objections to be raised when you are reasonably sure they* will *be raised.*

On the other hand, don't try to answer them *all* before the prospect gets to them. Maybe he never will!

When you weave the answer to an objection into your sales talk, never admit that you are dealing with an objection. Bring in the answer casually and incidentally.

4. *Don't fail to repeat the prospect's objection in your own words immediately after he gives it.*

Say something like: "Oh I see, your feeling is that . . ." or "As I understand it, your point is . . ."

When you restate the objection in your own words, you compliment the prospect and you let him know you understand the point he has raised.

Listen—you *might* learn something

5. *Don't fail to listen.*

Actually *hear* and *understand* what the prospect says when he raises an objection.

William B. J. Martin said in the *Arkansas Baptist Magazine*, "Listen with a genuine desire to understand not the question only, but the question behind the question and be at one with the questioner."

6. *Don't make the mistake of thinking that an objection from a prospect means, "No, I don't want it."*

What the prospect really means is, "No, you haven't made me want it yet."

7. *Don't ask banal, trite, idiotic questions.*

Says Derek Sones in *The American Salesman:* "Salesmen should be careful about the kind of questions they ask. For example, 'Do you want to save money?' or 'Do you want to get ahead faster?' are equivalent to: 'Are you opposed to sin?' Questions like this make the prospect lose confidence in the salesman."

If an objection "sounds good," watch it

8. *Don't let a prospect fool you with an objection that "sounds good," but is not his real reason for not buying.*

And remember, to paraphrase a remark by Dr. Jude L. Rosenstein, "The more noble the objection the prospect raises, the less likely it is to be the real reason."

One question I have heard salesmen use to smoke out the

real reason is, "If I answer that question to your satisfaction, will you give me the order?"

If he says, "No," then insist that he give you the real reason why he does not want to buy.

Always try to find the prospect's real reason, especially when he tries to put you off with the "not interested" rebuff.

This example was given by my friend, James D. Monson, director of sales training, The American Hardware Company. He said:

One of the big mistakes salesmen make when they try to answer objections is that they do not always find out why the prospect objects—what's underneath or behind the objection.

I saw an example of this recently when I worked with one of our salesmen in a Southern state. We made a call on an architect to acquaint him with our hardware for hospitals. Our purpose was to get this man to specify our hardware. After the salesman had talked awhile, the prospect said, "Well, I wouldn't want the thing anyway."

Our salesman, instead of smoking out the prospect's reason, disregarded the objection and went into a heavy sales talk. He brought in more evidence and went on and on for ten or fifteen minutes. Near the end of the talk, he was running out of gas! Fortunately for the salesman, the prospect did what the salesman should have asked him to do: he gave the reason why he was not interested in hospital hardware. He cleared it up in one five-word sentence: "I don't do hospital work." The salesman then switched to school hardware and got a favorable reaction. That was lucky, because he had wasted about fifteen minutes of the prospect's time, and hence had jeopardized the sale.

You can't argue with an example

9. *An example may be the right way to answer an objection.*

Suppose the prospect says, "Our customers would never go for a high-priced item like this." You might answer, "John Smith, who runs a store about like yours in Smithdale, thought just the same as you do, but I persuaded him to give it a trial and what happened was this..." (Then go into your example.)

Answering objections with examples is an argument-proof method.

10. *Don't neglect the "unsatisfied want" of your prospect.*

Don't talk much about objections—talk about *wants*. A good example of what a salesman can accomplish by switching from the objection to the prospect's wants was given in a magazine article by Lois Landauer (slightly shortened here):

"An excuse is frequently used to cover a restless fear or an unsatisfied want," explained Paul A. Norton, Vice President of the New York Life Insurance Company. "A salesman is often so busy trying to tell his prospect about his product that he misses the opportunity to learn the prospect's real need.

"I learned this lesson a good many years ago. A wealthy farmer who wanted to retire to Florida in ten years was in the market for a retirement policy. The policy he wanted was large enough to attract plenty of competition. We all had practically the same contracts, so everyone talked price. Confused by this barrage, the farmer kept objecting, always on the question of return per dollar.

"One day I rode out to the farm and learned he'd decided to get the whole thing over by signing with one of my competitors. So I stopped trying to sell him and started chatting. I said, 'Well, the important thing about the annuity you're getting is that you'll be able to go to Florida in ten years.' His eyes lit up and we started talking about Florida. As we talked he got more and more enthusiastic. Abruptly he asked, 'Do you have your contract with you?' I was so surprised that I could only nod. He said, 'Come on; I'd better get that policy into force right now.'

"All of us had been doing the worst selling job possible. We had accepted the price excuses without question. We had forgotten that the real reason he wanted a policy was to retire to Florida." *

11. *Don't expect to be able to overcome every objection.*

This one from *The Wall Street Journal*, for instance, would be hard to overcome:

* Reprinted with permission from the December 1959 issue of *The American Salesman*, New York, New York.

Fascinated by the dispatch with which the youngest mother on the block got rid of pesky salesmen, a neighbor asked for the secret. "Oh, it's simple," the girl smiled. "I tell them I'm so glad they've come because I want to show them my latest line of greeting cards."

_____ CHAPTER 19

Choice bits of sales wisdom about how to answer prospects' objections—culled from books by selling experts

*Some salesmen don't seem to know the difference
between an argument and an agreement.*

To make sure that I had not overlooked any rules or principles that might help you to overcome objections, I went through the "how to answer objections" chapters of over 100 books on selling. Each quotation contains some wisdom. Here they are:

* * *

*One of the fine points in handling objections is not
to go at your customer as though you were a better or
wiser man than he.... Approach the prospect in a
modest spirit.*
                    —SAUNDERS NORVELL (SLIGHTLY AMENDED)
* * *

*Salesmen must recognize that a sincere objection is
always evidence of sincere interest.*
    *A salesman must believe in the value of his product
to his prospect—a belief based upon the thorough
knowledge (a) of the product's merits and uses, and
(b) of the prospect's needs.*
            —DAVID B. OSBORNE, *Salesmanship
            for Today for Sales Managers of Tomorrow*
* * *

Real objections are often merely questions about the merchandise that the sales person has failed to answer. . . . The technique, then, of answering objections lies in analyzing the objections to discover the questions behind them. When the question is answered, the obstacle is removed.

—ROBINSON, BLACKLER AND LOGAN,
Store Salesmanship

*   *   *

You throw your prospect for a loss when you:

   (a) weigh his objections in silence.

   (b) appear to think before speaking.

   (c) disarm him with a smile.

   (d) restate his objections.

   (e) dominate him by (apparent) submission.

—HOWARD CARRAWAY,
Goodbye Failure, Hello Cash

*   *   *

The very essence of all the thinking on the subject of how to answer objections is contained in the four principles that follow:

(1) Never attack a buyer's viewpoint. Ask him to explain his side. You thus accomplish three things: (a) You assure the buyer of your willingness to listen to his views, (b) You learn exactly what is biting him, and (c) You let him get it off his mind.

(2) If you can puncture your prospect's objections by interjecting a word, don't say it—for two reasons: First, the prospect will get sore because you interrupted him; and second, he'll keep right on talking anyway.

(3) Don't raise your voice.

(4) See that the buyer thoroughly understands every explanation you make before you proceed to the next hurdle. Don't go on unless he expresses himself as satisfied with your answer.

—SOMEWHAT CONDENSED FROM MICHAEL GROSS'
Money Making Salesmanship

*   *   *

Never show by your expression that an objection has bothered you. If you wilt before some little objection

*that the prospect makes, he will instinctively feel that
you do not believe half of the things you are saying
about your proposition.*

—JAMES S. KNOX AND JOHN KNOX,
A Modern Course in Salesmanship

*   *   *

*Sales people should meticulously avoid any suggestion
of argument when meeting with objections.*

—RAY MORTON HARDY,
How to Succeed in Retail Selling

*   *   *

*When the objection is based upon lack of knowledge,
fear, desire to protect himself, or even when it is
founded on prejudice, the use of accurate information
is most likely to remove or neutralize the objection. . . .
Remember, the prospect will believe only what is in line
with his previous experience and present knowledge.*

—BEN D. HENTHORN,
How to Be a Star Salesman

*   *   *

*It is often a good idea to let the prospect establish
some minor objection, if it is valid, but not controlling.
Let him have it. You can always offset it by citing more
important advantages. . . . If you grant his point, he'll
feel better about granting yours.*

—*Let's Sell!* BY JOHN L. BECKLEY

*   *   *

*"Objections" are [often] not objections, but queries.
"That's too much money" could mean "What do I get
for all this money?"*

—WALLACE K. LEWIS,
How to Make Yourself a Born Salesman

*   *   *

*The prospect who states an honest objection does the
salesman a favor. That objection is (or may be) a key
to the prospect's mind. When a prospect states an objection, he practically says, "Here is a barrier that keeps
me from buying your goods."*

—*Salesmanship for the New Era,*
BY CHARLES W. MEARS

*   *   *

*To be able to answer the prospect's objections . . .
requires good humor and tact, and above all, a real
appreciation of the prospect's point of view.*
—Constructive Salesmanship,
BY JOHN ALFORD STEVENSON

* * *

*Don't try to do all the talking . . . don't interrupt. . . .
In the first half of the argument, inquire rather than at-
tack. . . . Restate . . . in your own words the gist of each
argument your opponent advances.*
—How to Win a Sales Argument,
BY RICHARD C. BORDEN AND ALVIN C. BUSSE

* * *

*Successful salesmen often ignore excuses completely.
They make no response . . . or they comment on it briefly,
and continue their sales presentation. [For example] if
the buyer interrupts with the excuse, "Business is too
bad to buy now," a salesman may simply say, "Yes, business could be better," and go on with his presentation.*
—Salesmanship—Practices and Problems,
BY BERTRAM R. CANFIELD

* * *

*You can't openly disagree with any man, woman or
child and get away with it.*
—How to Make People Buy Hard-to-Sell Things,
BY JAMES MARETTA

* * *

*Nearly always, objections can be turned into powerful
sales points, if you will take the trouble to find out what
the real objection is.*
—How Power Selling Brought Me Success in Six
Hours, BY DR. PIERCE P. BROOKS

* * *

*As part of your answer to an objection, or imme-
diately after answering the objection, stress an already-
mentioned sales point, or bring out a new one that has
application to the objection raised.*
—Big League Salesmanship,
BY BERT H. SCHLAIN

GREAT PROBLEM 4

Salesmen lack self-motivation— they don't know how to force themselves to do the things they know they ought to do

The "root of all evil" in selling—is what—?

Most salesmen, like most other human beings, lack the ability to motivate themselves to do the things they ought to do.

Few of the salesmen who answered the New York Sales Executives Club's questionnaire even mentioned the fact that one of their failings was "inability to motivate themselves."

They did admit they lacked perseverance, industriousness, resourcefulness, initiative, and "willingness to find the facts."

I have arbitrarily lumped all these weaknesses in this section because I know that salesmen who can motivate themselves can and probably will cure themselves of all these selling ills.

———————————————————————— CHAPTER **20**

No wonder salesmen fail in self-motivation —it is one of the world's hardest jobs!

Sales executives believe that one of the five great problems of salesmen is: they lack the ability to motivate themselves. Tell this to a salesman, and he may fairly ask, "What do you mean by 'self-motivation'—*motivation to do what?*"

Most salesmen lack whatever it takes to force themselves, or to inspire themselves, or to spur themselves to do everything they know they ought to do and to refrain from doing things they know they ought not to do.

Self-motivation is what salesmen need to drive themselves to observe the rules of good selling, good human relations, and good living.

Self-motivation means taking command of yourself. It means that you have the power within you to *incite* yourself to do what you know you ought to do, even when you don't want to.

Self-motivation isn't something that stands by itself like *sincerity* or *enthusiasm.* It is tied up with what you want yourself to do or to refrain from doing, because of the ultimate benefits to you.

You will find, in *The 5 Great Rules of Selling,* twenty-two pages devoted to the problem of "How to motivate yourself to do the things you ought to do to become a top-ranking professional salesman." In that book, I suggested twelve ways to accomplish this. (For convenience and clearness I have assumed that you know the rules of professional salesmanship. If you don't, you better learn them!)

If you are smart, you will work on one of your failings at a time. You will keep in mind that what you are trying to do is to form a habit of using the rule regularly—which usually means replacing a bad habit with a good one. (Who was it who said, "Why is it easier to break a good commandment than a bad habit?" Anyhow, it is!)

I say again, it isn't enough merely to force yourself occasionally to do certain things you know you ought to do. To make motivation of any lasting value, you must force yourself to do the things you know you ought to do until you have established the habit of doing them.

Habits are about the only servants that will work for you for nothing. Just get them established and they will operate even though you are going around in a trance.

Here's a place where you use "mind pictures"

Since you are what you think you are, you must begin to think of yourself as one who already possesses the good habits you want to acquire. Carry in your mind a picture of yourself doing things the way you want to motivate yourself to do them.

Frank Bettger, famous as a ballplayer, salesman, orator, and author, in his book *Benjamin Franklin's Secret of Success and What It Did for Me*, says that Miller Huggins, when he was captain of the Cardinals, always kept in his memory a mental picture of each player at his best. When a player's morale was low, Miller would try to get the player to see in his own mind a picture of himself when he was really playing good baseball.

Frank's comment on this plan was, "It worked."

You can use mind pictures to advantage in two ways: (1) picture yourself doing the job you want done the way professional salesmen do it; and (2) picture yourself enjoying the fruits of successful selling which come from using the rules. (We take up the latter on page 69.)

"Yes, it's hard—but don't let that scare you"

This exercise of your imagination will help you to motivate yourself, but it will not do the whole job.

This is no simple problem—this problem of motivating yourself *to do right,* and *not to do wrong*—in selling and in living. It is a problem that has stumped the sages and the philosophers, the religious leaders of all the world, and us common folks too, through recorded time—and probably before!

Here now is the substance of the many rules which appear in *The 5 Great Rules of Selling.* Literally hundreds of successful salesmen have told me these rules helped them to motivate themselves. Give them a chance to help you!

1. Determine to use self-motivation.

"Yes," some salesmen will say, "but suppose I am deficient in determination and weak in will power—what do I do then?"

The best way a salesman can bolster his determination is with imagination. Every time the question, "Will I do what is right or what is wrong?," comes up, just flood your mind with pictures of yourself as you enjoy what you have gained through observing the rules of good selling. See yourself as you drive a better car, live in a better home, take more luxurious vacations. You can see all this in a couple of seconds.

Then ask yourself, "Would I give up all these things I want for a trifling bit of self-indulgence?"

I know this plan works, because I use it successfully myself —in my weight-reducing battle. (To be quite truthful about it, let's say that I use it more or less successfully at widely spaced intervals. I'm just as human as anybody—maybe a little more so.)

To sum it up, if you use your imagination, you don't have to depend entirely on will power.

Imagination helps more than will power

So you can almost disregard Rule 1 ("Use your will") if you depend mainly on Rule 2, which is: Flash on your mind a clear picture of yourself using a rule and profiting from doing it.

Especially see the "profit"! Picture yourself as you take a

cruise on a luxury ship or behind the wheel of "that car" (maybe it's a Rolls!) or fishing on your favorite lake. Just flash the picture—that's all.

If your question, for example, is whether to quit early or to put in a full day's work, translate in your mind the question of an extra hour of rest *vs.* a vacation in Hawaii. If you can see yourself and your family on Waikiki Beach, you will have no trouble in making the right decision.

3. Start! Don't put it off.

4. Allow no exceptions. Use the rule every time—accept no excuse for failure.

5. Remind yourself constantly of the rule.

6. Sign a pledge or make an oath that you will observe the rule every time. Notify your wife, family, boss, and the other salesmen in the organization that you have made this pledge. Then, you will be ashamed to turn back.

If you are the only person who knows of your promise to use the rule, you have not supplied yourself with any penalty except remorse if you break that promise. However, if a lot of people know about it—and then you break your promise—the penalty is not only remorse, but shame also. (If that isn't penalty enough, agree with yourself to donate one dollar to the Salvation Army every time you break the rule.)

7. Get others to remind you to use the rule—"heartless" others like your wife, your boss, your mother-in-law, and your fellow salesmen.

8. Put in writing this agreement with yourself to use the rule. Make it a formal contract between you and yourself.

9. Keep a box score. Record it every time you use the rule. If you break your promise, record that also.

10. Report each morning to your wife and your boss your score for the previous day. (Be sure you tell the truth—all the truth.)

11. Use affirmation. Tell yourself repeatedly that you will observe the rule, that you have the strength to do it and the faith to believe you can. Keep on affirming. But remember, a

good resolution is like enthusiasm—unless it is fed daily it dies daily.

These self-motivation rules are as good now as they were the day they were written—and some of them date back to Ben Franklin's time. They have been used by hundreds of salesmen I have known personally who will testify that they work.

Practice them and note the improvement in your ability to force yourself to do what you *know* you ought to do.

—————————————————————— CHAPTER 21

To force ourselves to do the things we know we ought to do is hard—we'll never score 100, but we can improve

> *They fail, and they alone, who have not striven.*
> —THOMAS BAILEY ALDRICH

Let's think now of some additional ways we can make up for our "lack of self-motivation."

You will note that I amplify in this chapter some of the rules listed in the previous chapter. Also, that I give here some of the rules which we consider also in the "slump" section—especially rules which treat the problem of how to regain our lost morale.

This duplication of rules between *morale* and *motivation*—and the fact that this subject is taken up also in the section on "slumps"—is not surprising when you consider how these subjects are hopelessly and happily tied together.

Isn't it always true that the higher your morale the easier the self-motivation, that is, the easier it is to make yourself do what you ought to do?

All right, here are some more suggestions and rules we should observe to help us supply our "lack of self-motivation."

As a starter, sell yourself on yourself

Rule 1. Use faith talks—affirm.

To motivate yourself to do those things that will make you a successful salesman, you must see yourself in your own mind as a man who can motivate himself. You must look at yourself as a man who always does what he determines to do, then work to live up to what you have pictured yourself as being.

How do you build up this belief in yourself? With affirmation. Tell yourself that you have the qualities you want—that you can do the things you want to do. As you know, you don't have to *believe* what you tell your *subconscious* mind.

Tell it to yourself enough times and you will make it come true.

If, as Paul Yukon says, "A good sales manager can make a bad salesman feel hopeful, by simply selling him the idea," surely an unsuccessful salesman, by the same method, can make himself feel hopeful.

So sell yourself success.

Rule 2. Make what you affirm specific.

When you tell your subconscious mind what you want it to think, be sure to make the command specific! "I'm going to be a better salesman" is little help—too vague and general. But "I am going to make ten calls today" is specific—it's something you can bite into!

A popular writer recommends that you say to yourself "I can" as often as is practical.

Make this specific, too, as "I can make ten presentations today." Keep pounding "I can" into your subconscious mind.

Rule 3. Use mind pictures.

Norman Vincent Peale, in *The Power of Positive Thinking*, says, "Formulate and stamp indelibly on your mind a mental picture of yourself succeeding." That is, see in your mind *a picture of yourself* doing the things you are trying to motivate yourself to do.

You will realize the importance of this rule if you will consider that you rarely think in terms of words but usually in terms of pictures.

If someone had told me a few years ago, "Whiting, you think and remember in pictures," I might have wondered as to his sanity.

Now that I have thought about it a bit, I admit that most of the things I think about are translated in my brain into pictures. And in yours, too.

Exceptions? Why, of course. For example, I don't remember the multiplication table in pictures—when I do remember it (I'm a bit uncertain past the sixes). But anyhow, put the kind of man you want yourself to be into your mind in pictures. See yourself as you make that tenth call, or as you keep your temper when you tangle with an ill-mannered prospect. One picture like that is worth a bale of slogans.

Leave "brooding" to hens

Watch out that you don't put that rule into reverse. That is, don't see yourself as a salesman who does a lot of things wrong. Especially don't brood over your failures. If you make a blunder, find out how and why. Then consider how you will keep yourself from doing it again. Then kick it out of your mind and replace it with thoughts of success.

Rule 4. Use your eagerness to achieve your goal in life as a motivating force.

For example: It's near the end of the afternoon. It's hot. Your feet hurt. Your legs are weary. Your back aches. Yet you still lack two calls of your daily quota.

At that critical point, think of your goal in life. Bring it up as a vivid picture. Almost at once your eagerness to achieve that goal should sweep away fatigue and low morale, and keep you calling.

Of course, to make this rule work, you must not only have an attainable goal, but you must also be able to bring into your mind a vivid picture of yourself in full enjoyment of this goal. The clearer the picture, the stronger it will be as a motivating force.

Rule 5. Use the approbation of others as a motivating force. Dale Carnegie brought home to six or seven million people—maybe more—the significance of a "feeling of importance."

One of the best ways to make a man feel important is to give him approval. You can use that same force to motivate yourself. To do it, tell yourself to do the things you ought to do because it will please your wife or your boss or the other boys on the force—and will prompt them to give you the commendation and the feeling of importance you so much desire.

This rule is easy to apply. When you come to a point where you have to decide whether to do something the easy wrong way or the hard right way, just tell yourself, "I'm going to do it the right way because it will please the boss at the office and the boss at home."

You may point out, if you hate your office boss and aren't married, that this rule will not help you. That's no excuse for not using it. Surely there are some people whose approval you crave—people who will rejoice when you prove your ability to force yourself to do the things you know you ought to do.

After you have been engaged in selling for six months or so, if nobody cares whether you succeed or fail, you do need a friend—and "self-motivation."

CHAPTER 22

Next some minor rules and some "don'ts" to help you to motivate yourself to be a better salesman

> Some men have hundreds of reasons why they cannot do what they want to, when all they need is just one reason why they can.
> —*Uplift,*
> STONEWALL JACKSON MANUAL TRAINING SCHOOL
>
> * * *
>
> Selling is, for most of us, a continuous process of getting used to the things we hadn't expected.
>
> * * *
>
> Salesmen shouldn't quarrel with human nature— they've got it, too.
>
> * * *
>
> Always remember that money isn't everything—but also remember not to talk that sort of nonsense until you've made a lot of it.
> R & R *Magazine,* RESEARCH & REVIEW SERVICE

The rules for motivating yourself which follow are not the great big ones, but they are worth remembering and observing.

Rule 6. Develop courage.

You must realize that many times you are unable to motivate yourself because you are afraid.

The subject of how to get rid of fear is so important that I give it a whole section in this book. (See page 224.)

Rule 7. Hear inspirational speakers, read inspirational books —especially books about people who have done big things.

Get from them the inspiration that will help you to motivate yourself to do big things.

Rule 8. Associate with people who are self-motivators.

Maybe a little of their spirit and work habits will rub off on you. Study these self-motivators. Try to determine how they do it. Ask them questions; ask them for help. They'll love it!

Rule 9. Don't just *think* about it—*do* it!

Too many salesmen, when the time comes to motivate themselves, get into a mental argument with themselves as to whether or not to do what they know they ought to do. Take your own case. If it is 3:00 P.M. and you have made eight calls, and your daily stint is ten, don't stop to argue with yourself whether or not to make the ninth call. Go ahead and make it. Don't think at that point—just act!

Rule 10. Don't do the following "don'ts."

A. Don't let your body dictate to your mind. If your legs are tired and they shout to your brain, "Let's quit!"—just don't listen. Your mind is superior to your leg muscles. Make it control them!

B. Don't try to motivate yourself with booze. The motivation you get from John Barleycorn just doesn't last—and neither does the salesman who depends on it.

*   *   *

If you have trouble motivating yourself—and most of us do—try the rules in this section. I have seen them in action, and I know they work. However, don't expect too much too fast—of the rules or of yourself. If you get to be 50 per cent perfect, you are in the top group—and if you attain 75 per cent of perfection, you have set a new world's record!

Keep trying. You haven't failed until you quit!

GREAT PROBLEM 5

Salesmen lack the ability to communicate effectively

Maybe the inability to communicate effectively is your worst weakness

It is surprising and alarming that salesmen pay so little attention to the art of effective communication, since all selling—including advertising and direct mail selling—is necessarily based on communication.

If you can't communicate, you can't sell.

Yet not one salesman in a score has ever given any thought —much less any time—to making his conversation correct, clear, and forceful.

Let's consider what we can do about it.

_____ CHAPTER 23

Since salesmen communicate so much, it will pay them to learn to do it effectively

> *Talk is cheap because the supply is so much greater than the demand.*
> —*Virginia Methodist Advocate*

When salesmen and sales managers voted that "how to communicate" was one of the top problems of salesmen, they must have realized that the word "communicate" takes in more territory than Soviet Russia.

I worked out a definition of the word "communicate" from those offered by two dictionaries, as follows: "*To communicate* is to exchange information, thoughts, or opinions by talking, writing, or public speaking."

Of the many kinds of spoken and written communication indulged in by a salesman, the following are the most common and the most useful:

—Sales talks with his prospects.
—Talks with his boss.
—Talks with his family and friends.
—Group selling.
—Letters to prospects.

Let's consider the last one first—business and selling letters. Write lots of letters to customers and prospects. Write such letters as:

—Letters of thanks for orders, for advice, for tips, for any kind of help given you by anyone. These letters may pay big dividends.

—Letters to keep prospects warmed up between calls.

—Letters to pave the way for calls.

—Letters designed to make the recipient feel important— such as letters to congratulate a prospect because he won a golf tournament, because he became engaged or married (or maybe divorced!), letters on the birth of a child (such letters are doubly important if it's a first child). These letters help you to sell yourself to your customers and prospects.

—Birthday letters. The smart salesman keeps cards in his "tickler" with the birth dates of his good customers.

My friend, Roy Lockhart, a successful insurance broker in Birmingham, Alabama, is one salesman who constantly sends courtesy letters, and who gains friends and sales as a result. He said in a recent letter:

I have made several important insurance sales as a result of my courtesy letters. In many cases I did not even call the prospects for an appointment—they called me. I also made numerous sales by calling people after they received the letters. I found them more agreeable to granting an interview because of the letters.

Two examples:

1. In 1952, I mailed a newspaper clipping to a college football coach whom I did not personally know—but who had the same last name as a fellow officer I served with in World War II. I later phoned him, used this slim "point in common," and got an interview. He bought insurance from me and referred me to others at his school. Several of them bought from me.

2. Recently I sent a clipping to the public relations director of a large corporation here in Birmingham. Then I called and tried to sell him insurance. He turned me down with a couple of objections as old as insurance—(a) "I'm loaded with insurance, and anyway, (b) I have several friends in the business."

Undaunted, I sent him several clippings over a period of two or three months. Finally he phoned me one day and said, "You're such a good public relations man yourself that, when I had an insurance need, I naturally thought of you."

He bought!

The matter of selling to groups (public speaking) is discussed in a later section. (See page 82.)

This brings us back to our primary subject: How to talk.

You don't learn fast to talk well

All it takes to learn to "communicate effectively" is a mere lifetime of study. To communicate, we use the English language—or some reasonable approximation thereof! You can learn all you need to know about English in a generation or two—if you study quite steadily.

Seriously, considering that language—the spoken word—is the chief tool of salesmen, it would seem reasonable to believe that salesmen would try to learn how to use that tool effectively.

Alas, too few of us do!

Unless you are sure you speak with reasonably acceptable

grammar and diction, you should do something about it. Bad grammar is as offensive to many prospects as bad breath.

If you speak sloppy English, if you say "I seen it" or "He done it" or "I can't hardly," or if you commit similar atrocities, get in touch with some school or college which offers a course in remedial English.

By the way, if you want to know whether or not you need radical treatment, consult your boss or maybe some friendly and frank customers.

Even if you speak fairly good "business English," you still have a lot to learn about that broad subject. So keep reading and studying English—a little at a time—all your life. Don't make hard work of it. If English still troubles you, I recommend the McGraw-Hill *Handbook of English*.

The process of learning from any of the better-English books is practically painless. This is one way to do it:

Keep a book on English handy. Each time you sit down to read, run over a page or two in this book. Mark all the points you are uncertain about. Go through the whole book this way. When you have finished the first trip through, start at the front again—to review what you have marked. When you are sure you have in mind a rule or a principle which you have marked, check it. When you have run through the book on this basis, go back and study those you have marked but not checked. At the end of the third trip through the book you have probably either learned what you want to, or have given up hope. Then move on to the next book. This is the way I do it.

An interesting, pleasant, and at times even exciting way to correct bad errors in English is to make a game out of it. Maybe you can make it a family game. If you pay your wife and children a nickle or a dime every time they catch you in an error, you will make improvement and they will make money. Or challenge one or several men in your office.

Be careful, however, not to get into any grammar contest for money with anybody's private secretary. Maybe she really studied English and would murder you financially. Still, you learn so fast that way that maybe it's a good investment.

After correctness—maybe even before it—come the two great subjects of *force* and *clearness*. Your speech in a sales talk should be forceful and it should be clear.

The book on English that I studied in college (I hesitate to mention the name of the college—Harvard has had enough dubious publicity of late without dragging me into it!) had an even sixty pages on the subject of how to make your English forceful.

It contained such suggestions as:

—Stick to short, familiar, and specific words.

—Use repetition, but, as A. S. Hill says, ". . . provided each form (that is, each word, phrase, or sentence you repeat) is so different from every other as to have the freshness of novelty."

—Don't use more words than are necessary to express an idea.

—Put your strongest words and phrases in a sentence where they will make the strongest impression—usually at the beginning or the end.

If your prospect doesn't understand you, why talk?

Many salesmen apparently think that anything they say about their product is clear to everybody who listens. Often it is not!

There is no easy way to do this job

"Whiting," you say, "about all you do is to recommend that we take courses and read books to tell us how to communicate better."

I admit it, and believe that is about all I *can* do on this subject, and keep this volume under 1,000 pages. If I don't, nobody will buy it.

If somebody said, "Please tell me all I need to know to be a doctor," you would think that he was either joking or crazy. Yet it is not a bit more preposterous to say, "Tell me all there is to know about how to write and speak clear, correct, and forceful English."

Good English is the subject for a lifetime of study. But don't let that discourage you. Even if you study it only a little —and *practice* what you learn—you will be pleased with your progress, and so will your boss and those of your customers who appreciate good English. And, what is more, you will be on your way to a higher standard of salesmanship—which means more money and more of the things you want out of life.

Don't be the kind of salesman who never learns anything because he is sure he knows everything now.

_____ CHAPTER 24

Eloquence can do more for many salesmen than a rich grandmother or an oil well, and is much easier to acquire

> *When the salesman begins learning to sell to groups he is entering the field which may eventually lead him to the executive's chair . . . to the sales manager's job. This is the gate to real advancement.*
> —RICHARD LORING SMALL, IN *Salesmanship*

Every salesman should know how to make an effective sales talk to a group. In other words, he should know how to make a speech. He never knows when he will be called on to make one.

An example of what may happen to a salesman appeared in the *American Salesman* magazine in an article headed, "A Rival Had the Order—But Mack Rapp Got the Sale." This was taken from the book, *Great Sales by Great Salesmen*, by

Lasser A. Blumenthal. The article told of the efforts of salesman Rapp to sell baggage-handling equipment to a new airline
terminal.

The order had already been placed with another salesman,
but Rapp managed to arrange a forlorn-hope meeting to present his story.

The next morning when Rapp walked into the meeting, his eyes
took in the long table, the blackboard and some 20 Worldwide
executives.

"My blood ran cold," he said. "I'd expected about five people and
here I was, addressing a small army."

How did the story end? Buy the book and find out for
yourself. But this gives you an example of what may happen
to almost any salesman who has not learned how to speak
to groups.

If a salesman wants advancement he should know how to
make speeches.

Just for a wild estimate, a salesman who can speak effectively in public has five times as good chance to advance to
a sales executive job as one who can't. Also, he is at least
twice as likely to make good on the job after he gets it.

How the ability to speak in public helps a salesman

The ability to speak in public will benefit you in many ways,
including these four:
1. It gives you the necessary courage to talk to people—
   especially important people.
2. It gives you a master method to get prospects.
3. It increases your effectiveness when you sell groups.
4. It enables you to take an active and effective part in sales
   meetings, conventions, and civic group meetings that
   make you favorably known and give you prestige.

Benefit No. 1. Elsewhere in this book I tell you that perhaps the best way to cure fear is to take a course in public

speaking. Any *practical* course in public speaking will help you, will usually cure you. By a "practical" course I mean one taught by a well-trained instructor in which every class member speaks at every session. Several such courses are available. After you have taken a course in public speaking, accept every invitation to speak. In fact, go farther. Get yourself invited to speak—promote yourself. This is surprisingly easy to do because so many service clubs, women's clubs, church groups, and the like are always looking for somebody who will speak to them—free!

In fact, after you get a bit of oratorical reputation, you can even delude organizations into paying you to speak. Beginners sometimes ask me, "What should I charge to make a speech?" I tell them, "At the start ask $10—how do they know you aren't worth it?"

Public speaking helps a salesman to get prospects

Benefit No. 2. For some salesmen, all their prospects are found for them in advance and come neatly wrapped in a route book. For others—insurance salesmen or mutual fund salesmen, for example—prospects don't "come" at all. The salesman has to go out and find them—and they are often scattered like dandelion seeds after a hurricane, and seem no more eager to be found than the FBI's ten most-wanted men.

Salesmen of securities have three choices: (1) to locate prospects, (2) to marry a rich wife, or (3) to starve.

To locate many prospects fast, speak in public. People who hear you speak in public feel that they know you personally. Any public speaker will testify to that. Sometimes it is embarrassing. Quite often, after you have made a speech, some man or woman will stop you on the street and say, "You remember *me*—I heard you talk last night." Maybe thousands of other people heard you, too. All of them feel that they know you.

For example, my wife and I moved to Montrose, Alabama,

after I retired. A couple of months after we arrived, I spoke to the Kiwanis Club of Fairhope—an adjoining town where we do most of our shopping. Sixty-five people heard the talk. Afterward, when I met almost any one of the sixty-five on the street, he would bow and smile. It was embarrassing—I never knew to whom to bow. I solved that problem, though. Now I bow and smile at everybody in Fairhope!

I have nothing to sell the people of Fairhope except my friendship, but suppose I had? I am certain I could have obtained an interview with almost any one of those sixty-five people.

Maybe you'll have to sell a large group sometime!

Benefit No. 3. The ability to speak in public is insurance against a catastrophe if you have to make a sales talk to a group.

A real estate salesman in New Jersey lost a good commission because he couldn't talk when he faced a group. This man was the star salesman of his organization. The company had a plot of land that it wished to sell to a country club for a new golf course. It assigned this star salesman to the job.

The salesman was asked to present his offer one night at the clubhouse. He expected to talk to a couple of officers or, at worst, to a small committee. When he arrived, he found that he was supposed to make his pitch to the membership of the large club. They had assembled to hear his offer and that of a competitor. The salesman had never spoken to a group. He was terrified beyond his strength. I wasn't there, so I can't testify, but I am told that he took the easy way out. He fainted! The competitor made the sale.

An incident like that is not likely to happen oftener than once in a couple of million years—but again and again salesmen are called on to make their sales talks to groups, perhaps a board of directors, a buying committee, or prospects assembled by advertising.

My advice to you is: be ready for such a situation—learn to talk to groups.

If you want a better job, advertise—by making speeches

It is important that salesmen who are ambitious to become sales managers should remember that the sales manager is the executive who, in most companies, is the one primarily called upon to do any public speaking which may be necessary.

—A. C. HAZEL, MANAGING DIRECTOR, GULF RADIATORS, LTD., IN *Professional Salesmanship* BY ALFRED TACK (ENGLAND)

Benefit No. 4. If you are ambitious to become a sales executive, you need the ability to speak in public. The higher your position, the more often you need it. Without it, your chances are poor.

I'll admit I have known men in the executive branch of selling who weren't any better speakers when on their feet than they were on the flat of their backs, but I am certain these men could have gone twice as far twice as fast if they had known how to handle themselves on the platform and in conference rooms.

I have said in books, magazine articles and from platforms hundreds of times how public speaking helped me to talk my way out of a small job in Augusta, Maine, into a big one in New York City. This big job was manager of the Customer-Ownership Division of the Securities Department of Henry L. Doherty & Company (Cities Service Company) with a comfortable salary and a favorable commission arrangement.

Why did a billion-dollar company (then in the public utilities field as well as in oil) reach 'way north to a small company in Maine and pick an unknown man for an important job?

Ray C. Russum, then manager of the Securities Department, who was my boss, asked that question of Milan Bump, then

Mr. Doherty's right-hand man. Mr. Bump said that Mr. Doherty had turned the job of finding such a man over to him, and that, when he surveyed the field, he recalled that a man named Whiting had spoken about customer ownership at a couple of national conventions, and had taken an active part in meetings of the Customer Ownership Committee of the National Electric Light Association. So he offered the job to that man. The ability to speak at conventions and to committees got me the job, slight as the ability was.

Perhaps you are one of those who say, "Oh, I don't need to make speeches to call myself to the attention of my superiors. I've been doing a good job for years—someday they'll promote me."

Are you sure?

Look around any big company and you will see men who "have been doing a good job for years" but have never been promoted to anything important—and never will be. They are the "silent strong" type, who stay put, while the men who have called themselves to the attention of top management by speeches at conventions and meetings get the prize jobs. It may not be fair, but it's life!

Has it ever occurred to you salesmen who expect to be noticed because you always do a fairly good job that the reason you never get a raise is that the boss knows you will never quit and that his competitors will never hear of you? The men they give raises to are the men they fear they will lose if they don't.

_____ CHAPTER 25

If you can't speak in public you may miss the chance to make money and gain advancement to a sales executive job

Any salesman who thinks he can slip through his selling life without selling to groups has either aimed low or guessed wrong. Therefore, every ambitious salesman should prepare himself to sell to groups.

Maybe you ask, "How many people does it take to make a group?" Certainly the sales talk you would make to two people differs from that you would make to an individual; and, to that extent at least, a talk you would make to two people qualifies as a *group sales talk.*

When you make a pitch to three or four people, you have certainly embarked on a group talk.

If, when you talk, two or more prospects can hear you without the aid of a telephone and can see you without the aid of a telescope, it is a *group sales talk.*

How Dale Carnegie sold to a "group" of 7,300

As an example of big-group selling, I once heard Dale Carnegie make a regular sales pitch to 7,300 people—a pitch which was aimed at getting them to enroll in the Dale Carnegie Course in Effective Speaking. (In those days, Dale used this plan to get most of his classes: he would advertise a meeting in the daily papers—and sometimes by mail—would make a sales talk to the group thus gathered, and would then ask them to enroll at tables in the back of the hall. I know, because I enrolled that way!)

The meeting where 7,300 people gathered to hear a sales talk—and incidentally look at Dale Carnegie, who was then a world celebrity as a result of his amazing book, *How to Win Friends and Influence People*—was held in the New York Hippodrome, an oversized building that long ago went the way of the hairy mammoth. Except for three or four rows in the top gallery, every seat was filled. I know because I watched the show from that uppermost gallery.

Authorities differ as to how many enrollments we took that night—Dale said one, I say two! The reason for this apparent failure? After the meeting was over, the huge, crushing crowd swept would-be buyers right past the enrollment tables and out into the street! Anyway, the meeting paid off. Within a few days we filled several classes from that "group meeting."

It is hardly likely that you will be called on to make a group pitch to 7,300 people, but, no matter what you sell, you may sometimes be asked to make a sales talk to a group of prospects, a buying committee, or a board of directors.

Richard Loring Small, in his excellent book, *Salesmanship*, says:

As the salesman becomes more proficient and more professional in his selling, he naturally seeks broader and more profitable fields. ... He discovers that, as the unit of sale becomes larger, more people will be involved in the buying side of the table. So, as more buyers are involved, and the expenditure of larger sums of money, a salesman must learn to handle more than one buyer at a time, perhaps a group of buyers. He must learn, in other words, how to sell a group.

Talk to a big group much as you talk to a small one

Perhaps you think you should make one kind of talk to a group of three, and another entirely different one to a crowd of three thousand. If you do, you are only about 10 per cent right.

Of course you would speak louder and with somewhat more animation when you faced a big group, and you would use slightly more formal language (but don't overdo the formality).

A little audience participation is useful when you speak to a large group, but don't overdo that either, or some smart boys in the audience may try to take the platform away from you.

As to questions from the floor—I discourage them if I am making a formal platform talk to more than a dozen people. Also I discourage the practice of having a question period after the talk.

Questions from the floor are likely to be of interest to only a small part of the audience. They are likely also to be poorly worded and so involved that nobody understands them, including you. Often they are mumbled in such a low tone that few can hear them.

Then, too, the invitation to the audience to ask questions is also an invitation to them to heckle you. Generally they don't, but I can tell you from experience that if they do, you will wish you were far, far away.

I remember that sometime ago, before I had learned better, I was talking to a group about the Dale Carnegie sales course (which I wrote myself, and about which I presumably knew all the answers). In the question period, a pompous prune of a salesman arose to ask what a man of his superior attainments could possibly expect to acquire from a course in selling that was obviously designed for halfwits. He made quite an oration of it!

When he had finished, I said, "Nothing," and turned to another questioner. He wanted a feeling of importance—and he got it! Or did he? An argument would have fully inflated his ego. The one-word dismissal, however, left him nothing to heckle over.

The rule is: don't encourage hecklers!

If I had not invited questions on that occasion, I would not have wasted that time. If you must answer questions—and I know that sometimes you must—don't do it until you finish your formal talk.

Of course, when you are trying to sell a group, you have to welcome questions. So be ready for them.

Until you know how your product will both benefit and serve your listeners, you can't make an effective group talk

Let's consider now how you should prepare to make a sales talk to a group.

I assume that you already know all the general facts about your product, or "service," or whatever it is, that a reasonably intelligent and industrious salesman can be expected to know. Generally speaking, all you need to know about your product is everything!

Sandford and Yeager, in their book *Principles of Effective Speaking,* tell the story of a man who was trying to train a mule, but was having some difficulty. The would-be trainer asked a friend who was standing nearby for advice. The friend said, "First of all, in training a mule, you have to know more than the mule."

Even if you do know more than your prospects about your product, the question still remains, "Do you know exactly how this product fits the needs and wants of this particular group?"

Your first step, of course, when you prepare to talk to a group, is to be sure you have earned the right to make the talk to this particular group. To qualify, you must be able to answer the following questions:

1. What are the special advantages of my product for this particular group of prospects?
2. What are the advantages of my product for this group over those of my competitors?
3. What objections are the people in this group likely to raise against my product? Which of these objections should I answer in my talk? What should I say in answer?

Unless you have "earned the right," don't talk

The next step you take to "earn the right" to make a sales talk to a group is to know all important facts about the group you are going to try to sell.

Some of the facts you need to know are these:

1. How much does the group now know about my product? It is awkward, for example, to make a sales talk about a sales course to a boss and his men, and to have the boss stop you in the middle of your talk to say, "Don't bother to tell me that —I took the course myself."

2. Get as much advance information as you can about the people in the group, as to their: ages, education, social status, goals, sex, and ability to buy. If the group numbers over three or four persons, about all you can hope to get are estimated averages or galloping guesses. These, however, are better than nothing.

3. How does the group feel toward my product: friendly, unfriendly, or indifferent? Remember, a talk suitable for a friendly group might not do at all for one that disliked you or your product.

I don't have to theorize about this—I went through it many times back in the days when I conducted customer-ownership preferred-stock selling campaigns. In those drives, we asked all the employees of a power company, for example, to offer the preferred stock of the company to its customers. We held a series of meetings to sell this idea to employees. The first round of meetings were as happy as a disarmament conference. We were asking power company linemen, meter readers, and book-keepers to sell preferred stock. They hated the idea and they hated me.

When the second campaign came along, the attitude had changed. Many employees had made money in the first campaign by selling stock. Those who hadn't made money were hopeful. At all meetings, after the first round, I was received like a rich uncle. Those campaigns taught me the difference between selling to friendly audiences and selling to hostile or indifferent groups.

To sell an unfriendly audience, try this method

"How did you handle unfriendly audiences?" you may ask. In general, I tried to start with a couple of laughs at my expense. Then I used a formula similar to the one for handling prejudiced prospects, to wit:

A. Treat their attitude with respect. Agree with your listeners about something.

B. Don't argue with them.

C. Suggest tactfully and indirectly that their present feeling is inconsistent with something they believe or do.

(These three rules, which will work in handling prejudiced audiences if anything will, are from *The 5 Great Rules of Selling*.)

Here are some more questions to ask about the people you are going to talk to:

4. If the group is unfriendly to me and my product, why?

5. Who are the influential men in the group? Which man or men must I win over in order to make the sale?

6. Can I hope to get a decision at the end of my talk?

*   *   *

I have tried to give you in this chapter some ideas as to how you can earn the right to make a sales talk to a group.

George Rowland Collins, in *Platform Speaking*, hit the mark when he said, "I fear that the primary cause of poor speech-making is poor preparation." That goes double-and-a-half for group selling!

If *you* aren't "sold," how can you sell?

If you don't believe in your product, you are a "dead salesman," because no man can sell unless he is sold. To quote Matthew Arnold, "The persuaded persuade."

I assume that you honestly and sincerely believe that your product will benefit the members of the group or the company the group represents. If you don't, your failure is assured.

There are few sights more tragic than a man who stands in front of a group of people to sell them something he does not believe in! I think it was Albert J. Beveridge who said, "If you do not believe what you say, you are only a play actor after all —a poor mummer reciting your lines."

Maybe you ask, "What am I supposed to do when I have to try to sell something I don't believe in?"

The answer to that one is: "Get another job!"

To sum it up, if you learn to speak effectively in public, the chances that you will get better pay and a better job are vastly increased.

In the next chapter, let's consider some lesser, but still important rules that will help you to make an effective sales talk to a group.

_____ CHAPTER 27

To make an effective talk to a group, follow many of the rules you use when you are making a talk to one person

Use the rules which follow. They will help you to make a group sales talk that will really sell.

Rule 1. Build your talk around the four steps of the selling process, as follows:

Attention Step—Start by talking to the group about something in which they are interested.

An almost sure-fire attention getter is an *example* (or incident). If you start your talk to a convention of retail grocers with "Six months ago Mr. ——, a grocer in Y-ville, learned something new about merchandising groceries. He ...," your listeners know that you have started a "story" and they pay attention.

However, please remember these two cardinal principles when using examples in a sales talk or a speech: (1) never make yourself the hero of the example, and (2) never invent an example. Somehow the imaginary ones never sound quite real and are never quite convincing.

Interest Step—Get your listeners to listen by talking to them about how your product will benefit them.

Don't go into details at this time about your product or try to prove any points. Just make your claim. You *prove* in the "conviction step" what you *claim* in the "interest step."

Don't spend much time on the first two steps. As Mark Hanna said in *Public Speaking Without Fear and Trembling,* "In a love affair or a speech, a lot of preliminary only wastes time and bores people."

Conviction Step—Give the facts about your product and try to make them interesting.

Now is the time to prove your claims—with facts, benefits, examples, testimonials, and charts. Now is the time for showmanship and excitement. Bring out your visuals; if possible, demonstrate your product. Be very sure that every time you mention a fact about your product, you follow it immediately with the related benefit to the prospect.

Desire Step—Do these three things to arouse the desire of your listeners to own your product:

1. Point out to your listeners their lack (or their company's lack) of what you are selling.

2. Remind your listeners that what you are selling will fill that need.
3. Paint a word picture of your listener (or his company or organization) as he uses your product and benefits from doing so.

If you can visualize, you can arouse desire

This "painting a word picture," or "visualization," is a vital factor when you sell a group. Again, I remind you how important it is to develop and use your *imagination*.

Please note what John A. McGee said in his book, *Persuasive Speaking*:

... this process which we term *visualization* ... is a projecting of your audience into the future and portraying for them the successful realization of their desires as a result of adopting your proposal ...

Visualization is a prize weapon of the successful speaker. [If the speaker was trying to get his listeners to vote in favor of a bond issue to build a new park] ... the audience might be made to see the beautiful green lawn, hear the children's happy shouts, feel the impact of golf club and ball, taste juicy steaks, smell the fragrance of flowers.

Please don't tell me that the desire step will not sell people in a group. I used it for fifteen years in a speech designed to get people to enroll in a public speaking course. When I came to the desire step in that speech, I (first) pointed out something I had already told them, of what they missed by not being able to make speeches, then I (second) reminded them that they could learn to make a speech in the course I was selling, and I (third) painted a word picture of their triumph with their first speech.

It's "ham," but it's high-grade "ham"

Call it "ham" or "hokum" or what you will, it is still a fact that audiences listened breathlessly and many of them stopped on the way out to enroll. Is this evidence that I am a good speaker? Not a bit, because scores—yes, hundreds—of other speakers successfully used substantially the same desire-rouser to sell the same speech course.

Use this desire step in the semifinal stage of your speech or your sales talk—it works miracles.

"Word pictures may be wonderful," you say, "if you are talking to a big group and are selling something that is suitable for word pictures. But suppose I have to talk to a buying committee of four or five men, and I want to sell them on stocking my brand of coffee—can I possibly use a word picture there?"

To answer this question I say: If you know the "end use" of the product you sell, if you know what the purchaser will use it for, of course you can paint a word picture of the prospect using the product and profiting by it or enjoying it.

The end use that stores would make of the coffee is to sell it to users, to housewives. Here are some of the words you might use, for example, in the three steps of arousing desire:

Step 1. "Today people who have read our XYZ Coffee advertisements walk into your stores, ask for our coffee, find you don't have it, and then walk across the street to a store where our coffee is sold."

Step 2. "When you stock our coffee, this bad condition is remedied."

Step 3. "Then people who now trade elsewhere will stream into your store, buy XYZ Coffee, and at the same time buy all the other groceries they need."

Step 4 (Closing Step). Take the following two steps to close the sale and get the order:

A. Weigh the advantages of your proposal against the disadvantages and show that the advantages outweigh the disadvantages.

B. Ask for the order on a minor point or an alternative proposal.

Don't tell me that you can't sell a group with the same formula you use to sell an individual. I have done it at hundreds of meetings. Men I have trained have done it literally thousands of times.

You just can't afford to argue with what works, and that formula does work.

Rule 2. Write out your talk and work over it until you have fixed it in your memory.

Directions for writing out your sales talk (which apply equally to the writing of a sales speech) will be found beginning on page 132.

Tell your listeners what you want them to do—and make it specific

All the way through your talk—and especially at and near the close—be sure you have in mind exactly what you want your listeners to do. If your objective is to get your listeners to join a club or contribute to a cause, approve the purchase of a fleet of trucks, or vote for a candidate, be sure to tell them. Make it specific. (Not "Join the Club," but "Stop at the tables at the rear of the hall, sign an application, and write a check for $175.")

If you are talking to a committee or a group which is to consider your proposition, be sure that what you ask group members to do is something that they can do, something within their power. (It's idle to end with the plea, "Buy my product," when the group is empowered only to report to the boss. In that case, you should, of course, ask them to report favorably on your product.)

Rule 3. Try to sell one or more of the individuals in the group in advance. It works magic—especially if you sell the influential people.

Rule 4. If the deal you work on is a big one—and if you have the time—rehearse your talk at least a couple of times before you face the group—once to yourself in front of a mirror and once to your sales manager or some salesman (or maybe a group of them, if they will listen to you).

Rule 5. Be sure you know how to pronounce correctly every word in your sales talk. Of course, you should aim to pronounce, according to accepted standards, every word you use in a sales talk or in conversation or anywhere else. If in doubt about the pronunciation of any word, consult a dictionary.

Rule 6. Eliminate from your talk any words which are hard for you to say. Words I always try to avoid are "linoleum," "narrower," "formerly," "familiarly," and "forwarding." They get tangled in my teeth, so I try not to use them in a speech.

Don't bother to be "impressive"—just be clear

Rule 7. Never try to impress your listeners with the idea that you know more than they do about anything.

I once heard a man say in a speech at a direct-mail convention, "I always throw into my mail-order letters a couple of words I know the prospects never heard of. It impresses them with the idea that I know more than they do; hence, they are likely to look up to me and believe what I say."

That technique may work in direct mail, but not in direct selling.

For example, I know a man who stayed away from a talk on "The Eleventh Commandment" because, as he said, "I never even heard of the first ten."

Rule 8. Talk with animation. Gesture—with your arms, your body, your head—but don't do it consciously. That sounds contradictory, doesn't it?—and maybe it is. However, it is a fact that, if you are really trying to get your listeners to buy your idea or product because you sincerely believe it will help them, you will talk with animation—and that means you will gesture.

So think about your main project—which is to get your message across to your listeners—then animation and gestures will largely take care of themselves.

George Rowland Collins, in his book *Platform Speaking,* supports that idea as follows: "When you speak, forget action entirely—be enthusiastic, sincere, dead-earnest. Some action is bound to result."

The unanimated salesman is usually a bore, no matter how well he knows his subject. The best informed insurance salesman I ever knew made only a moderate living, partly, I believe, because he was no more animated than a sofa pillow.

Just as an experiment, when you make your next pitch to a group or an individual, why not try to be twice as animated as you normally are?

Rule 9. Look at your listeners. Look at them all the time you talk.

If you really have that eager desire to get your message across to your audience, you can't help looking at your listeners.

If a speaker doesn't "contact" his audience as he speaks, he might about as well send a handbill.

CHAPTER **28**

Now that you know what to do to make an effective talk to a group, I shall tell you a lot of things not to do

Here are some "don'ts" that apply to sales talks made to groups, whether large or small:

Don't smoke while you talk to groups (or to a single prospect for that matter).

Don't drink water or anything else. If your throat is dry, it is because of nerves—and water is no cure for nerves. Besides, if you have to gulp water every few minutes, your listeners may wonder where you were last night!

Don't *read* your talk. Of course you wouldn't do that when you were speaking to a small group, but you might be tempted to if you were addressing a big one. Don't do it! A speech which is read is an abomination.

Don't give the audience anything to read or look at while you talk. When they start reading, they stop listening.

Don't yell—and even more important, don't whisper. Just "speak up." If you don't make your listeners hear you, why bother to speak at all?

Don't tell a joke unless it is the best possible illustration of the point you are trying to make.

Don't try to show off. Just be natural. Most people who show off do it because they feel inferior and want to compensate for it. If you talk on a subject you have earned the right to talk about, you will not feel inferior to anybody, because you will know as much about the subject as the best of them—and a lot more than most of them.

Don't talk too rapidly. If you have to finish at a given time and find yourself running late, don't try to gain time by talking fast. Instead, leave out something. Nobody will miss it, except you.

Don't use profanity or stale language

Don't use profanity. Some of your listeners may object to it —and anyway, it's the poorest form of emphasis.

Don't use clichés, stereotyped language, and worn-out slang. Some folks hate and resent stale language. I do, for example! (See my book, *How to Speak and Write with Humor*, McGraw-Hill Book Company, $4.95.) When a salesman says "get with," "falls flat on his face," "so right," "the hard way," "Let's face it," I writhe.

People who use stale slang and clichés merely try to be smart like a parrot.

Don't use "word whiskers." "All right," you say, "but what are they?"

The question is answered in the book, *Public Speaking as Listeners Like It*, by Richard C. Borden (Harper & Brothers,

$1.95). I strongly recommend this book to any salesman who wants to know how to sell to groups. Mr. Borden says in part:

When you pause, pause cleanly. The worst foe to vocal composure is the pause-wrecker—the deadly "Er-r-r."

Listen to the typical er-addict bewhisker his pauses: "One of the ... er-r-r ... most effective ways to ... er-r-r ..."

Attack it—the "er-habit"—directly ... agree to give fifty cents to a charity every time you catch yourself "er-ing." Have your friends help you keep score. At the end of a week you will be broke but cured.

To surprise yourself and your audience, use understatements

Don't make wild claims about your product or what it will do. Don't use a lot of superlatives. Prospects hear so much from salesmen about "best," "strongest," "longest-wearing" that they discount such claims.

Understatement in selling is always stronger than overstatement. (I have been preaching the virtues of understatement for years and, as far as I know, I have not converted one salesman yet!) Why don't you try understatement, just for one selling day, and find out for yourself the miracles it performs?

Don't use long sentences. Your listeners may be stuck to stay in their seats, but they don't have to pay attention! Long sentences are hard to follow—often hard to understand. So put in "full stops" often.

Don't apologize—about your speech or your oratorical ability or anything else. I have rarely seen a platform situation so bad that an apology didn't make it worse. I like the old Scots maxim: "Never apologize, never retract, never explain —get it done and let 'em holler." (Some discretion should be exercised in following that advice!)

Don't run over your time limit.

Don't lean on a desk, rostrum, or chair. Stand up.

If you have to use notes, and I hope you don't, put them,

printed in big letters (at least ½-inch tall) on 8½ by 11-inch sheets of heavy paper or light cardboard, and place them on a card table beside you. If you use a card table to hold your notes, you are not likely to lean on it because the card tables they supply for speakers are usually not strong enough to support a politician's promise.

Don't put your hands in your pockets. Oh yes, I know that lots of good speakers do, but I beg to be excused for believing that they would do a still better job if they didn't. This hands-in-pockets habit strangles gestures before they start, and signals the audience that you are nervous.

As Mark Hanna once wrote, "Did you ever see anybody win anything with his hands in his pockets?"

Talk about people rather than things.

Mark Hanna, in his book *Public Speaking Without Fear and Trembling*, said, "Describe things in terms of people . . . if you must recreate the din of a canning factory, talk also about the people who work there. Tell about Mollie Swenson who has had her rough, capable hands in vegetables for over thirty years. What does she think of life and love? Have too many string beans warped her outlook?"

It's bad business to use bad English—so don't

Don't use bad English.

"Yes, it's all right for you to talk," you say. "You were taught English in school and college. Of course, good English is easy for you."

You're wrong, brother, on the last count. Good English isn't easy for anyone. If you study it all your life, you will still fall far short of perfection.

"All right," you say, "I had none of the advantages you had —how can you expect me to speak nearly perfect English?"

I don't. You or anybody else!

Luckily, however, anyone who is willing to work hard can learn to speak and write well enough to be accepted.

Salesmen often ask me, "When I talk to people who are illiterate and speak bad English, should I drop my language down to their level?"

My personal opinion is "no." When you talk to people who use bad English at home and at work—I mean the "I-seen-it and you-done-it" boys—don't think about the elegance of your language, think about its clearness. (Anyway, many of those guys *know* better grammar than they *speak*, and they won't appreciate being "talked down to." They are not stupid —just ungrammatical!)

I wish I thought that one salesman out of a hundred who reads this book would be stimulated by it to try to improve his English—but, alas, I don't.

Why not?

Horace Greeley gave the answer when he said: "Education bores people. It implies that they do not know everything, which is very humiliating!"

Don't try to imitate some other speaker or salesman. Just be yourself. Remember, a real "you" is a better salesman than an imitation "somebody else."

PART TWO

How you can turn your five "next-to-worst" problems into valuable assets

Problem 6. *Many salesmen are afflicted with the wrong attitude. They grab when they should serve.*

Problem 7. *Too many salesmen quit before they have heard "no" seven times.*

Problem 8. *Sales talks are rarely as good as they should be.*

Problem 9. *Salesmen spend too much time in sales "slumps" because they do not know how to get out.*

Problem 10. *Salesmen lack the kind of courage it takes to sell successfully.*

Let's tackle now your "second-string" problems

The purpose of this book is to suggest ways for salesmen to substitute right methods of selling for wrong methods, and make more sales and more money.

You will remember, of course, that the Five Great Problems I tackled in Part I were those that sales executives and salesmen considered the biggest problems of salesmen.

Unfortunately for salesmen, these are not the only selling enigmas that harass them. So in Part II I consider the five problems that, in my judgment, rank next in importance to the Five Great Problems.

CHAPTER 29

All salesmen—from "near failures" to natural-born successes—can learn in this section how to sell more

To determine the five "next-to-worst" problems of salesmen, I thought for a long time as to just what had held back the salesmen I had known in my experience as a sales executive. I made a list of these mistakes and weaknesses. It was quite a list!

Then I switched from the negative to the positive, and asked myself, "Whiting, in your forty-four years of teaching and drilling salesmen, and in working with them in the field, what rules, techniques, and sales principles did you learn which will convert pretty good producers into top producers?" I made a list of those rules, too.

Next, I narrowed the list down to five. The five rules I selected have increased sales for thousands of salesmen. This I know from experience—my own, and that of salesmen who have worked under my supervision. So learn these rules and put them to work to make money for you.

Specifically, the purpose of most of these rules is to help you *make* the sales you now *miss*.

I heard Leonard L. Lyons, when president of Sales and Marketing Executives, International, sum it up neatly in a talk before the Mobile Sales Executives Club. He said, "I would like to have the commissions on the unmade sales that untrained salesmen missed."

Do you really want to become a "trained salesman," and to stop missing sales? Are you willing to do something about it—willing even to be educated a bit? (I hope you do not fall under the definition of "education" which appeared in the *Indianapolis News* in these words, "Education is the process of changing blissful ignorance into some other kind of ignorance.")

Be honest now—just how hard are you willing to work?

I hope also you are not one of those salesmen who goes through life looking for something "easy to sell."

George Mather of Babson Brothers Co., Chicago, wrote on this subject:

I am willing to agree that all men were created free, but I won't agree that they were all created equal . . . not when it comes to selling, anyhow. Some men *are* better born than others, but the real difference is not so much in some God-given native ability as it is in some inner compelling force that drives some men to learn *how* to sell while others stumble and blunder their way through life hunting for something *easy to sell*.

For some unknown reason God didn't see fit to make very many natural-born salesmen, but what is even more pathetic, He didn't even see fit to make many men who are willing to work hard enough to *learn* to be salesmen. There are so few thoroughbreds and so many, many scrubs who just can't seem to spur themselves into learning and practicing the methods that cause the winners to succeed.

One further point—the five rules I give you in this section will help you whether you are a beginner or a veteran salesman who has a long record of sales honors. Don't think that because you lead your sales force, or are a seasoned oldtimer, you can't benefit from this section:

The magazine *Instrumentalist* says: "At the age of 75, his international reputation as a virtuoso long since assured, Pablo Casals was asked why he continued to practice the cello four hours daily. 'Because,' he answered, 'I think I'm making some progress.' "

Maybe you, too, can "make some progress," no matter how good you are now! Try it, anyhow.

Successful salesmen should remember the sage remark of "Red" Motley, perhaps the best-known salesman in America. Red said: "No one is smart enough to remember everything he knows, and just as we need basic training for techniques, we need sales refresher courses, too. I read every new book on selling as soon as it comes out. I don't find new things, but I am constantly reminded of things I did know at one time—and have since forgotten to use."

Let's see now how we can cure the five "next-to-worst" errors that beset salesmen in their work

The five problems that, in our judgment, rank sixth to tenth in diabolicalness in the salesman's chamber of selling horrors are:

6. Salesmen have the wrong attitude.

7. They quit before they are "licked."

8. They don't perfect their sales talks.

9. They get into "slumps" and can't get out.

10. They are afraid.

How many of the problems listed above complicate your selling? On how many of them would you like advice and help?

Maybe you don't need advice on any of the five, but don't be sure until after you have read what this book says about them—and about how to solve them. After you have done that, go ahead and solve the five problems as they apply to your selling, and, other things being equal, you will sell more. It is inevitable.

Attitude is more important than aptitude

This aphorism is not only pleasantly alliterative, but it contains one of the great truths of selling—and of life.

To put it another way, "*What you think* has more bearing on your success in life than *what you can do*."

The attitude of most salesmen is, "I gotta sell because I gotta eat."

Salesmen are not in the least out of line in this respect with other men and women in the business world. Most of them work because they "gotta eat."

In the sales field the men who make the most astonishing sales, however, are usually men who sell, not primarily to eat, but rather to serve.

Let's put this great truth in the form of a rule, to wit: "Develop toward your prospects an attitude of helpfulness, of altruism, of unselfishness, of chronic empathy." That is, develop what we salesmen call the "missionary spirit."

Or, to put the rule in three words, "Sell to serve."

To paraphrase John A. McGee in his book, *Persuasive Speaking:* "You must have the urge to communicate something which you feel will benefit the prospect. This urge is perhaps the most important element in mental attitude that makes for effective delivery of your sales talk."

Some of my readers may say to themselves, "Here now, Whiting, when did you start to be a do-gooder, a soul-snatcher, and a psalm-singer?"

It is a fair question, and it gets a fair answer: "I started to preach service when I found that salesmen with the right attitude, with the missionary spirit, could sell perhaps twice as much on an average as salesmen who lacked it."

Wouldn't figures like that convert you into a man who preached "service?"

It did me.

One salesman with "missionary" spirit can outsell a half dozen who lack it—why not let it work miracles for you?

The semi-salesman sells to eat—the super-salesman sells to serve.

"How can I develop this 'missionary spirit' that can make me a miracle man in selling?" you ask.

If I knew the whole story, it would take a whole shelf of books to tell it.

However, when you know all there is to know about the product and the prospect, and believe that the product fits the needs and wants of the prospect, you have laid the foundation for developing in yourself the "missionary spirit." You are likely to build up within yourself an honest, sincere, unselfish desire to sell the prospect. You can honestly tell yourself: "This is what he needs. It fits his needs better than any other product. If he buys it he will be doing himself a favor."

In your mind's eye you must see your prospect using your product and benefiting from it. You are excited, you are eager, you feel that it is your mission to help him enjoy these benefits.

The rest of the solution of this problem is: live the Golden Rule. That is, learn to sell to others as you would have others sell to you. To give you detailed directions I would have to preach—and that is out of my line.

You have half-earned the right to make a sales talk to a prospect when you have learned all you possibly can about your product. The other half is to learn all you possibly can about the prospect, and his need or want for what you sell.

Naturally, the amount you have to learn varies with the product. For example, the amount a brush salesman has to learn is considerably less than what a computer salesman must learn.

Whether your product is big or little, simple or complicated, you have to learn what the prospect's need, or want, is and how your product will supply his need or want.

It is a darned good idea, just before you go in to see a prospect, to ask yourself, "What will my product do for this man?" If you can answer that question, you can talk in your prospect's interest.

How you get "prospect knowledge" is a question all beginners should ask—and, I regret to report, also a lot of more experienced salesmen.

What you should look for is information which will tell you why your product will supply some lack or want on the part of the prospect. The facts you need to know depend so greatly on the prospect and the product that it would be idle to try to give you rules for getting them.

I shall feel I have done my duty if I convince you of the tremendous importance in scientific modern selling of knowing your prospects' needs and wants.

Undoubtedly you have known of the importance of "prospect knowledge" since the day you started to sell. It was one of the first things your sales course teacher told you.

So we come back, as always, to the critical question: "What are you doing about it?"

It's always easier *not* to do it!

To dig out adequate information about a prospect is usually hard work. It takes time away from calls. The information you get may not be of any immediate service to you. It is a lot easier not to do it.

So, in too many cases, you do nothing about it. You walk in blind on your prospects and take a chance. That may be the more sporting way, like drawing for an inside straight, but you can't afford it unless you are a born millionaire.

Even when your call is on a prospect you have called on often, it usually pays to do a little pre-approach question-asking. You want to learn if there has been any change in his family situation. You want to know if there has been any change in the financial, competitive, or personnel situation of the organization. A few well-considered pre-approach questions may help you to avoid embarrassment and to make a more effective sales talk.

Any useful information you get about the prospect should be recorded on his card, or elsewhere. Don't depend on your memory—that would be asking too much of it.

CHAPTER **30**

Every salesman knows where *to look for product knowledge—the trouble is, most of them don't bother to look*

Nobody knows one-millionth of one per cent about anything.

—THOMAS A. EDISON

Often I am asked, "How much must I know about my product to have 'earned the right' to sell it—and what else must I know?"

The best possible answer, to paraphrase a famous remark by a famous actor, "Know *all about your product,* and as much about everything else as possible." Or, as Vincent F. Sullivan said, "A good salesman knows a little bit about dam' near everything."

How do you learn all you need to know about your product? Here are seven suggestions that apply.

1. *Read books about your product.* Borrow books from the public library or from the company library. It might be a good

investment to buy one now and then. Books about the product you sell should be as interesting to you as a detective story.

If you sell a lot of different items, probably you say, "This is not for me. How could I possibly read about all the items I sell?"

The answer is, maybe you can't. You can, however, begin to get information about one item or one group of items, or about your company or something connected with your business. Ask your boss to suggest a starting subject.

2. *Read the magazines of your industry*, and magazines in the field of selling.* It is possible, but not in the least probable, that there is no magazine which covers your field, or any field near it. If you don't know, ask your boss or the public library.

B. C. Forbes said, in *Forbes Magazine*, "Progressive business leaders (and salesmen) cannot afford not to read about business. The man who has no time to read about business has no time to succeed in business."

3. *Read—yes, study—the matter put out by the manufacturer of your product.* He wants you to know all about it. You ought to want to, too.

4. *Talk with satisfied users of the product.* In this way you can get practical information that will help you to sell. Also, you may get some examples of how your product has rendered a real service—examples you can perhaps work into your sales talk. (Also, as we pointed out elsewhere, an interview with a customer who is pleased with your product is (A) an almost perfect "slump-overcomer," and (B) is likely to make a "missionary" of you.)

5. *Ask questions of factory representatives.* They will be glad to help an enterprising salesman.

6. *Talk with other salesmen who are selling the line.* They may know something that you don't.

---

* Elsewhere in this book I have recommended *The American Salesman* and *Sales Management*. Salesmen who do door-to-door selling will find two magazines, devoted to their interest: *Specialty Salesman*, 307 North Michigan Avenue, Chicago, Illinois, and *Salesman's Opportunity*, 850 North Dearborn Street, Chicago, Illinois.

7. *If the manufacturer's plant or home office is not too far away, visit that.* Find out how the product is manufactured and distributed. This visit will give you confidence, and perhaps add to your prestige.

Once when I was helping a Canadian bond house do some customer-ownership preferred stock financing, the company was about to float a bond issue to pay part of the cost of financing a dam and a generating plant.

The senior partner of this bond house took his salesmen, by private railroad car, to the site of the proposed plant. He gave them a banquet. He had talks by the chief engineer and the contractor. He took us to the river and showed us where the power plant and dam would be built.

I still remember that day. It was in the late fall in Canada— cold, rainy, windy. And I don't drink. All I saw was a piece of river that was by no means scenic and a piece of land that looked to me about like all other pieces of land along that part of the river.

The next day, by which time I was thawed out, I asked one of the partners, "Does a junket like this really pay?"

"It does pay," he said positively—and that meant something coming from him, because he was a Scot and made no practice of spending money foolishly. "Largely as a result of this junket, our salesmen should sell this issue in about half the normal time."

They did! Because they knew so much about the company and its plans, they believed in the bonds. Because they believed in the bonds, they could sell them with enthusiasm.

As Harry Auesel said, "Most sales are closed, not because the buyer believes, but because the salesman believes."

The smart salesman knows more than he tells

Remember, however, this great rule: "*Know* all about it, but don't *tell* it all."

One day in a sales meeting one of my salesmen said, "I am so excited about this company and its preferred stock that I am

going to take a home-study course in electrical engineering."
"If you do," said my sales manager, "I'll fire you. You talk too dam' much now."

To talk too much is common—to know too much is rare.

You don't have to make hard work out of acquiring product knowledge. Read fifteen minutes before you go to bed at night. Read a book or magazine that deals with your product or with selling. Get up a quarter-hour earlier each morning (a dreadful thought!) and read for fifteen minutes. You will be astonished and pleased with the progress you will make in a short time.

Acquiring product knowledge can be good fun

Because you will be reading about the product you sell, you will find it easy reading, and interesting.

Again, I say, know your product.

Books on salesmanship have long contained the rule, "If your prospect asks you a question you can't answer, get the answer, then go back and tell the prospect." That's a good rule, too. But how much better to know the answer *before* your prospect asks the question. To get the answer after the prospect has asked the question shows that you are conscientious; to get it before the customer asks shows that you are smart.

Too many salesmen are in the classification in which Macauley placed Lord Brougham, of whom he said: "He is indeed a kind of semi-Solomon. He half knows everything."

I beg of you, be the exception. Study your product. Know so much about it that you are regarded as an expert. Be so good that when you say, "This is true," people will believe you, because they know you know more about it than they do.

Study and read as long as you live. Never let up. Edward A. Filene, owner of a great store in Boston, said in *New Outlook:* "Once upon a time, we used to read in the obituary column that so-and-so 'completed his education' at such and such a college. But the phrase has about gone out of use. We now know that if a man's education is finished, *he* is finished."

Arthur "Red" Motley, president of Parade Publishers and past president of the U.S. Chamber of Commerce, said, "We want our salesmen to establish some sort of a doctor-patient relationship, so the prospect will feel, 'This guy knows what's good for me.'"

Surely the basis on which such a relationship can be established is a knowledge of your product and of the prospect's wants and needs.

An alert, ambitious salesman should be like the witness, "Red" Williams, who testified in a trial in New York City. Williams was being questioned by District Attorney Tom Dewey as to his literacy. "Williams, how much of the alphabet do you know?" "Only from A to Z," came back the mental bombshell.

Two other advantages which a salesman gains when he has product knowledge were pointed out by C. B. Larrabee, publisher of *Printers' Ink*, in his "39 Tips to Better Salesmanship:"

1. The salesman who knows his product never has to misrepresent the thing he has to sell.

2. The more the salesman knows about his product, the more conviction he will have in selling.

Ollie F. Minor, sales manager, New York Division, Shell Oil Company, in an article in *Sales Management*, "How to Wind Up Run Down Salesmen," said: "Eliminate fear. Ninety percent of fear is caused by lack of complete knowledge of the salesmen's products or proposition."

Lack of product knowledge is the cause of a lot of low-grade retail selling. You have all heard the old joke: Question— "What's the difference between these two shirts?" Answer— "A dollar." That's not only old, it's not even a joke—it's a tragedy. I suppose it happens tens of thousands of times every day. It has happened to me dozens of times. I encourage it because, when a clerk offers me two items at different prices, I ask him, "What's the difference?" Try it. You will get little information, but a lot of laughs.

Get product knowledge and prospect knowledge, or you fail as a salesman

Unless you are willing to dig out all the knowledge you possibly can about your product, you are never likely to become better than a tenth-grade salesman. If, on the other hand, you acquire enough product knowledge to make you an expert on your product, nothing except stupid sales methods can long hold you back from becoming a successful salesman.

Here are two examples of the value of knowledge to a salesman. The first shows the value of *product* knowledge, the second the value of *prospect* knowledge:

Once, when Henderson E. McPherson was investigating a piston-pin plant that used a competitor's steel, he saw that the prospect's product was being made with a low-carbon, low-sulphur steel. Said McPherson, "I told the purchasing agent that their production would go up 20 percent with a low-carbon, *high*-sulphur steel, and I got the account."

As to his experience with an old-fashioned purchasing agent in another company, McPherson discovered that no rule should ever be followed blindly, even the one, "Never go over a purchasing agent's head."

"For eighteen months," said McPherson, "I'd been making unsuccessful calls on the purchasing agent of a small screw-machine outfit in Kalamazoo, Michigan. I was getting one stall after another. Once or twice it occurred to me that I ought to see someone else, but I didn't dare.

"Finally I chanced in on a day when the purchasing agent was home with a cold. I went in to see the president and told him that in a year and a half I hadn't been able to sell him a single pound of steel.

"'And you never will the way you're going,' he told me. 'I run this company. I buy all the steel around here because it's the most important thing we use. Any salesman who hadn't the initiative to find that out doesn't deserve an order.'" *

* From an article by Richard Osk, reprinted with permission from the *American Salesman*, 51 East 42 Street, New York 17, New York.

CHAPTER 31

If you are honestly convinced that you have a product that will really benefit the prospect, you are a hard man to stop

A "missionary" on the rampage can sell anything to anybody.

As I look back over my long experience as the Whiting family's assistant purchasing agent, I can recall one salesman— and only one—who ever sold me with real "missionary" spirit, who really wanted to sell me primarily because he felt that the machine he sold would benefit me.

At that time I was the majority stockholder and general manager of a successful security selling organization on Wall Street. A salesman would hardly pick me as a prospect for a Kitchen Aid beater and mixing machine—and he would hardly consider it appropriate to tackle me in my Wall Street office.

However, this salesman felt that he had a mission. He had learned from somebody in my office that, in spite of the fact that the Whiting family could then afford servants, we preferred to do without them. This convinced the salesman that we needed a Kitchen Aid machine—and he sold it to me. I had no chance—he was there to help me. Objections meant nothing to him—he had me hypnotized.

I bought the machine, and everything that could be attached to it—slicers, beaters, whips, mashers, a knife sharpener, an ice-cream freezer, a big storage cabinet.

I well remember what was said that day by our chief purchasing agent when the truckmen unloaded that shipment of Kitchen Aid equipment and packed it into our kitchen. My wife didn't like machinery and she didn't like clutter, and besides she was short of space in the kitchen, anyway.

When the shipment was unloaded into our kitchen, it filled it practically solid. My wife didn't wait for the truck crew to withdraw before she started a speech on the acute unwisdom of buying junk we didn't need and had no space for, and that wasn't any good anyway, and would just make work harder and scare away cleaning women!

However, by that time I, too, had caught the "missionary" spirit—I was certain that the machine would benefit my wife. So in time I convinced her—with a lot of help from the machine.

That all happened thirty-seven years ago, and the Whiting family is still using a Kitchen Aid. I think my son's family is still using the original machine. I am glad that salesman had the "missionary" spirit!

If *you* believe, *your prospect* is likely to believe

Marvin L. "Pat" Jones, sponsor for Dale Carnegie & Associates in northern Ohio, gave me this example of what a salesman can do if he believes his product works miracles for owners:

Several years ago, the most enthusiastic member of a Dale Carnegie class in Hamilton, Ohio, was a salesman named Gil Williams. This enthusiasm came from Gil's tremendous belief in the product he was selling and the benefits it would render users.

This product was a mechanical device which was not sold outright, but which was rented to users. It was part of Gil's job to pick up the device at the end of the rental period. The rousing testimonials which users almost invariably gave him when he came for the pick-up, built in him a wild enthusiasm for the machine and the miracles it would perform.

I never made any sales calls with Gil, but I am told by men who have seen him in action that he made sales because he converted prospects by his wild enthusiasm and his missionary spirit. Naturally, he was tremendously successful.

Oh yes, the product he sold?

It was a mechanical device to cure bed wetting!

Note: I don't know the address of the manufacturer or the name of the product, so don't bother to ask me.

To sum up this subject:

1. Know your product.
2. Have an earnest desire to sell it because you believe you will thereby benefit the purchaser.

"Shucks," you may say, "I don't have that kind of product."

Maybe that belief is what ails you. Probably you need to re-study your product. Surely you need to talk about it with your sales manager, with satisfied customers, with enthusiastic salesmen.

If you still don't believe that your product really benefits the buyer, and hence you can't sell with the "missionary" spirit, then brother, you'd better change companies or jobs. You will never be a really successful salesman until your attitude is right.

Emerson said, "There is no strong performance without a little fanaticism in the performer." If you have a fanatical belief that your product will greatly benefit your prospect, you will rarely fail to come up with a strong selling performance.

If I could make all salesmen realize the importance of these two rules, and could persuade them to use them, I would do about as much for the selling profession as the inventors of the printing press and movable type did for the advertising business.

If salesmen would observe these two rules, they would convert many of each day's sales failures into smashing successes.

Unfortunately, one of the rules calls for work and the other calls for faith—both of which are abhorrent to many salesmen!

But observe them anyway, and earn more money. This is one of the few sure ways.

Don't quit until your prospect says "no" seven times

One of the hardest rules for salesmen to learn is: Don't believe your prospect when he says "no."

The less attention you pay to your prospect's first half-dozen "no's" the more successful you will be. A good general rule is: Don't give up on any good prospect until he has said "no" at least seven times. Some salesmen could at least double their sales if they would observe this rule.

———————————————————————————— CHAPTER **32**

If you are naïve enough to believe prospects mean it when they say "No," you will lose sales that belong to you

Just when you are beginning to think pretty well of salesmen, you run across one who quits on the first "No."

* * *

Fall down seven times, get up eight.
—JAPANESE PROVERB

* * *

Expect no—don't think anything of it.
—CY BERG

* * *

Seven thousand dollars of my insurance I bought at seven different times from seven different agents. Why

didn't the first agent get all the business? Because, when
I said, "No," he thought I meant it.

—GENE CRANE, PAST PRESIDENT, SALES
& MARKETING EXECUTIVES OF MOBILE, ALABAMA

To start a verbal fracas among sales executives, ask them to discuss this question: "What one weakness causes salesmen to lose the most sales?"

One point they will usually agree on, the one basic bobble in selling, is: *salesmen quit too soon.*

I can think of a dozen men who tried to sell insurance to me who quit like a tenth-rate preliminary fighter when I solemnly pointed to the place where I then supposed my heart to be and said with pathos, "My heart has an abnormal beat."

It has, too! Doctors have shown me electrocardiograms to prove it.

What I didn't tell these insurance salesmen was that this odd heart beat of mine, though an interesting medical phenomenon, was as harmless as goat's milk. As evidence, my company once bought, in spite of my off-beat heart, a quarter-of-a-million-dollar policy on my life. (I was then clearly over-insured for the value of the property! In fact, during the Depression, I never got near an open window when one of my partners was around. They knew a quarter of a million dollars would do more good for the company than I would!)

If any of those salesmen who retreated quickly when I mentioned my "queer" heart had refused to be turned away so easily—if he had said, for instance, "An abnormal heart, Mr. Whiting? You certainly look stout-hearted enough. Has any reputable insurance company ever turned you down for a policy?" or had asked, "What do the doctors think is wrong with your heart? Is it serious?"—they undoubtedly would have sold me a lot more insurance.

I wish they had.

They failed because they quit on the first "no."

It's hard to hang on—but it helps

When I was at Vanderbilt University, I took a course under
the impressive title of "Systematic Zoology A." The title was
deceptive. The real purpose of the course was to give instruc-
tors and students an excuse to go out once a week to collect
dragonflies.

Our instructor, E. B. Williamson, was then one of the
world's leading authorities on the names and addresses of
dragonflies.

As a hobby of the moment, Williamson collected snakes—
not because he was especially interested in snakes, but because he liked to turn them loose in the dining room of
Wesley Hall where he and the theological students ate. The
"theologues" didn't like snakes!

One day we were working near the edge of the Cumberland
River at a point where the banks are high, steep, and slippery.

Williamson carried more equipment tied, strapped, and
buttoned to him than a big-league catcher in full uniform:
butterfly net, field glasses, cyanide bottle, lunch, camera, and
a half dozen cigar boxes to hold dead dragonflies and live
snakes. The boxes were held together by a strap slung over
Williamson's shoulder.

We had had a bad day for dragonflies, but a good day for
snakes. Most of the snake boxes were full of writhing
specimens.

We were working along the top of a steep river bank when
Williamson whispered excitedly, "I see two black snakes right
together at the edge of the bank. I'm going to get them both
with one grab."

He jumped, lunged forward, and grabbed a snake in each
hand. At that instant the river bank crumbled under Williamson's weight and he slid down toward the river, feet first.

As he started down, the strap came off the snake boxes,
which let out a large assortment of harmless snakes.

Down the steep bank they slid—snakes, sandwiches, net, field glasses, bottles, and Williamson. The bank ended in the river—and so did Williamson! He came out of the river disheveled and dripping.

The point of this story? Williamson came out of the river *with a snake still in each hand!* He had held on!

An easy-quitting salesman who does not see how the moral of this tale applies to him doesn't *deserve* to make any more sales!

Apply the rule with some judgment, of course

Let's admit that sometimes it would be tactless and stupid to ask again and again for an order. Such occasions are rare, but not unknown.

One man who didn't agree with my view that it was ever a waste of time to make a presentation even in a hopeless selling situation was Austin Brown, one of the best salesmen I ever knew.

Once when he was selling a preferred stock, Austin said to me, "Even if a man tells me that he is in bankruptcy, I go right ahead and make my sales talk. Then I say, 'I know you can't buy this stock now, but do you know anybody who can?' "

"You'd be surprised," Austin continued, "how many good prospects I get from poor prospects and how many sales I make as a result."

Don't quit until your prospect knows what you sell!

A common fault with beginners, and, alas, with some experienced salesmen, is that they accept a "no" and quit before the prospect even knows what they are selling. As any salesman can tell you, "Whatever it is you are selling, nobody wants it." That's one of the challenging facts about selling.

To meet this situation one of my salesmen sometimes used this odd opening: "I know you don't want to buy any Cities Service Preferred Stock today, but do you mind if I tell you what you're missing?" This approach worked for him. He told his story and closed many sales.

Prospects don't *want* any of anything

You will sell more, and be happier doing it if you will admit to yourself that this "I don't want any today" complex is natural and normal. "No's" are a natural reaction and seldom mean that a prospect will not buy.

Suppose you stick a boy gently with a pin. Ten to one he will say "Ouch!" It doesn't mean anything—any more than many "no's" from your prospects. Both expressions are often mere ejaculations. "No's" are not always refusals to buy. Let's quit taking them for what they are not!

Get over your delusion of persecution, if you have one!

"What am I to say to a prospect after the first 'no'—or the sixth?" you ask.

My answer is, "Pile on the benefits."

After the prospect has refused to buy, you should introduce another benefit with some such statement as, "Another thing I forgot to tell you . . . ," or "Here's one thing that interests a lot of folks I talk to . . . ," or "I haven't done my duty by you or the company if I leave before I tell you . . ."

If, as "no" follows "no," you can't think of any new benefits, repeat some of the old ones—but do it in different words.

However, the salesman who knows both his product and his prospect is not likely for a long time to run out of benefits.

Here's where your own enthusiasm for your product is helpful. You should not only (1) answer each "no" with one or more benefits, but (2) you should do it with an enthusiasm that will convince your prospect that your product must be good and worth buying, or else you couldn't be so enthusiastic about it.

So remember the rule: Overcome the "no's" with benefits stated with enthusiasm.

Observe this rule and sell more

Make up your mind that from now on you will not quit after the first six *"no's."* Wait for the seventh—it might be "yes." Do this and you will walk out with more orders and you will make more money.

Why shouldn't you wait for seven "no's?"

Well, admittedly it takes courage. It takes knowledge of your prospect and your product to keep piling up benefits, reasons why the prospect should buy. It takes tact and politeness and good nature to keep from offending the prospect.

On the other hand, stick for seven "no's" and you will make more sales—which is the object of the game. Your prospects will have greater respect for your courage, and so will your fellow salesmen and your boss.

It's your decision.

I wish I were a more persuasive writer. I'd make such a stirring appeal to you that you would never fail to observe this rule: *Keep selling until you have heard "no" at least seven times.*

This interesting example of the value of partial deafness when the prospect says "no" was written by Louis H. Brendel, merchandising director of Chirurg and Cairns. It appeared in *Sales Management.* A condensation of that article follows:

Years ago I had a crew of missionary men introducing a new line of valves. Everything was going fine . . . with one exception. One of these "missionaries," a Swede named Carlson, could get more orders in a day while working with distributors' salesmen than I could. So I went out to Chicago to see first-hand how he did it. I arranged to accompany him on his first day's calls, which were to be made on a group of the most impossible prospects the distributor had.

The first name on this list was the Blank Candy Company, which had never bought a valve from our distributor.

The receptionist at Blank Company was not particularly encouraging. She told Carlson he could *not* see the master mechanic. Bang!

I pulled out the list to see where our next prospect was located. But I had failed to evaluate properly my friend Carlson. This Viking apparently hadn't heard the Sweetheart of Southside Chi. For he instantly pounded determinedly on the gate and when the receptionist glared at him, he inquired where the master mechanic went for lunch and at what time. A nearby lunch room at 12:30 P.M., she grudgingly told him.

We were in the lunch room by half past twelve. Carlson barged up to the master mechanic and asked for an appointment. "Not a chance," the man blustered, but Carlson seemed to have lost his hearing. "Would two o'clock be convenient or would you rather I came later?"

As the clock indicated two, the Swede knocked confidently on that receptionist's door. When she peered out, he said, "You go tell the master mechanic he has an appointment with me here at two o'clock. Go ahead!"

Nothing happened for the next five minutes—and Carlson repeated his knock and instructions.

Shortly thereafter, the master mechanic stormed out into the lobby, glowering at us, "Let's sit down here," said Carlson. "Do you have any leaky valves?"

"I can't buy valves," the master mechanic barked, "The chief engineer buys them."

Again Carlson's hearing failed him. "Where do you have the most trouble with leaky valves?" he demanded.

"On our caramel steam kettle," the master mechanic reluctantly admitted, "but as I told you, I can't buy any."

"What size valves do you use on those steam kettles?" Carlson queried.

"Three-quarter inch," answered the master mechanic, "but as I told you, I can't buy any."

At this point, Carlson went stone deaf and gave this order to the master mechanic, "You write out a requisition for *one* three-fourth-inch Hardhearted Valve, and go in and get an order from your purchasing agent. Then you will see how to get rid of leaky valves. Go ahead!"

Don't ask me why or how it happened, but the master mechanic went in and got the order for the single trial valve. Carlson had done in one day what our distributor had been unable to do in twenty-five years.

I tried to analyze what Carlson had that I didn't have, and all I could come up with was that his ears could not hear the prospect telling him *"no."*

Everything worth doing calls for hard work

Success in selling has a price.

The price that salesmen must pay for success isn't expressed in terms of money. It is expressed in terms of work—the kind the Irish refer to in their saying, "Hard work isn't easy!"

Sam Walter Foss said it in verse thus,

> The path that leads to a loaf of bread
>   Winds through the swamps of toil,
> And the path that leads to a suit of clothes
>   Goes through a flowerless soil,
> And the paths that lead to a loaf of bread
>   And the suit of clothes are hard to tread.

CHAPTER 33

You can develop a sales talk so worded as to give you the best possible chance to get a favorable decision every time

Sometimes a man thinks he is ahead of his times, when the fact is the times are really not going in his direction at all.

I can tell you an absolutely certain way to increase your sales!

If I do, will you give it a fair trial, even though it will cost you some hard work?

Alas, most of you will answer "no," without even asking "What's the deal?" When you read those hateful words "hard work," you probably will skip over to the next section.

Still, at the risk of losing my audience, I am going to tell you "the deal"—tell you, that is, how you inevitably can increase your sales.

Here is the secret in eight words: *Standardize all important parts of your sales talk.*

"Oh," you say, "is that all?"

It is all—and it's plenty!

You probably have standardized parts of your sales talk already without realizing it. This is especially likely if you sell only one, or only a few articles. In that case, you present your sales talk over and over until you memorize parts of it in spite of yourself. That means that you have automatically started yourself on the road to a "standardized sales talk."

"Exactly what do you mean by a 'standardized talk?' " you ask.

"Well, "standard" means "that which is established as a model."

So, a standardized talk is a model talk.

Perhaps your next question is, "How do you produce a standardized talk?"

That is what I plan to tell you right now.

Few can standardize all their talk—all can standardize part

Don't say "This is not for me" until you have read this entire section. If you sell a product or line that does not lend itself to a completely standardized talk, you can standardize parts of it, as I shall explain.

A standardized talk will give you a real advantage over your competitors who still depend on luck and heavenly guidance to supply them with the right words.

One of my salesmen once said to me, "When I am about to call on an important prospect, I always ask heaven to give me the wisdom to say the right thing in the right way."

Once, after he had gone a week without a sale, I told him in all reverence that I thought it was selfish to bother heaven with his sales talk problems. I suggested that instead he buckle down and prepare for himself a standard sales talk so he would always say the right thing in the right way. He did, and his sales increased.

Again I say, any salesman who depends upon impromptu, improvised, unplanned sales talks can, by standardizing his talk, increase his sales—and sooner or later his earnings.

I agree with Eugene Whitmore who said, in *American Business* (now *Administrative Management*):

Salesmanship is ever so much more than making calls.

If any salesman or sales manager wants an increase in sales, let him begin to make an effort to get more results per call, rather than try to increase the number of calls. Worry about the calls which result in failure rather than those we did not have time to make.

If the thought of real hard work frightens you, don't *think*—just start

Don't underrate the difficulties of this talk-writing job. You might believe from the casual way most salesmen throw their sales talks together, that a sales talk is as simple and easy to make as a noise!

Let's think a minute about what goes into a successful, professional sales talk.

Such a talk combines all that should be said about:

1. The prospect and his needs.
2. The product.
3. How the product will benefit the user.

All this should be presented according to the applicable rules of good salesmanship. It should be worded in correct, clear, and concise English.

A sales talk "simple?" Yes, about as simple as Einstein's Theory!

Yet the average salesman walks in on his prospects with no standardized talk, and little idea of what he is going to say, and less of how he will say it!

As M. J. Butler, Jr., said in *Sales Management* magazine:

The reasons for the failure of a salesman haven't changed. Most salesmen do not give, within any month, more than a dozen sales presentations which are truly organized statements of why the prospect should buy the product.

The reason lots of salesmen never present a well-organized talk is that they never have a well-organized talk ready.

CHAPTER 34

Any sales talk you write for yourself is flexible—you can change it as you go along

Let's consider the objection of the salesman who says, "Every one of my prospects is different, so of course I couldn't use a standardized talk—even if I wrote it myself."

I welcome that objection, because it gives me an excuse to clarify two points:

Point One. You can modify your talk as you go along to fit it to any prospect or any normal situation. Exceptions? Oh yes, of course. Some situations and some prospects are unique. However, you can modify your standardized talk as you give it. Haven't you heard comedians do it? They break out of their prepared lines, ad-lib awhile, then jump back into the script without a jolt.

A salesman should always be ready to depart from his standardized talk. He may need to do it because of some outside interruption or to take advantage of a lead the prospect gives him.

Here's a recent example from my own experience:

Early in 1961 my wife, Gene, and I bought a home on Mobile Bay in Montrose, Alabama. The salesman, Connie Council, must have done a good job, because he showed us the property at 12:30 P.M.—and we owned it at 2:30 P.M. the same day.

Before Connie had shown us many homesites, we made it clear to him that we did not fish, did not swim, and did not sail; that we despised motor boats, and were not crabbers, shrimpers, or flounder-giggers.

Immediately Connie dropped out of his talk all references to the points we were not interested in. Undoubtedly he did not change all the remainder of his talk. He mentioned the abundance of magnolias, dogwood, camellias, pines, and azaleas. Then he concentrated on the view. This was smart. We bought the view. They threw in the house and lot!

Some real estate men will protest that they have no use for a standardized talk. Admittedly, every piece of property is different. But, if you are selling homes or other property, for example, in one community what you say about schools, climate, churches, population, shopping facilities, and cultural advantages can be "canned" and repeated almost word for word.

Point Two. Few salesmen should standardize their *entire* sales talk, but almost all salesmen should standardize *part* of it.

"I have to modify my talk to suit my prospects," you say. Of course you do! You can make the quick switch just as Connie did when he sold us "the view," which I am enjoying as I write this book.

Granted, the man who sells big machinery, big installations —ten-million-dollar jobs—will not need to standardize his sales talk. At the other extreme is the newsboy (now largely extinct) whose whole sales talk was "Extra! Extra! Read all about it. Five cents." He standardized his entire talk. Most of us are in between these two extremes. Most of us can profitably standardize at least half of our talk. Nearly all of us can, to our advantage, standardize the "conviction step," and the answers to objections.

So please don't let that old delusion, "This doesn't apply to me," steal from your bank account. Standardize your talk. Your sales will be easier, and your bank account bigger!

CHAPTER 35

Don't get the standardized talk which you write for your own use confused with the "canned talk"

Don't confuse the standardized talk with the oldtime "canned" sales talk.

When I speak of a "canned" talk, I refer to the kind that probably was written by somebody in the advertising agency. Usually it was written in the language which people used in writing, not in talking. The salesmen were supposed to memorize it, then grind it out without change. It had no more flexibility than a gravestone inscription.

The "standardized talk" I advocate is a talk you will write yourself, in your own language. You will work it over again and again until you remember it. Then you can deliver it in the best possible way for you. You can change it to fit any individual prospect.

"Canned" sales talks are now almost extinct

I have checked recently to find out if any big companies ask their salesmen to deliver "canned" talks. I found only a few which still use them.

One of the men I asked was George Mather of Babson Brothers of Chicago. Mr. Mather wrote:

When I received your letter I thought long and hard and I couldn't think of anybody who was now using canned sales talks— that is, anybody of importance. Then I wrote and called the great Dr. McMurray who has, over a period of years, attempted to teach me something about finding and hiring men. He thought a long time and still hasn't found anybody. In the meantime, I called up some old heads around here who reach back to the days of the first Remington, when the boys spent two full weeks rehearsing their speech in front of a full-length mirror and then went out and knocked them cold. My conclusion is that you can say without fear of any very successful contradiction that the canned sales talk is a dead duck.

Mr. Mather was referring, I am sure, to the oldtime twelve-cylinder management-written "canned" sales talk, not to the standardized, flexible talk that the salesman writes for himself in his own words, for his own prospects.

We show you in this section how to develop the kind of talk that Charles Roth reports in his book, *My Lifetime Treasury of Selling Secrets*, when he says, "Have a standardized presentation, and stick to it."

One company which still has good success with a complete "canned" talk sells "Great Books of the Western World."

Many companies encourage their men to standardize parts of their sales talks or to build their own from a model submitted by the company.

For example, Electrolux Corporation wrote me: "Electrolux salesmen do not use canned talks. However, a basic demonstration is presented to each man which he may adapt or modify for his own selling needs."

Avon Products uses a standardized "opener"

Another direct-selling organization—and a highly successful one—Avon Products, Inc., uses a standardized approach.

David W. Mitchell, director of sales training, in answer to my question, "Do you use standardized talks?" said:

We don't teach canned sales talks either to our sales representatives or to our managers. We do, however, teach our sales representatives a suggested phrase to be used as an approach at the door. We are 100% sold on the fact that our sales representatives need some kind of canned phrase to use when they approach new customers. In surveys we find that representatives who stray from the suggested approach don't do nearly so well in gaining entrance to the home as those who do use it.

The Fuller Brush Company, which, as everyone knows, is one of the world leaders in the field of direct selling, does not ask its men to use "canned" talks, but does recommend *standardized openers*. The company recently wrote me:

In field training, Fuller Brush dealers are taught certain short, effective phrases to arouse interest in Fuller products.

For example, a dealer will open his sales approach by saying, "Good morning, Madam, I'm your Fuller Brush dealer. Which one of these free gifts would you like?" While he says this, he holds up a small card which pictures four or five gift items.

When the housewife indicates which gift she prefers, he says, "Thank you, may I step in and deliver it to you?" Once in the house, he opens his display case to remove the gift and at the same time exposes various pieces of merchandise which he carries.

The entire line of sales approach follows an extremely low-pressure technique.

C. A. Alseth, director of sales management of the Victor Adding Machine Company, answered my question, "Do you use a canned sales talk?" as follows:

We have a structured canvass approach for a man to use when he is seeking permission to show a machine for trial.

We use a canned demonstration, if you want to call it that, for demonstrating the piece of equipment to the prospect with whom we are going to leave the machine to try out. We definitely do not believe in a canned closing talk because this is something so personalized that anything canned along this line would not be practical.

The way we teach the demonstration is this: we have a man learn the demonstration verbatim, but once he has learned it and has given it to one prospect verbatim, we then want him to forget it *per se*.

We do know, however, that a man who has memorized the demonstration is going to benefit in three major ways during his selling career: (1) He is going to learn the correct terminology in showing the machine to the customer. (2) He is going to have a logical sequence in which to present the many fine features of his equipment to the prospect. (3) By having a canned or memorized demonstration, he is never going to be at a loss for words when he is presenting the equipment to the customer.

In answer to my letter asking about "canned" talks, John H. Kostmeyer, vice president and sales co-ordinator of First Investors Corporation of 120 Wall Street, New York City, wrote:

Our salesmen do not use canned talks. Our presentation might be described more as a flexible container-type talk. The salesman must master the general outline of the presentation, but he is not required to use a prepared script verbatim except where the regulatory considerations make it mandatory. However, a number of our representatives choose to virtually memorize the prepared script.

To sum up this point: few companies use a complete "canned" talk. Many, including some highly successful ones, "can" part of their sales talks.

If you can't "can" all, then "can" what you can

Many salesmen, who do not standardize their entire sales talk, do "can" certain important phrases, sentences, and paragraphs.

Frank Bettger, in his book *How I Multiplied My Income and Happiness in Selling*, tells of a magic phrase that enabled him to close a sale. His prospect for life insurance already had $76,000 worth of insurance. When the prospect told Frank this, Frank said, "You'll never be satisfied until you get it up to $100,000." So the prospect bought $24,000 more.

Though Frank does not say so in his book, I'm sure he used this exact phrase again and again, changing only the figures.

CHAPTER 36

The best reason why you should standardize your sales talk is—you will sell more and earn more

A planned call which concisely musters a complete set of facts, told in an interesting way, supported by proof and followed by a request to buy is exactly what the buyer wants to hear.
    —M. J. BUTLER, JR., SALES PROMOTION MANAGER, THE DIVERSEY CORP., IN *Sales Management Magazine.*

Probably I haven't entirely convinced you that you should go to work to polish up your sales talk. Probably you ask yourself, "Why should I do a lot of work when so little work satisfies me?"

NOTE: I say again—Don't back away from this section because you sell a product which does not lend itself to a completely standardized talk. Remember, whenever you sell and whomever you sell, parts of your sales pitch can be standardized, and should be.

So don't say, "This business about standardized sales talks is not for me," because it is. Read on, please, and find out for yourself.

Here are eight reasons why you should standardize all or parts of your sales talk:

1. When you have a standardized talk that you can rattle off with no strain on your memory, your courage in any sales situation is better. It is most comforting to know exactly what you will say next and the best possible way to say it.

2. Since you know your talk verbatim, you always remember every important fact and benefit about your product.

A sales manager once told me that he gave his salesmen a new product to sell and asked them to state in each interview all seven ways it would benefit the prospect. Then he sent field managers to call with the salesmen to see how they presented their new product. Every field man reported that every salesman they called with failed to state all seven ways in at least 90 per cent of the cases.

3. You can be sure your talk is clear and understandable.

4. When you write out your talk and go over it again and again, you can cut out unnecessary material and thus make it briefer. As Pliny the Younger (who lived in the first century) said, "Nothing pleases as much as brevity." He didn't say that about sales talks, but he could have—if they had had sales talks in his day, and maybe they did!

5. You increase your enthusiasm for the product you sell.

I saw an example of that once when I had a force of investment security salesmen under my management.

I put on a new man who looked promising, but he did not live up to his looks. So I told him either to work up a standardized talk that fitted him or quit.

Up to that time, his enthusiasm for the preferred stock we were selling was far from warm. This, no doubt, explained the poor sales record, for he was really a natural salesman.

To prepare this standardized talk he had to read printed matter about the stock and the company behind it. He had to interview minor company executives. As so often happens with a good product, the more the salesman learned about it, the more excited he became.

This enthusiasm put him, not only "over," but "on top," where he stayed for several years, then advanced to an executive job.

6. As a result of working your talk over and over, you automatically learn it word for word. This is different from "committing it to memory." Because it's your talk and expresses what you deeply believe, you say it naturally and easily.

You trick yourself into *knowing* your talk *"by heart"*

I realized the advantages of a standardized sales talk many years ago when I learned the advantages of a standardized public speech in group selling.

When I took the Dale Carnegie course in effective speaking, over a quarter of a century ago, Dale Carnegie repeatedly told my class, "Never memorize your speeches."

A few months after the end of the course I heard Dale deliver one speech several times, and I noted that each time he used exactly the same words. I thought he had memorized his talk, and I was horrified. How could a man of his integrity teach one way and practice another!

When I knew Dale better, I realized that his preaching and his practice were in accord. He did not commit his talks to memory—*he just accidentally remembered them,* which is different.

Why did Dale remember his talks? It was because when he started to work on a speech, he would go over and over in his mind what he wanted to say. He would add or subtract sentences and phrases, change and rearrange words until he had them to suit him. Now here is the secret:

He worked this talk over and over so many times that he *fixed it in his memory.*

When I began to teach men and women to sell, I recommended that salesmen use the same plan to prepare their sales talks. I found that when salesmen followed this plan, their sales increased.

So will yours!

7. When you write your talk, you have the courage to put in some understatement, something that few salesmen have the hardihood to do in an impromptu talk.

The standardized talk forces the salesman to be accurate, to be exact in his statements—to put it brutally, it forces him to tell the truth. This helps because, as some forgotten sales manager stated, with slight exaggeration, "All salesmen are born truthful, and die liars." (I don't subscribe fully to this statement, but I do admit that a lot of salesmen I have known were mighty careless with the truth.)

_____ CHAPTER 37

Are the objections you raise against standardized sales talks real reasons or plausible reasons?

The one way to be prepared to do your best when you are on that center-stage spot in front of a prospect is: know what you are going to say and exactly the words you will use to say it. This is a sales talk.
—HARRY H. DANIELS, EASTERN DIVISION MANAGER,
ROBERT PALMER CORP., SANTA BARBARA, CALIFORNIA

You may still think that you would not gain enough from standardizing your sales talk to compensate you for the time and effort it will take. You have "objections."

All right, let's see what these "reasons for not buying" this idea are, and how valid they are. Here are, I suspect, some of your objections to the use of a standardized talk:

That old favorite, "My business is different." You state this fact as though it were as original and as epochal as the discovery of gravity, relativity, or soluble coffee.

As soon as I advised you to write your own sales talk, I could hear the clamor of stricken salesmen who moaned, "A standardized talk is all right for mutual fund salesmen or book agents or brush salesmen, but it would never sell *my* prospects."

Let's admit, as I have already, that there are a few exceptions to the rule, "Write out your own standardized talk, and use it." A jobber's salesman who makes nothing but routine calls on grocers will not often need a standardized talk—but then, often he isn't selling, anyway. In many cases, he is merely a traveling order blank with a speaking attachment.

The salesmen for hardware jobbers or grocery jobbers, for example, will tell you that they don't need any sort of "canned" talk because they do not sell. The truth is, however, that any enterprising house in those lines has deals, special promotions, and the like that call for selling. And selling of that kind, to be most effective, calls for a standardized talk.

The reason a lot of order-takers do not learn to sell is because they have no conception of how it would benefit them, so they don't bother!

Once I tried to teach the principles of salesmanship to some men who took orders for a wholesale grocery house in Texas. I am convinced this was my worst educational failure. These men resisted education with almost superhuman pertinacity. Their belief was that in their line of work they never had to use salesmanship, so why bother to learn how to sell.

At one of our class sessions I ran into a dialogue which went like this:

P. H. W.—Sometimes a new grocery store opens in your territory, doesn't it?

Order-taker—Yes.

P. H. W.—You want that business, don't you?

Order-taker—Yes.

P. H. W.—Please tell me now what you would say to the grocer who is about to open in your territory to convince him he should buy from your company rather than from your competitors?

They couldn't tell me—not one of them! They not only didn't have a good, smooth standardized talk to meet this situation; they didn't have any talk at all!

I'll bet those lads are still making up to $35 a week—and earning every cent of it!

Even the old-fashioned "canned" sales talk will work sometimes

Now let's look at the next reason you are not willing to use a standardized sales talk, which is: You are prejudiced against it.

If I asked you why you were prejudiced against it, probably you would say, "Canned talks are stiff and clumsy. They *sound* canned."

Is that a true reason or is it a rationalization? Don't justify your attitude by claiming motives that are, to quote the *Merriam-Webster Dictionary*, "plausible but untrue."

How a "canned" talk sold an old settler

"Nobody with any sense will buy from a salesman who uses a standardized talk," you say. Well, let me tell you what happened to *me*. Recently I subscribed to another magazine. I didn't subscribe for one year—I *subscribed for four!* My wife and I needed another magazine about as much as we needed another virus. I, who rarely do more with a magazine than look at the pictures, was only about twelve or fifteen magazines behind in my scanning, but my wife, Gene, who insists on *reading* the darned things, was, as of that date, 102 magazines behind.

"Why," you ask, "did you buy something you didn't need, want, or have time to use?"

A "canned" sales talk got me! Not only was the talk "canned," but so were the salesman's smile, his compliments, and his thanks. There I was, after forty-odd years in selling and sales training, after teaching over 100,000 men and women to sell, after writing a successful book on selling, and a successful sales course, falling like a tree for that venerable I'm-working-my-way-through-college "canned" talk—something so old that Ben Franklin probably used it when he was selling *Poor Richard's Almanac* back in 1732–1757.

Why did I collapse in the face of a "canned" sales talk? It

was partly from sheer admiration for the way the salesman delivered it and partly because I was hypnotized.

Don't tell me a "canned" talk never works! If it works on an old settler like me, it is likely to sell anybody anything!

When you prepare a standardized talk, keep it natural and convincing—just *say* your talk, then write down what you said

You think you can't prepare a good standardized talk. "I'm a salesman," you say, "not a writer."

A little later, when we come to the place where I tell you how to prepare your talk, you will see that it is mostly done by "talking," and that you are fully competent to do that.

Don't tackle this job of preparing your own standardized talk unless you are determined to become a professional, big-league salesman. If you are satisfied to drag along and make a comfortable living—and get nowhere and take life easy—and live on your children or social security, or both, in your old age, then you should not bother to build a completely effective sales talk.

You love your own talk, even though you know it can be improved. As Ian Harvey said, slightly changed by me, "Bad sales talks, like idiot children, are often loved by their authors."

If, however, you want to be the best, to lead the sales force, to make enough money to enjoy life in your productive years, and still put enough away to support you in retirement, do what I suggest.

In the next chapter I shall tell you how to build a sales talk that may not be exactly irresistible, but close to it.

Most salesmen can increase their earnings a thousand dollars a year, and many have more than doubled their income, merely by doing what I suggest in this section.

To sum up: the reasons you give against a standardized talk are feeble and unconvincing; the reasons why you should use one are convincing and compelling.

So let's find out now how to write all or part of your sales talk.

_____ CHAPTER 38

How to whip your standardized sales talk into such shape that it will increase your sales

> *You must take it [your standard sales talk] into con-*
> *stant study, ceaseless review, until it becomes an insep-*
> *arable part of you. Then you can relax with the pride of*
> *a job well done, and be yourself when the curtain rolls*
> *up and you are on the stage.*
> *Does this sound easy? It isn't.*
> *Only the failures and mediocrities will differ with me.*
> *You won't have time to listen to these bleeding hearts,*
> *if you've dedicated your life to the greatest career and*
> *opportunity in the world today.*
> —HARRY H. DANIELS, EASTERN DIVISION MANAGER,
> ROBERT PALMER CORPORATION, SANTA BARBARA,
> CALIFORNIA, IN *Sales Management*

Soon I shall ask you to stop reading for a while and to start writing your standardized sales talk.

Let's assume that you use the five steps of the selling process set forth in my previous book on salesmanship, *The 5 Great Rules of Selling*, and given here on page 36.

"I don't use those steps—I use only four and they have different names," you say. Don't let a little difference in names or numbers disturb you. If you are following any recognized selling process, you are close enough to ours so that you can apply to your formula what I say about the "Five Great Rules."

Of course, you are not going to try to do the whole job of writing in one great, big tiresome sitting. Instead, if you are smart, you will work on it for a while each day until you finish it.

Here are the six steps to
develop a good sales talk

Step 1. Decide which part of your sales talk you will standardize first. I recommend that you start with the Conviction Step—the part in which you give your prospect the facts about your product, together with the benefits related to each fact.

Step 2. List on separate pieces of paper every fact or sales point about your product or service that is of importance to the average prospect.

Step 3. Write under each fact the related benefit.

Step 4. Decide whether or not you will need any evidence to support your claim about your product.

For example, if your point-and-reason is, "Because this pen is light, it does not tire you to write with it," you do not need supporting evidence. It is obviously true. If, on the other hand, you say, "This equipment will save you $50 a month," you will need some evidence that it actually will save $50 a month.

Step 5. Go back over your points and see which ones you can omit.

For example, if you were selling an automobile, you might take a list of specifications and find twenty-five or fifty selling points for your car. You would probably want to eliminate all but a few points—those that would most help you to close sales.

Step 6. Arrange your points in the most effective order. Since you have written them on separate sheets of paper you can arrange and rearrange them, until you have them to suit you.

Be sure to put your points and reasons on paper in easily spoken salesman's language. To do it, speak each point and reason over and over—aloud.

You can get a world of ideas about the best way to construct your sales talk by reading *How to Write a Speech,* by Edward J. Hegarty, published by the McGraw-Hill Book Company. Nine-tenths of what Ed says about speechwriting applies equally to sales-talk writing. Incidentally, if you ever have to write speeches, this book is a true friend. I consider it the most practical book on the subject ever written.

_____ CHAPTER 39

Ask yourself the questions presented in this chapter—they have helped many salesmen to improve their talks

Salesmen may be able to do things, know things, understand things—but most salesmen find it difficult to give clear, logical explanations.

—AUTHOR UNKNOWN

For almost a half century I have used the questions which follow in this and succeeding chapters to check sales talks. They will help you to be sure your talk is headed in the right direction, that it omits unnecessary things, and includes all necessary items.

We will give you questions to ask yourself: (1) as you write; and (2) as you check your talk for errors and omissions after it is written.

Ask yourself these questions before you start to write your talk:

1. Am I sure exactly why the prospect should buy my product or service?

John M. Wilson, formerly vice president, sales, of the National Cash Register Company, said in *Creative Selling*:

To do more third-dimensional selling it is necessary to:

(a) Uncover the need.
(b) Prove the need.
(c) Prove that your product or service is the answer. In fact, you do not know whether or not you have a prospect until you uncover the need ...

To sweep away the prospect's sense of complacency with the situation (of doing without your product) is to show him the specific shortcomings of his present product or service ... When the prospect is convinced he may suffer a loss by failure to act, he is immediately eager to take the action.

2. What am I going to say in answer to my prospect's inevitable double-barreled question about my product: "What is it, and what will it do for me?"
3. What can I say to convince my prospect that I am not just an order-grabber, but that in addition to being a salesman for my company, I want to be a sort of assistant purchasing agent for him?
4. What can I say tactfully to convince the prospect that his present situation is unsatisfactory? How can I make him dissatisfied—without offending him?

Don't neglect this step. As Ernest Jones said in the *American Salesman Magazine*, "A contented man can't be sold a damned thing."

A man who is satisfied with his present method of dictating letters will never buy a dictating machine. Once you have shown him a better way, pointed out his lack, made him discontented, you can begin to sell him.

So make your prospect discontented with his present situation. Point out his lack. Have you been doing this—consciously and invariably? If not, this failure could account for some of your lost sales.

A standard sales talk is not delivered like a commencement address

Put *questions* into your pitch. This gives your prospect a chance to talk and gives you a chance to listen and learn. As

Elmer G. Leterman said, "A respectful listener not only makes a good impression—he stands a chance to learn something." Especially try to get your prospect to talk about his wants and needs.

5. How can I get the prospect to *do something?*
  A. How can I get him to look at some exhibit?
  B. How can I get him to read a testimonial?
  C. How can I get him to pick up and handle the article I'm selling?
6. How can I put some showmanship into my talk?

Don't say, "Oh, I sell bonds (or coffee or wheelbarrows)." No chance to get any showmanship into that! Brother, if you *sell,* you can use showmanship.

7. Have I figured out what my competitors may say and do to get the business away from me? Have I decided how to counter their arguments?
8. How can I bring into my talk any available sales helps?
9. Have I decided what objections I should answer *before* they are raised?
10. Have I answered the question so often in prospects' minds, "Did you just drop in because you were going by or have you a real reason for being here?"
11. How can I work a demonstration into my talk?
12. How can I get in step with my prospect—what can I say that will get him to say, "Yes, that's so"?
13. What suggestions can I make that promise to solve the prospect's problems?
14. I want to be able to change my talk as I deliver it so that it will appeal specifically to the dominant buying motive of the prospect I am "pitching." How can I so word my talk that this will be practicable?

For example, if you were writing a talk to sell a mutual fund, you might cover points like management, history, past record, then leave a gap. If your prospect's dominant motive was greed, you could then stress in the "gap" the great possibilities of profit. If his motive was safety, you could point out the protection provided by good management, diversification, and the policy of investing in blue chip stocks.

15. What evidence can I use to support my claims about my product? Do I have any examples or incidents which would help to support my main claims? For example, suppose you say, "This dingbat is made of steel, and hence is strong"—then you could add an example such as, "John Smith tells me that . . ."

Remember that every important sales point, every important claim in your talk, should, if possible, be supported by some kind of *evidence*. One of the most practical kinds is an example or incident.

16. Will my prospect be convinced by my examples? Test your examples by asking:
    A. Are they real   did they actually happen?
    B. Are they specific—do they give facts, names, figures?
    C. Are the examples believable?
17. Have I testimonials that will support my claims?

My friend, Mrs. Ethel Knight "Polly" Pollard, gave me this suggestion for telephone testimonials:

If your testimonial is from someone the prospect knows personally or by reputation, sometimes it is effective to say, "Just pick up your telephone and talk with Mr. Blank. Let him tell you what our product has done for him." If the call is long distance, be sure to add, "Of course, I'll pay for the call!"

Naturally, you must have asked in advance for your customer's permission to use him occasionally for a "telephone testimonial." The mere fact that I suggested the call often convinced the prospect. Often, he would say, in effect, "Oh no, I won't bother to call him—I'm convinced."

I've used this technique in selling everything from educational courses, real estate and insurance to soda pop. I know it works!

18. Have I any books, magazines, statistics, charts, and diagrams which will serve as evidence to support my claims?

Have them handy, but show only enough to support your claim.

CHAPTER **40**

Questions asked in this chapter will help you make your sales talk interesting, convincing, and productive

> *A prefabricated plan [to sell] is your best assurance against straying off your course . . .*
> *A planned sales presentation . . . is as necessary as any other phase of your selling program. Perhaps even more so . . .*
> —WALLACE K. LEWIS IN
> *How to Make Yourself a Born Salesman*

As you plug along on this talk-writing job, please remember that *your objective is to turn out a talk that will get the orders so you can get the money.*

To keep your talk from running off the track as you write it, ask yourself these questions:

1. Are my words too stiff, stilted, or high-flown, or, on the other hand, are they cheap, boorish, or slangy? Remember, before you write any paragraph in your talk, you should think it through, then say it aloud at least a half-dozen times. Then write it the way it sounds best.

2. Am I trying to be too clever or too humorous? Humor can be as dangerous in a sales talk as a firebug in a lumber yard.

3. Do I talk in terms, not of what the product *is*, but of

what it will *do* to benefit the prospect? Not "This pen is light," but "Because this pen is light, it will not tire your hand."

4. Do I picture the prospect as already owning the product I am trying to sell him? As, "When you are behind the wheel of this car," or "As you finish a hard day's typing on this machine . . ."

5. Do I understate rather than overstate? Is what I say true—and does it *sound* true? Not, "This car will go 100 miles an hour," but "Calvin Smith, the banker, told me he chased a robber in this car at over 100 miles an hour."

6. Have I used concrete language? If it is concrete, it brings a picture to the mind's eye, or a sound to the mind's ear, or a sensation of touch, taste, or smell. Remember that concrete language—picture language—makes your sales talk more vivid and compelling.

Substitute specific facts for vague general claims

7. Have I avoided loose, general, non-specific statements? Don't say, "It's the best." Nobody believes a mere claim of that sort. Be specific—explain what you mean by "best." Tell why you think it is best. Give evidence.

8. Do I avoid such thin, flabby statements as, "It will outwear our competitor's product?" "Prove it," says your prospect. "People around here have been using them satisfactorily for years." "Name the people," says your prospect.

The trouble with most of the claims a salesman makes is that they are general rather than specific. Claims don't have to be in loose language. For instance, an automobile salesman might say, "This car is guaranteed to give you twenty miles per gallon or more." That's specific. It is easier for most of them to say, "This car is light on using gasoline"—so they say it, and expect the prospect to be satisfied with that.

9. Is my language specific, as opposed to general? Is it explicit? Does it state things exactly as did the back-country hillbilly, whose son had been brought into court and sentenced

for a breach of the peace? Part of this "breaching" was his use
of a knife on his adversary. "Can't figure where that boy gits
his meanness. Now you take me—I never stuck a knife *deep*
in nobody!" That statement "specified" exactly.

Another fine example of exactness in diction comes from
the retail field, via the *Saturday Evening Post*: "Floor manager
to adjustment clerk as angry complainant waits: 'The customer
is always right, Benson. Misinformed, perhaps; inexact; bull-
headed; fickle; ignorant; even abominably stupid; but *never*
wrong.'"

The salesman who is addicted to generalities falls into the
classification that I think Don Raihle had in mind when he
said, in "Harry Thompson's Scratch Pad Column": "Quiet
people aren't the only ones who don't say much."

Now for one last question:

10. Does my talk tell my prospect what my product will
do for him? If it does, it will hold him in his chair indefinitely;
if not, it may drive him to excuse himself "for a minute,"
sneak out, and never come back.

Tens of millions of dollars of commissions are lost by the
salesmen of the United States each year because they talk
about what the product *is* when they should talk about *what
it does* for the prospect.

CHAPTER 41

When you *"work over"* your talk, you not only improve it, but also you fix it forever in your memory

Some salesmen never make a mistake because they never make a move.

I have suggested a couple of times that you "work over" each sales point in your talk until you get it in the most effective possible language for you. For instance:

Suppose you are selling a dictating machine, and that you want to make the point that it has a device which enables the user to play back the last few sentences he has dictated, just by pressing a button.

Here are some of the ways you could stress that point:

1. "If you want to listen to what you have just dictated, you don't have to set the needle back—you just press a button and get a rerun."

2. Or, "Sometimes, when you are dictating, you are interrupted, aren't you? Then, when you are ready to resume dictating, you don't know where you left off. In that case, press the button right here (point to it) and you hear the last one or two sentences that you just dictated."

3. Or, "If you want to hear what you have just dictated, press this button and back it comes."

All right, suppose you decided that you liked No. 2 best— then you would start to work on it. You would begin with the first sentence, "Sometimes, when you are dictating, you are interrupted, aren't you?"

You would say it aloud a couple of times. Immediately you would see that the two "you ares" should be made into "you'res."

Then that word "interrupted" is too long and too vague, too general. How about, "Often, when you're dictating, your phone rings, doesn't it?" That's specific—and, alas, true!

Now let's take the next sentence, "Then, when you're ready to resume dictating, you don't know where you left off." What can be done with that sentence?

To start with, "resume" is too fancy. How about "start back dictating"? Then, "where you left off" is hardly specific. Let's say, "what you said before the phone broke in." That leaves us with "Often, when you are dictating, your phone rings, doesn't it?" Let's see again—that word "dictating" bothers me. I hate anything ending with "ing." So try again with, "Sometimes, when you dictate, the phone rings, doesn't it? Then, when you start to dictate again, you don't know what you said before the phone broke in."

Then you decide the last sentence suits you okay. This is what you have worked out:

"Sometimes, when you dictate, your phone rings, doesn't it? Then, when you start to dictate again, you don't remember what you said before the phone broke in. In that case, press the button right here (point to it) and back comes your last sentence."

To test your talk, say it aloud

Now you give it the "say-it-aloud" test. To do it, say aloud what you have just written a half-dozen times.

The first sentence doesn't "say" just right. How about, "Sometimes, as you dictate, your phone rings." That is shorter and leaves out the "doesn't it?"—which isn't necessary because anyone will admit that when he starts to dictate the phone almost always rings!

Then take the next sentence, and say it aloud at least six times. What's wrong? Well, to begin with, it sounds as though you had tried to write blank verse—and failed.

That's bad. So, let's try it this way: "Then, when you start to dictate again, what happens? You've forgotten what you said."

Anyway, that is shorter, and it is in the spoken language—mine anyway!

All right, try the last sentence aloud a half-dozen times. It "speaks" all right. But I have forgotten one of the big rules: "Always let the prospect demonstrate for himself." So you say, "In that case, Mr. Blank, press the button right here (point to it) and back it comes." Then pass the mouthpiece over to the prospect and let him try it.

Let's assume that now we have a paragraph that is a finished product. Here it is:

Sometimes, as you dictate, your phone rings. Then when you start to dictate again, what happens? You've forgotten what you said. In that case, Mr. Blank, press the button right here and back it comes.

Say it over again a half-dozen times to see if it still sounds all right. It not only sounds all right, but presto, you have remembered it! Never again will you have to make this point the second-best way.

I told you before you started it would be hard work!

At this point, you are probably aghast, and saying to yourself, "Does this man, Whiting, think I have time to go through my whole sales talk this way?"

All I ask is that you try this technique on just one point—your most important one. When you see how much you have improved your talk on this point, you will have the courage and inspiration to work on the next most important one.

CHAPTER 42

After you finish writing your talk, "work it over" again to make certain the bugs are out and the juice is in

> *The old-fashioned sales talk isn't coming back—it just never went away.*

It is better, I think, to check parts of your talk as you go along. The most practical way for most of us to "work over" our talk is to write as much as we have time for at one sitting, then correct it. Let it cool off a day or two, then check it again with these test questions:

1. Does my talk sound as though I expected to get the order? It will if you continually picture the prospect as owning the product. As: "Your drives will average twenty yards longer with this club."

2. Have I too many "verys?" Remember the old newspaper rule, "Don't use 'very' oftener than once a week."

3. Should I cut out a lot of unnecessary adjectives? Avoid the "adjectives habit." It will weaken your talk.

4. Have I dragged in any clichés, bromides, or stereotyped, hackneyed, lifeless expressions? If so, drag them right out again!

Especially avoid clichés. A cliché, according to the *Thorndike-Barnhart Dictionary*, "is a worn-out or trite expression." For example, "each and every," "in the foreseeable future," "in depth," "image," "frankly," "right," "the hard core of."

These, and ten thousand other clichés, have been damaged by over-use, and should go into the garbage pail along with a lot of tongue-worn slang. Stop using clichés and you will force yourself to discover brighter, fresher language. Have I warned you before against clichés? I have. I don't even guarantee not to do it again. I hate them and so should you.

Now then let's get back to the questions you should ask yourself:

5. Does my talk sound as if I were more interested in grabbing the order than in benefiting the prospect? If it does, change it!

6. Does my talk sound sincere? Weed out anything sly, tricky, or too smart. Good, old-fashioned honesty pays in a sales talk—as elsewhere.

7. Is there anything in the talk that would irritate the prospect? Or is it courteous, good-natured, frank, friendly?

8. Have I dragged in any statistics that I can leave out?

9. Can I use charts instead of figures? They are easier to understand and are usually more interesting.

10. Have I tried out on several people what I propose to say, to get their reactions and suggestions? If not, I advise you to do it. As John Dolman, Jr. says in his *Handbook of Public Speaking*, "To develop thought most effectively for sharing with others, he [the salesman] must seek the reaction of others to his talk."

11. Do I give or imply all the facts my prospect will want to know about my product? For example, the old Packard slogan, "Ask the man who owns one," implied that the car had many good qualities, without saying so.

12. If I took the name of my product out of my sales talk, and inserted the name of my competitor's product in its place, would my sales talk then be as good for him as it is for me?

Surely you can find some exclusive features of your product or service that can't truthfully be said about products that compete with yours. If you can't, then you need a new advertising agent, a new sales manager, or a new product.

13. Does what I say sound as if I were talking to a friend or to an enemy? Is it argumentative or belligerent? I hope not.

14. Have I written any part of my talk in the lingo or jargon of my business? Recently, I said to a friend, "This matter

should be set l.c." His jaw fell; he just looked at me. He didn't know that "l.c." was a printer's abbreviation for "lower case," and it would not have helped him if he had, because he didn't know what "lower case" was either! I could so easily and clearly have said, "This matter should not be set in all capitals."

Try to standardize your questions as carefully as you do the other parts of your talk. In many cases the questions should bear on the prospect's business. Here is where knowledge of your prospect and his company are most valuable. You certainly can't ask intelligent questions about a business you know little about.

Take, for instance, this one:

> A professor of physics was crossing the border into Mexico at Tia Juana to see the bull fights one Sunday afternoon when the Mexican guard stopped his car. After the professor gave his name and address, the guard asked:
> "What business are you in, please?"
> "Physics," replied the professor.
> A few moments elapsed while the Mexican guard pondered this development. Then he suddenly spoke up:
> "Wholesale or retail?"
> —David Castle in the magazine *Quote*

CHAPTER 43

You'll find it a bit of a problem to ask helpful questions

Here are some suggestions about asking questions summarized from Roy Garn's book, *The Magic Power of Emotional Appeal*:

1. Word your questions so that you will get the answer you

want. (For instance, "Wouldn't it be wonderful if you could get your desk cleared every night by five o'clock?")

2. Be sure your prospect knows the answer to your questions. ("Wouldn't your salesmen sell more if they knew the prospect's dominant buying motive?" would be a stupid question if your listener had never heard of a "dominant buying motive.")

3. Ask questions that deal with the prospect and his needs and desires. (For example, "Wouldn't you like to cut ten strokes off your golf score?")

4. Would I be willing to turn my talk over to the Big Boss to read? (If not, change it so that you would.)

5. Are my sentences short enough? (If they are too long, they are harder to say and harder to understand. If you have a sentence that runs much over fifteen words, leave out something—or if you can't, split it into two sentences.)

6. On the basis of my sales talk, would I buy from *me*?

*   *   *

Well, those are the check questions. Now, what are you going to do with them?

The least you can do is to check the talk you now use—or the parts of it you have standardized—against the questions given in this and previous chapters.

What I hope you will do—for your own profit and success—is to write a new talk, one point (or one paragraph) at a time. The formula is:

1. Get in your mind the material you want to put in that paragraph.
2. Say it over a half-dozen times. Try different ways.
3. Write it out.
4. Test it with the questions.

At first, this testing is slow work. However, after you have tested a few paragraphs, you will find you can do it quite rapidly and easily.

As soon as you finish checking one paragraph, work it into your talk, and use it. Don't wait until you have finished the whole job.

Don't put off the job of standardizing your talk, or such parts of it as are suitable for "self-canning."

The job is not too hard, if you take it a little at a time, and it will make your selling easier and your earnings larger.

What more can you ask of one idea?

Now, turn back to Chapter 41 and read again—carefully and thoughtfully—about how to "work over" your talk. Do it without delay. Please, for your own sake!

――――――――――――――――――――――― CHAPTER 44

Sage thoughts by the sages on an unpopular subject: hard work!

Since I have been recommending to you for many pages past that you tackle a job that calls for hard work, perhaps it would be wise to give you now some remarks—mostly frivolous— about work, some by philosophers, some by mere writers.

*   *   *

To youth I have but three words of counsel, "Work, work, work!"

—BISMARCK

*   *   *

His whole concern with work was considering how he might best avoid it.

—ANATOLE FRANCE

*   *   *

I go on working for the same reason a hen goes on laying.

—H. L. MENCKEN

*   *   *

I like work; it fascinates me. I can sit and look at it for hours.

             —JEROME K. JEROME

*   *   *

If any [man] would not work, neither should he eat.

             —THESSALONIANS

*   *   *

There is no substitute for hard work.

             —THOMAS A. EDISON

*   *   *

Work is something to do when you can't sleep.

How to cure "slumps" and solve other problems that bedevil the poor salesmen (and also good ones)

Probably you expect to find toward the end of a book like this nothing but "leavings."

Happily, that is not true of this book.

One single rule given here revolutionized the life of a salesman I know.

It may revolutionize yours. So try all the rules presented in this section. They work. The time to start is today—as soon as you lay down this book.

———————————————————————————————— CHAPTER 45

This one section may help you more than all the rest of the book

This section on "slumps" is a serious (and I hope successful) attempt to show you why you get into selling slumps and how you can get out of them.

If you are a chronic victim of slump sickness, this section is important to you.

However, even if you are one of those slumpless salesmen—which I have heard about but never met—you will find it worth while to read this section. It contains ideas that will help any salesman—good, bad, or mediocre—to sell more.

My purpose, when I started to write this section, was merely to tell salesmen the cause, control, and cure of slumps.

As I gathered together the slump cures, I realized that I had in them a lot of the rules of good selling, as well.

Just about any rule that will help you cure "slumpitis" will help you to be a better salesman. Equally, any rule which will help you to build up your morale, will help you to build up your sales.

So, read on.

_____ CHAPTER **46**

If you are now in a selling slump, cheer up —"slumpitis" can be cured and I tell you here how to cure it

> *Plato said, "Nothing in human affairs is worth any great anxiety," which proves he was never in a selling slump!*

If I can tell you how to get out of your selling slumps, and how to stay out of them, I shall, I'm sure, have done you a service.

If I can also tell you and other salesmen how to *avoid* slumps, I shall indeed be a benefactor to all selling humanity, and shall deserve a medal struck off in my honor. (P.S. I won't get it. PHW)

You know exactly what a slump is, or do you?

Let's be sure first that we all agree what a "slump" really is. The verb "to slump" means "to drop suddenly and hard, or to fall in a heap." The dictionaries do not say so, but we salesmen know that a slump is also a period of low morale.

We all know what morale is, too, even if we can't define it. A striking definition was given by a veteran sergeant who said of morale, "It's what makes your legs do what your head knows ain't possible."

What we really need is a definition of the phrase "low morale." "I may not know how to define it, but I sure know it when I feel it," a friend said to me. Most of us are sure of only one thing about low morale: to wit, it's the state of mind we are in when we are in the selling "doldrums."

The best way I can think of to get a definition of "low morale" is to reverse the dictionary definition of "morale." That gives us this definition: *"Low morale* is a state of individual psychological ill-being, low spirits, gloominess and depression, based on such factors as physical and mental ill-health, a feeling of uselessness, a lack of sense of purpose and a loss of confidence in yourself and your future."

This modified definition is based on *Webster's Third International Dictionary,* copyrighted 1961 by G. C. Merriam, publishers of the Merriam-Webster Dictionaries (by permission).

One other thing we know for sure about slumps and the accompanying low morale is that they are as debilitating as the flu and as slow to cure as an ingrowing disposition. My late irreverent and agnostic friend, E. B. Williamson, used to sound this slogan, "Cheer up, there is no Hell." He was a scientist. If he had been a salesman, he would have known that there is a Hell, and that for salesmen Hell is a slump, and a slump is Hell!

Sales slumps come in cycles

Most salesmen will tell you that low morale is always due to poor production, and that the only way to cure it is to sell more. Heaven knows, in most cases this is true. However, sales managers have noticed that low morale tends to come in cycles. I read recently in *The New Yorker* that "The emotional state of sane adults varies in cycles of from . . . sixteen to thirty-three days, depending on the adult."

A writer who recognized the existence of cycles in human lives was the late Paul Specher, who wrote, in his book, *154 Messages from Paul Specher:*

Give yourself the courage to meet the valley days when they come. We have learned that the cycles in the business chart are a part of a program, a swing of the pendulum that is inherent in life and in its affairs. The ups and downs in a man's state of mind likewise are a part of the scheme of things.

We have hilltop days and valley days, and the trick in life is not to be discouraged when the valley days come, not to believe that all of life ahead is to be a valley day.

Never forget that discouragement is a part of the plan and that if we will only take to the road fearlessly, walk on, one step and then another, so hilltop will follow valley as surely as day follows night.

To convert that scientific fact into salesmen's language, "Low morale comes in cycles." Even the best salesmen have periods of depression. Somehow the good salesmen manage to "live above their slumps." So will you, if you heed the suggestions in this section.

To keep up your morale is a job that never ends

As Horace Russell Smith said in *Manager's Magazine*, "To keep up the high morale of the individual life insurance agent is a never completed job."

With the successful salesman, slumps are spaced far apart and are relatively harmless. With the unsuccessful salesman— well, to modify an old Spanish proverb, "A salesman is always right who suspects that he will soon be in another slump."

"Slumpitis" is as natural, normal, and human as colds and corns. Your objective is to make the visits to "slumpland" few and brief. If you have too many slumps, and stay in them too long, you will inevitably lose your job—unless you're the boss' son-in-law!

Here is, in substance, though not in exact words, something interesting on this subject that Harry Simmons wrote for the magazine, *Advertising and Selling*:

Salesmen are not fired because they lack skill. They fall into slumps and fail because they are human beings who permit human weaknesses to develop. Finally, they reach a point where they have to be fired. They become lazy or dishonest—or both. They develop fears and frustrations. They sulk.

The mistakes and human frailties that cause slumps can be detected and corrected. Correct them, and you cure the slump.

Writers of popular psychology tell us that it is natural and normal for people to run into periods of depression and self-doubt.

Don't consider that you are a unique character because you occasionally lose confidence in yourself and in your ability to sell.

So, to sum up this chapter:

1. Admit that slumps—poor morale and depressions—are natural at times.
2. Start to work to learn how to cure them. And remember always this great truth: A *slump is not a fact—it is a state of mind.*

_____ CHAPTER 47

If you are the victim of a slump, your first step toward a cure is to find out what causes the slump

If you were so sick you called a doctor, and if that doctor merely glanced at you and said, "I don't know what's the matter with you, but take a couple of aspirin, go to bed, and you'll feel better . . . ," well, you wouldn't call that doctor again, because he didn't bother to find out what was the cause of your distress.

So, when you suffer from selling distress, your first job is to find out what ails you.

Maybe it's a slump, maybe not —anyhow, find out for sure

Nobody can give you wiser advice than yourself.
                                        —CICERO

So, to make a quick check, ask yourself:

1. Is my morale moribund, if not stone dead?
2. Am I depressed, moody, sullen, short-tempered, quarrelsome?
3. Do I refuse to take an active part in sales meetings? Do I even refuse to ask questions?
4. Do I avoid any discussion of what's wrong with me?
5. Do I dread to face prospects?
6. Do I feel that it is better for me to go to a picture show than to make more calls?

If you have these symptoms, you don't need to hire a practicing psychologist to tell you what's wrong with you.

You, my friend, are in a "slump."

If you have these symptoms, you don't need a diagnosis—you need a cure!

The first step toward more sales and higher morale is for you to find out exactly *why* you have these symptoms—to look for causes.

Now, let's analyze a bit

Let's consider now how to conduct this analysis of yourself, your selling habits, and, in general, your plan of life. Do this, and with no further thought you may solve your slump problem and your morale problem. Before you do this, I want to give you one warning:

Don't think it is easy to get out of slumps—so my advice is, stop looking for easy and painless ways to get back into production, and try the hard but sure way which I am going to suggest.

As the *American Salesman* said, "The reason many salesmen never get anywhere in life is because, when opportunity knocks, they are out in the back yard looking for four-leaf clovers."

And remember the old New England saying: "Of two courses of action, choose the harder. It always proves the easier in the long run."

CHAPTER 48

Here we face the critical questions—"Why do I get into slumps, and what can I do to get out and stay out?"

You are ready now to face the problem, "Why do I get into slumps and what can I do about it?"

Lois Landauer, in the *American Salesman,* suggests six causes for fading sales and ebbing morale. Ask yourself regarding each of the six "Is this the cause of my slump?": (1) Financial problems? (2) Domestic problems? (3) Staleness? (4) Complacency? (5) Loss of confidence? (6) Pressure from above?

If you are a salesman who sells to wholesalers, jobbers, or retailers for redistribution, you might ask yourself the five questions that follow. I have changed them slightly from the original list, which was written by Porter J. Henry, Jr., and which appeared in the *American Salesman*:

1. Has my territory changed? (For example, have drug stores in my territory lost business to supermarkets?)
2. Do I use these changes as alibis for lost orders, instead of basing my sales approach on them?
3. Do I make fewer calls than I once did?
4. Do I make a higher percentage of calls on big customers?
5. Have I changed my standard sales "pitch"?

Analyze your situation fearlessly

Please answer the questions in this chapter honestly and fearlessly. Don't rationalize—that is, don't "attribute all your actions to motives that are creditable and worthy." Instead, make an adequate analysis to determine the true motives that prompted the actions.

In an article in the magazine *Sales Management* entitled "The Ten Biggest Mistakes Salesmen Make," George N. Kahn pointed out that, when a salesman loses a sale, he is always ready with an explanation. It is never his fault. To quote Mr. Kahn:

> The salesman doesn't often bother to test the validity of his rationalization. He accepts it at face value. He automatically excuses himself from any personal responsibilities.

Did you find in this chapter the reason why you have slump trouble? Well, whether you did or didn't, let's now approach your problem in another way. Let's ask ourselves some additional penetrating, scrutinizing questions that may give us the answer to the question, "What'n blazes is wrong with us?"

_____ **CHAPTER 49**

No matter how well you are selling—or how badly—you will profit if you answer the questions in this chapter

All right, we have discussed some of the broad, general reasons why you are in a slump.

"I'm not in a slump," you say.

Cheers for you!

In spite of your sales success, however, please read the questions in this chapter. They suggest ways you can sell more.

Before you ask yourself the questions that follow, write in detail your answer to this question: "Why am I not making as many sales as I feel I should?" Do this even if you are on a sales binge and leading your sales force. (Remember, you can always sell more, right up to the time you sell the entire output of your factory—which is hard to do if you sell insurance, investment securities, or educational courses, especially!)

If you will write carefully and completely this list of reasons why you are selling below par, you may in this way solve the problem of why your sales sag and your morale wobbles (if such is the case) or, if you are selling well, what you need to do to increase sales and income. Now, get paper and pencil and start.

When you have completed this list, ask yourself the questions that follow:

1. "Have I discarded a successful sales talk for one not so good?" Salesmen often do—I've seen them do it.

Don't rush along without giving this question some thought. You say, "I haven't changed my talk at all." But are you sure? Think back carefully to the talk you used and the sales methods you used when you were selling successfully. Have you perhaps added anything? Have you dropped anything? Do you deliver your talk with the same force and enthusiasm? Do you believe in your product as you once did? Do you demonstrate it as often and as well as you did in the good old happy days when you were really selling?

And here's some good advice: Learn why you slumped today—and you'll know how to avoid slumps tomorrow.

If you find that you have changed your sales talk—for the worse—try to recall the one which was successful for you in the past, just what you said and how you said it, just what you did and how you did it. Recall your words, your tone, your manner, and your attitude—then say it and do it in tomorrow's selling as you said it and did it when you were at your sales peak.

Remember, the sales talk you want is the one that sells, and the sales talk that sells today is probably much like the one that sold last week and last year.

2. "Is the tone of my talk right or wrong? Is it an 'I' tone or a 'you' tone?"

As you deliver your talk, do you think of the benefits your

prospect will gain when he uses your product, or do you think only of the commission you will be paid if this prospect buys from you? In other words, is your attitude right?

If you honestly believe that the product you sell will benefit the prospect—if you think, as you talk, about what *he* will gain, not of what *you* will gain—your tone will be right.

If the tone of your talk is a selfish, money-grabbing one, you can easily correct it. Just think of yourself as an assistant purchasing agent for your prospect, figure out what the prospect wants and needs, then tell him how your product will supply his wants and needs.

3. "Do I talk too long? Is my pitch practically endless? Do I bore my prospects with sales conversation?"

The cure for long-windedness is to write out your talk, then boil it down.

4. "Would my sales talk sell *me* if I were the prospect?"

That is a good question for you to ask yourself about once a day. Go back over your talk, sentence by sentence, and ask yourself, "Would I 'buy' that statement if I were a prospect?"

Try this analysis. You will be astonished what it will do to improve your sales talk.

A good golf score or a good sales score—which?

5. "Do outside interests interfere with my selling?"

A salesman I know who has everything a successful salesman needs except the right attitude puts golf first, sales second. So he fails at both. Another salesman who tried to sell a sales-training course for us also had a jack-leg sideline of insurance. You know what happened to him—he failed—on both jobs!

I suspect that many salesmen who have low sales morale have it because they can't put all their efforts into one thing—sales-making.

Because sales work is so demanding, you can't successfully share it with any other serious occupation. Also, if you have to carry a sideline—just to eat—then your primary line is the wrong one for you.

What would you think of a physician who had a sideline of plumbing, or a lawyer who dabbled in ditch-digging?

Before some physician friend becomes annoyed by that statement let me explain that some of my physician and surgeon friends raise Palomino horses and Black Angus cattle, but not for profit. Quite the contrary! This is a hobby—often an expensive one—that gives them some needed relaxation and recreation. It is not a secondary job.

To sum it up: Don't have a sideline, and don't have an unrelated job.

_____ **CHAPTER 50**

Don't hesitate to change your talk so long as the change improves it, but don't drop successful techniques

> *Big men become big by doing what they didn't want to do when they didn't want to do it.*
> *Supervision, 1–64*

Our aim at this time is to find out what you are doing that you ought not to do, or what you are failing to do that you ought to do. These are important points, whether you are in the depths of a slump or at the height of sales success. So here goes more probing to find out why you do not sell more:

6. "Do I lose my morale and sink into slumps because I fail to do some of the things I know I ought to do?"

Lots of us fail to cure low morale as we fail to cure obesity. We know that the cure for excessive corpulence is to eat less, but we go right ahead and eat more, and die before our time —and deserve to!

This excerpt from *Human Relations in Management* I believe supports my point:

It would seem that the man who wants to succeed would study, drill, drive himself to do the things necessary for success (or to get himself out of a slump). But too few men have the necessary drive within themselves. They *want to,* but they don't *want to enough.* ... As A. E. Smith says, "People very rarely fail because they intend to. They fail because they fail to do what they intended to do."

So ask yourself, "What do I now fail to do that I formerly intended to do?"

7. Do you want to know how to cure laziness and shiftlessness? So do I. So have all the employers since people started to hire out to do work which was undoubtedly long long ago.

Nobody can cure a man's laziness but that man himself.

So remember this—if you continue to be lazy and a "nogood," it is your own choice.

Let's be optimistic for a change

If you are depressed by this long string of questions about what is wrong with you and your selling, cheer up. In the next chapter we'll indulge in an exercise in optimism.

_____ CHAPTER 51

It will cheer you up to consider your good points as a salesman and why you should be successful—even if you aren't!

We have talked so far in this section about the negative side of the morale problem. We've considered why salesmen get into slumps. Perhaps you needed this. As Barney Baruch said, "Failure is a far better teacher than success."

We know, though, that it is dangerous to think only of what is wrong. So now let's list the reasons why you should be selling normally, why your morale should be high and your sales volume satisfactory.

Start with the reasons why you believe your product is better than that of your competitors'. Bring out your paper and pencil now and write them down.

Next, list your personal qualifications to sell this product. Here are some of your probable advantages and points of strength, adapted from a list in Louis E. Bisch's *Why Be Shy?* (List only those desirable qualities that you really possess.)

A. You have at least a reasonably active imagination—and sense enough not to let it run away with you.
B. You know how to use showmanship to enliven and strengthen your sales talks.
C. You do what you say you will—*when* you say you will.
D. You try constantly to improve yourself as a salesman by taking sales courses and reading sales books and magazines.
E. You have a "winning way." Your prospects like you and like to buy from you.
F. You handle orders and reports carefully and promptly.
G. Fear is not one of your handicaps.
H. You keep your clothes neatly pressed and your linen and your body clean. You never neglect to shave.
I. You try to think not only of the interests of your company, but also of those of your prospect. You are a salesman for your company and an "assistant purchasing agent" for your prospects.
J. You believe in the product you sell. You honestly feel that it is better than anything offered by your competitors.
K. In all your dealings you are strictly honest. You never try to take an unfair advantage of your prospects—or even of your competitors.
L. You probably don't know what your IQ is, but you are convinced it is high enough for the job you are doing.
M. You have a conscience and you keep it in good running order.

N. You talk fluently but stop frequently. You ask a lot of questions of your prospect and you give him a chance to talk.

O. You win friends because you have tact. You rarely say or do anything that offends people.

P. You are a "good loser." You don't sulk or get unduly depressed when you lose an order or a prospect.

Q. You welcome criticism when it is designed to help you to improve.

Next, list the advantages you have which are not mentioned above.

Quite a list, isn't it!

Since you have all these good qualities, you ought to be able to sell—easily and copiously!

"Yes, but suppose I don't have all these advantages?" you ask. Well, maybe that tells you why you are in a slump and what you should do about it.

CHAPTER **52**

Let's resume our study of what's wrong with your sales efforts

Now that we have thought a while on the cheerful subject of what's right with us and our selling, let's go back to asking questions designed to help us find out why we get into slumps. That should help us to learn what we can do to cure that dangerous selling disease, "slumpitis."

The next question as to possible reasons is:

8. "Do I get into periods of selling depression because I don't display enough pep and zizzer?"

If you fail in animation, it's because you don't try. Any salesman who isn't sick or paralyzed can be animated. You can turn animation off and on as you do electricity or draught beer.

Surely any salesman who wants to impress prospects favorably can be "sprightly and vivacious"—unless he's too all-fired lazy!

P.S. Don't confuse the word "animation" with the word "enthusiasm." Those two words don't mean the same thing. "Animation" is a surface manifestation—"enthusiasm" is something way down deep within you. The man who tells you to "be enthusiastic" as he would tell you to "take a deep breath" just doesn't know what enthusiasm is.

To sum it up, observe this rule: "Be animated when you sell." This is one real remedy for lost morale.

9. "Do I let ill-mannered prospects destroy my poise and make me ill-tempered?"

If you can't keep your temper, you'd better give up selling and try ditch-digging. The way to keep your temper is just to *keep it.* We all know how—we just don't always use what we know!

10. "Do I lack the quality of friendliness?"

Do you like your prospects, your customers? Do you like your fellow salesmen? Can you see even a few good points in your competitors?

An unfriendly salesman develops his own bad morale, pushes himself into slumps.

Do you want to attain a spirit of friendliness? Then read Dale Carnegie's *How to Win Friends and Influence People*, and follow his human-relation rules. It has done more to humanize salesmen, I think, than any book ever written.

11. "Am I in a slump because I am a self-made pessimist? Do I habitually expect bad luck today and worse tomorrow? Do I let past mistakes weigh down my spirits, then do I keep on making those same mistakes over and over?"

You can't make things "unhappen"

Remember Arnold H. Glasgow's statement, "We can't repair the past—but we don't have to repeat it."

This belief that the world is full of nothing but difficulties and disadvantages, and that life is pretty much a mess would drive any salesman into a slump. Fortunately, chronic pessimism is curable.

How to cure it? Replace pessimistic thoughts with optimistic thoughts. Read Chapter 77 on affirmation.

12. "Do I resist sales training, and all other education?"

> *Education is what you have left over when you subtract what you've forgotten from what you've learned.*
> —*Hartford* (WISCONSIN) *Times Press*

Some of you will say, in answer to Question 12, "How silly! Salesmen never resist education."

People who cherish that delusion will be startled to learn that a questionnaire put out in 1959 by the National Sales Executives asked, "Why do salesmen fail?" and that the answer that ran second in the voting was, "He couldn't (or wouldn't) assimilate sales training."

Take it from one (me) who has had a part in the training of tens of thousands of salesmen—some of them actually seemed to prefer death to education! They feel as Mark Twain said he felt, that "Soap and education are not as sudden as a massacre, but they are more deadly in the long run."

About all you can do with a salesman who forcibly resists education is, as Emerson said, "drown him to save his board."

If you resist sales training, this may explain your slumps.

If you are one of those who does not grab education as it whizzes by, I suggest you think about how much more the experts in your line earn than the ignorant salesmen.

Education—and especially education in salesmanship—has a high cash value.

Remember this: Only the ignorant despise education.

Sell only what you're "sold on"

13. "Have I complete confidence in my company and my merchandise?"

Note this rule: Believe in your company, or don't work for it; believe in your product or don't sell it.

I have had my share of experience with this rule.

When I was manager of the securities department of the Central Maine Power Company, my entire sales force (all five of them!) suffered from a sneaking belief—and so did I—that the preferred stock we offered was not quite as good as the preferred stocks offered by some of our competitors.

We were completely wrong about it, as subsequent events proved. Our distrust was the result of ignorance. We just couldn't see the future of the public utility business.

I am convinced that if our boss, Walter S. Wyman, had taken the time to tell us something about the future of power companies, and how our company would grow, and what the stock would do, we could have sold three times as much—with one-third the effort.

If you have doubts about your company and your product, don't be as stupid as I was. Instead, go to your boss, tell him your doubts, and get the truth.

Or, take another example out of my life. After I became manager of the retail division of the securities department of Henry L. Doherty & Company, our salesmen undertook the sale of Cities Service preferred stock. Now sometime in the dim and distant past, this stock had skipped a few dividends. This, in the minds of all the oldtime salesmen on the force, stamped the stock as strictly "no good." Since they felt that way, of course they couldn't sell it—at least not in any volume.

When I told them that, in spite of a bit of dividend-skipping back in the foggy past, the stock was now a good buy, they hooted and ascribed this belief to my ignorance, of which I had plenty! And when I mentioned this brief dividend failure in circulars, advertisements, and in our standardized sales talk, the veterans all but exploded. "You are ruining everything!" they said.

Once the salesmen found that it was best to face facts, and once I had convinced them that the stock really was a good buy, they began to sell in volume. If they had gone on being ashamed and afraid of the stock, they would never have sold enough of it to pay their car fare.

14. "Am I completely sincere in what I say about my product? Or do I try in a mild, gentle, and refined way to bamboozle and hoodwink my prospects?"

Don't. It pays best to tell the exact truth, and all the truth.

15. "Do I get into slumps because I am terrified by objections and resistances?"

If you do, that's tragic!

Fortunately, the fear of objections can be cured (see Chapter 17. If you will learn how to meet objections, your fear of them will depart, and maybe with it your low morale and the high frequency of your slumps.

16. "Do I think I am too big or too good for a selling job?"

If so, it's a wonder you have any morale at all. The cure is easy: either go to a head-shrinker, or quit selling and find a job that meets the status requirements of your inflated ego.

_____ CHAPTER 53

In this chapter we take up more of the possible causes of your slump—wife trouble, loquacity, insincerity

Here we go with some more questions which should help you to determine the cause of your slumps.

We start this chapter with a most serious problem:

17. "Does my wife believe I am in the wrong line of work?"

Boy, here's a morale-buster for you! If you battle stubborn prospects all day, and a mentally misguided wife all evening and Sunday, the wonder is that you are ever *out* of a slump!

Does your wife look down on selling as a low-grade occupation? When somebody asks her, "What does your husband do?" does she shudder and try to evade the question? Does she look around in the neighborhood at the homes of doctors, dentists, lawyers, and preachers, then ask you, in tones of reproach, "Why don't *you* have a high-grade job?"

Of course, it does little good to tell her that, when you are at your selling best, you make more money than any of them. Some wives are a little unreasonable because they expect you to have both a big income and a big hunk of status. (I'll bet they never tried to *eat* status!)

Have you ever tried to sell her on the vital part that selling plays in the prosperity of our nation? Did you ever try to make her understand that, if there were no salesmen, this country would head promptly into the worst slump in human history? Does she recognize, as did Joseph A. Hall, general sales manager of The Ruberoid Company, who said: "Without the sales part of our business we could not exist. Unless we succeed in this area, we don't even begin."

Here are four suggested cures for "wife trouble"

If your wife looks on selling as only one grade above driving a garbage truck or tending bar, and if you cannot sell her on the fact that salesmen perform a vital function in our economy, then you have three choices—or maybe four.

They are: (1) get a new job; (2) get a new wife; (3) both!

Of course, the fourth alternative is to sell your wife on your job, and what it can mean to her, to your family, and to the nation's economy.

How to do this I don't know. I am like the man quoted in the Southern Railway's magazine, *Ties*, who said, "It isn't that men don't understand women; it's just that they don't always know what to do about it."

Seriously, I don't know the answer to the wife problem. If you can't sell her the idea that you have a worthy job, maybe you ought to get a job in another field. If you are a successful salesman, I hope that alternative isn't the only answer. If you did get a job outside the selling field, your wife might not like that one either.

If your wife can't forgive you for being a salesman, consult a marriage counselor, or your minister, priest, or rabbi—or some older and more experienced friend.

Yes, even consult your wife. Tell her the problem and ask her help. Maybe, between you two, you can work out a solution.

Before you talk with your wife, sit down and ask yourself how much you are to blame for your wife's dissatisfaction with your job. Don't skim over this—really think. Do you tell her the good things about your company, your product, your job? Or, do you constantly regale her with its shortcomings and your annoyances? Do you invite her to enter into any of your activities such as district meetings and national conventions? Try to imagine yourself on your wife's job and her on yours. Then ask yourself what you do and what you fail to do that would annoy you if you were the wife. To put it in salesmen's language, "Get over on her side of the fence."

Then carefully think through the sales talk you will use on your wife. Don't skim over this, either. It may be one of the most important sales of your life.

18. "Are my slumps the result of ill-feeling between my boss and me? If they are, which of us is to blame?"

Neville Sharp wrote, "Children are basically good but are made bad by adults who mishandle them." If we substitute "salesmen" for "children," and "sales managers" for "adults," I suspect we could use this statement to explain why some salesmen get into slumps. I doubt if there is a sure cure for personality jams. However, I have one recommendation: talk the situation over with your boss.

Once when a sales manager who worked for me was making life miserable for one of his salesmen, I brought them together for a talk. They discovered that their ill-feeling toward each other had resulted from a misunderstanding. When we straightened that out, the war was over!

—————————————————————————— CHAPTER 54

I wasted nine years of business life because I worked at a job I didn't like—so read this and avoid the mistake I made

> *If you cannot work with love [for your job], but only with distaste, it is better that you should leave your work and sit at the gate of the temple and take alms of those who work with jobs they love.*
>
> —KAHLIL GIBRAN (SLIGHTLY AMENDED)

It is a bitter mistake for a normal man to waste a hunk of his life because he doesn't like his job.

Take my own case: when I left college I worked for eleven years as a sports editor.

My first two years as a sports editor were exciting. I learned a lot of useful things about deadlines, about rapid writing, about headlines and subheads, about dispatching work.

By the way, I know of few better schools for a young man than a couple of years as a reporter on an afternoon paper. Every edition of your paper closes at a set time. If your stories aren't in by that time, they're out! If they are out too often, so are you! The city editor's orders to his men are: "No alibis, we're not interested in *why* you failed. Just don't fail." It's brutal, but it's great discipline.

In the days when I was a sports editor, basketball was ignored by newspapers, professional football was unknown, golf stories were run on the society page. (One Nashville paper sent its society editor out to cover the first Southern Golf Association Championship in 1902. I know—I played in it.) Tennis was for sissies, wrestling was mostly crooked and almost completely ignored by newspapers, boxing was not worth attention except for an occasional heavyweight championship.

All this means that we covered regularly only one sport—baseball.

By my third year as a sports editor, I was bored with baseball. As year piled on year, the boredom increased. Toward the end of my inglorious career as a sports writer I reached a point where, if I could choose between a baseball game and a tooth pulling, I would have headed for the dentist.

Finally I wangled an offer from a magazine in Augusta, Maine—whereupon I borrowed $100, packed our few belongings and went into new and interesting work. I was moderately successful at it because I enjoyed it.

What I learned from the nine years I wasted as a sports editor (I didn't call the first two years "wasted" because I learned a lot) was, "Move mountains if need be to work at something you enjoy."

A good example of the fact that you can't do your best in any activity you don't enjoy I took from the writing of my friend, the late Grantland Rice:

A coach told me this story. "This kid was the sensation of his freshman team," the coach said. "I counted on him for the regular halfback post next year, and he made it all right. But he wasn't the player he should have been. Some days he would give off flashes of his freshman form, other days he was just fair.

"I sent for him one day and asked him 'Are you worried about anything?' and he laughed, 'No, do I look it?' 'No, but I don't understand why you aren't playing the kind of football you are capable of. I thought you might have something on your mind.'

" 'No, that's not the reason.'

" 'Well, what is the matter then?'

" 'Nothing much,' he said, 'except that I just don't like to play football.' "

I hope the reason I was a mediocre sports writer was that I just didn't like to write about baseball.

You may well ask, "If you didn't like sports writing, why didn't you get out sooner?"

I stuck for two reasons: (1) I didn't *know* that my distaste for the work was evidence that I was on the wrong job; and

(2) I had acquired a wife, a home, two kids, and some responsibilities—like debts. (It looked foolhardy to give up a secure job and go into a strange land, Maine, to work for a man I didn't know, at a job I didn't know how to do, but it was the smartest risk I ever took. That's one risk I "calculated" right!)

To get back to *your* case, if you hate to sell, even when you are not in a slump, then you have good evidence that you should quit selling and find something you like to do.

Note: I'm not talking about the man who hates every known kind of *work*. He's so hopeless, it matters little what kind of work he is evading!

Let's move along now with our self-analysis.

Love it or leave it!

19. "Am I in the right line of work? Do I belong in selling, or should I quit it?"

Let's split that great big problem into smaller ones by asking ourselves these questions:

A. "What do I want to get out of life?"

Ten to one you don't know—even money you never even thought about it much!

If you have not yet acted on my repeated suggestion that you decide on a goal in life, stop right now and do some thinking. This is one of the most important decisions you will face in your whole life. If you have not done it already, get out your pencil and make a list of your objectives in life: family, home, money, status, health, friends. If you spent a day on this question, it would not be too much—when you consider how important it is to you.

B. "What do I actually get out of life now?"

Make a list of what you get, and compare it with the list of what you *want*.

C. "Why do I sell? That is, why do I sell rather than keep books or teach school?"

D. "How did I get into selling in the first place? Did I get the job, or did the job get me?"

E. "Would I like some other kind of work better?"

"Move Heaven and earth to work at something you like," said Charles Schwab.

If your career as a salesman is just one long slump after another, if you are unhappy in your work, if you dread to make calls, maybe the solution of your slump problem is "Get out of selling."

I don't recommend that you quit just because you have an occasional slump. We all have them, just as most of us have colds now and then. Look for a new kind of work only if you are *unhappy* in selling, if you hate your work.

Weigh your likes against your "don't likes"

If you are uncertain whether or not you are in the right job, if sometimes you like it and sometimes you detest it, if you enjoy parts of it and abhor other parts, why not use the old Ben Franklin technique to determine whether or not you ought to give up selling? Do it this way:

Draw a line down the middle of a piece of paper. On one side of the line write the points you like about your job and on the other put those you don't like. If your "don't likes" greatly exceed your "likes" in number and in importance, then change your product or change your job.

Another way to analyze the situation is to write down all the requirements you have for an ideal job for you, then check to see how many of these requirements are supplied by your present job. Don't be surprised at what happens. Take an example which was given by my friend, the Reverend William R. Hill of Fairhope, Alabama, in a talk he made to an Inquirers' Group. Here is his story:

An unmarried friend of mine decided to approach the problem of matrimony in an orderly way. So he listed the requirements for a girl who would qualify to become his bride. He finally had twenty-two requirements.

Next, he bought a book in which he kept his records. On the first page he listed the twenty-two requirements. Then each time he went out with a new girl he started a page with her name at the top. Below her name, he put her standing in each of the twenty-two requirements.

He is still unmarried!

Now you know what's the matter with you—what's next?

This chapter finishes this part of our self-analysis. If you have answered all the questions we have asked, you now have a good idea of what is right and what is wrong with you and your selling—and what you have to do to restore your lost morale and get out of your slump.

In the next section you will get a set of rules which are designed primarily to help salesmen rebuild ruined morale and cure "slumpitis." No matter how low your slump or how high your morale, every rule in the next section is designed to benefit you. No matter how well you sell now, read these rules, observe them—and sell more.

In the following section I give you some magic rules of selling especially designed to cure slumps

Let's turn now from pestering ourselves with questions about what causes our slumps, and take up some rules designed to: (1) help the successful salesman sell more; and

(2) help the man in a slump to recover lost morale and get back into production.

These rules have worked for thousands of salesmen I have trained. They will work for you. So, if you are in a slump, remember that it is not the slump's fault, and that *you* can do something about it.

_____ CHAPTER **55**

Luckily, the rules for curing slumps work also to increase the production of those who are doing a good job now

In the pages which follow, you will find—if you look, and I hope you do—some of the best rules to increase sales that I have found in a half-century of search. Give these rules a fair trial and enjoy increased production and prestige.

Let's start with some suggestions designed to help you improve your morale, to get you in the right mental condition to sell successfully.

Rule 1. You must very much want to get out of your slump.

I have heard that no amount of AA-ing will cure a drunkard unless he is eager to be cured, and hence co-operates.

It is the same with a "slump-ard."

Don't tell me that every salesman in a slump will do everything possible to get out of it. I have known salesmen in slumps who, in a sour sort of way, seemed to enjoy it, to be satisfied to stay right there. It gave them an excuse for failure, an alibi for making fewer calls, an exemption from quota requirements, and a release from their responsibilities to provide for their families.

"I'm in a slump," they say. Then, as though that excused everything, they settle back to "enjoy financial ill-health."

Rule 2. Put failures out of your mind. Think success! Don't keep "warming over" your old failures.

Get used to the idea that you can't change yesterday. Put failures out of your mind. Stop living in last week.

To get these wrong ideas out of your mind, you must put right ideas there to replace them. Saturate your mind with success thoughts, and thoughts of failure will fade away.

The easy way to stop "thinking wrong" is to start "thinking right."

And remember always: if you believe you can sell, *you can sell.*

Rule 3. To get out of a slump, Tell yourself you are going to shake off this slump. Use affirmation.

It is so important for you to use affirmation to cure slumps and for a dozen other purposes, that I have devoted an entire section to it. It begins on page 246.

Rule 4. To build back lost morale, repeat your own name over and over. Say, "I am John Smith, I am John Smith, I am John Smith," and so on—and on and on.

Sounds silly, doesn't it?—and it may be. However, good practical psychologists recommend it and can give you examples as evidence that it works.

When you are in a slump, anything that builds up your morale, that improves your self-rating, is worth a try.

Psychologist Robert F. Mims said in the magazine *Salesman's Opportunity:*

There is magic in the sound of one's own name. Saying "I am John Jones" quietly to yourself can often give you a decided lift—and at times when you're most scared and most need it!

Novel as this idea may sound, scientific testing has demonstrated that it really works.

Try the "Good Samaritan" technique

Rule 5. Help others who need help.

A sure way to get your mind off yourself and your sales troubles is to do something helpful for somebody who needs it.

So look around until you find someone who has troubles worse than yours. After you find him, figure out some way to help him, then do it. For instance, do a half-day's work for somebody who needs it. (This is a good idea—even when you aren't in a slump!)

When you come back from doing a benevolent act, your spirits will be better and your morale higher. Then jump right back into your job. You may find yourself in such a favorable mental state that you can swing back at once into adequate production.

During World War I, we in the security-selling business were in what seemed like an endless slump.

The Army wouldn't have me, so I tried to help by working in Liberty Bond drives, Red Cross rallies, and similar fund-raising activities. When we finished a patriotic or charitable drive and turned back to selling, my morale was vastly better and the men in my sales force who had helped in the drive were much more effective in their selling.

No, I deny that I am a "do-gooder." This is not an effort on my part to convert you to the Golden Rule—not but that I heartily recommend it! I suggest that you be a Good Samaritan because I know from experience it will help you to get out of your slumps and into good production.

Rule 6. To stave off low morale, wear better clothing and groom yourself more carefully. Says H. R. Smith, in *Manager's Magazine*, "A salesman's clothes and his personal appearance influence his morale."

So, to cure a mild case of "slump-itis," buy a colorful necktie. If the mental illness is severe and of long standing, buy a new suit.

Rule 7. Imagine you are some friend of yours (or an enemy) who is a successful salesman—then go out and act as he does.

Does this method work? It does in sports.

Oldtime tennis enthusiasts will remember Sarah Palfrey. She played good tennis for thirteen years, and for thirteen years never won the championship. Twice she was rated second among the woman players of the U.S.A., twice third.

Then, at twenty-nine—rather old for championship tennis—
she won the championship. She beat Helen Jacobs in the
semifinals and Pauline Betz in the finals.

Here is how Sarah explained her victory: "One day, I told
myself, 'I'm not Sarah Palfrey, I'm Suzanne Langlen.' "
(Suzanne was perhaps the best woman tennis player who ever
lived.)

"It's amazing," Sarah continued, "what happens when you
decide you are somebody else. You actually acquire many of
the characteristics of that person."

Does that sound silly to you? Well, if you are desperate
about your selling situation, try to imagine that you are some
successful salesman—some champion—and then, as nearly as
you can, talk and act as he does. It can't do you any harm and
it may do you some good.

You may feel that this advice can't be reconciled with the
rule given you earlier in this book: Be yourself. Let me explain.
The "Be yourself" rule applies if you are selling satisfactorily.
The "Be somebody else" rule applies when your morale is low.

_____ CHAPTER 56

If you are in a slump, it isn't enough just to improve your sales pitch—you must also learn to think and act positively

*I am bigger than anything that can happen to me. All
these things, sorrow, misfortune and suffering, are outside my door. I am in the house and I have the key.*

—C. F. LUMMIS

Rule 8. Don't depress your morale by comparing yourself with
highly successful salesmen. "That," says Robert Tyson, Ph.D.,
"is the formula for remaining forever miserable."

Instead, compare yourself with your own past performances. "You are a success," says Dr. Tyson, "when you improve on your own record."

Don't try to get out of your slump by setting a new world's record. Be satisfied, for now, just to beat your own record.

Surely, if you made only one sale last week, you have an easy mark to shoot at. Then, if you make two sales this week, it's a big improvement—a 100 per cent improvement—and should be easy to attain.

Rule 9. Pretend that today is your last day to live.

If you knew you had just twenty-four hours to live, and if you were guaranteed life hereafter if you made some sales today, wouldn't you get out of your slump right now!

Hal Boyle, in his column, once wrote, "Julie Harris lives by a kind of Doctrine of the Last Chance." Julie said, according to Hal: " 'If you approach everything you do as if this were your last day—your last chance to do it right—everything becomes terribly exciting. You can't be bored.' "

You can't stay in a slump, either—not if you act every day as though it were your last.

"Sounds fantastic," you say.

It does, indeed.

If you are in a slump, try it. It may work, and if it does, it is worth much money to you.

Rule 10. Unless you are a frightened beginner, always tackle the tough prospect first.

That practice will build up your courage and your morale.

As G. H. Lorimer said, "Putting off the easy thing makes it difficult; putting off the hard makes it impossible."

Build up your ego a little

Rule 11. Cultivate a feeling that you are needed. Realize that when you sell successfully, you benefit not only yourself and your family, but also you benefit your prospect, your company, your industry, your nation and humanity.

Picture to yourself what would happen if every salesman in the nation went into a permanent slump. Business would fall off, production would have to be curtailed, unemployment would boom, and the United States of America would "go-bust."

Of course, you are only one of nearly five million salesmen in the country, but you are asked to do only your share. You can't do your share if you are in a slump.

Rule 12. Be resilient—bounce back. Get up fast every time you are knocked down. As the poet said, "The harder you hit, the higher you bounce."

"Yes," you say, with sarcasm, "that's easy to say, but how do you do it?"

One of the best ways to bring back faded morale (I repeat) is to give yourself a pep talk. Tell yourself over and over that you can sell. Picture yourself in your mind as making big sales. Fill your mind with thoughts and pictures of successful sales.

"Silly," you say. Maybe, but it works.

"If you wish to change your fortune, *change your thoughts,*" says *Rosicrucian Fellowship Magazine.*

Rule 13. Quit *looking* licked.

If you *look* like a "salesman in a slump," you are quite likely to *sell* like a "salesman in a slump." Shorten up that long face, turn up the corners of your mouth, force a smile, and hold yourself erect. Spruce yourself up—get a haircut and a shoeshine. Wear your best suit and your brightest necktie. If you look successful, it will help you to become successful.

Rule 14. Don't talk much about your slump.

That rule can be split up into these sub-rules:

A. Admit you are in a slump, but don't brag about it.
B. Don't use your slump as an excuse.
C. Don't expect sympathy.
D. Don't just talk about your slump—*do something.*

Let's consider the basic rule: Don't talk much about your slump. (The recommended exceptions to this rule will be found elsewhere in this book.) Too much talk about it will lower your morale, and make people avoid you. As some wise man has said, "Misery loves company, but after three days, nobody else does!

So don't keep your low morale fresh in your mind or in other people's minds by talking about it.

When your morale is low, and somebody asks, "How're things going?," don't tell him. As Bert Leston Taylor said, "A bore is a man who, when you ask him how he is, tells you." Don't be that kind of salesman. To put the rule in salesman's language, "don't squawk."

I liked what the magazine *Bluebird Briefs* said on the subject: "What a terrific din there'd be if we made as much noise when things go right as we do when they go wrong."

Now let's look at the first part of *Rule 14A*: Admit that you are in a slump.

I can argue for or against the rule: "Admit it." However, my money is bet on the policy of "Admit it, find the cause, then do something about it."

Few sights are more pitiful than the salesman who goes around saying, "I'm all right, no slump—just a little hard luck —I'll be over it in a few days."

Let's look now at the second part of *Rule 14A*: Don't brag about it.

Don't boast about your slump as though it were some rare disease or some major athletic feat. Maybe slumps aren't anything to be ashamed of, but certainly they aren't anything to be proud of! Don't expect people to be interested in your slump or to want to listen to long explanations as to why yours is the most wonderful and fearful case of low morale anybody ever had.

To handle this situation: Talk less, call more.

You can't excuse yourself out of a slump

Now let's look at *Rule 14B*: Don't use your slump as an excuse.

I have known salesmen—and so have you—who believe

that when they say, "I'm in a slump," they have excused everything. As I pointed out earlier, if these men make too few calls,
if they fail to report, or if they go to movies in business hours,
it must be all right because they have that old excuse, "I'm in
a slump."

When their boss says, "Yes, but . . . ," they seem shocked.

Here's an awful thought: maybe secretly and deep down in
their hearts, *they want to be in a slump* because it is easier
there.

To paraphrase Dr. David Mitchell, "Salesmen who say to
themselves, 'I'm in a slump,' save themselves the trouble of
working their way out."

If you are one of those strange and wonderful characters
who prefer failure to success, I hardly know what to suggest.

My inclination is to advise you to go jump in the creek.
However, I understand that it is against the law in some states
to advise a person to commit suicide—so that's out.

I do advise you, however, to do something drastic such as
consulting your family doctor for advice.

Nobody loves a "cry baby"

The salesman who goes about sobbing, "I'm in a slump,"
gets little sympathy, deserves less, and has few friends. Such
men give you the idea (to quote from a UP dispatch) that
"The only reason they stay alive is to see what the Hell is
coming next."

Don't be one of those slump victims who comes to sales
meetings primarily to have a good cry. Low morale is con-
tagious. Don't let anybody catch it from you.

Once I was drinking (water for me!) with some advertising
solicitors of national magazines and one agency man. One of
the salesmen was wailing over the deplorable condition of the
advertising business and moaning over his personal ill-luck.
Then the agency man spoke up: "Around our shop they call
you 'Lacey, the Wailer!' When we see you coming, we hide.

Everybody hates you because you never give us anything but songs of mourning."

I don't know whether or not that blast did Lacey any good, but I have remembered it through most of a long lifetime.

Recently in the *Mobile Register* I read an advertisement for salesmen for a mutual fund. Splashed across the bottom of the advertisement was a display line which read, "Weepers and wailers please do not apply." That gives you an idea of how employers of salesmen feel about salesmen who lament and bewail.

Walter Trohan, in the *Chicago Tribune*, gave a good example of business sympathy. He wrote, in substance:

Sen. Clinton Anderson (D—N.M.) tells of an employee who arrived an hour late at the General Accounting Office. He was in bad shape—he had a limp, an arm in a sling and a beautiful black eye. "What happened?" asked the boss, watch in hand.

"I fell out of the window," the employee explained.

"And that took you an hour!" the boss shouted!

Now, as to *Rule 14D*—Do something about it—well, this whole section is devoted to that point. I have given you rules that work for many salesmen. Your job is to put them to work for you.

Rule 15. Don't feel sorry for yourself because you are in a slump—or for any other reason.

At times, most folks get sorry for themselves, and always have. In fact, Terence, who lived from 185 to 159 B.C. observed, "Every man is sorry for himself." Why don't you try to be the exception and make Terence a liar.

My advice to you is, don't feel that you are an abused man, entitled to public sympathy, because prospects won't buy, or putts won't drop, or inside straights won't fill.

Don't be like the despondent rooster who leaned his head against the barn door and said: "What's the use of it all? Eggs yesterday, chickens today, feather-dusters tomorrow."

The cure for feeling sorry for yourself is: Stop feeling sorry for yourself.

It will help you to accomplish this if you will look around at the millions—yes, billions—of people on earth who are worse off than you are. It may help you to think that all these people have more reason to be depressed than you have.

If you let yourself get sorry for yourself every time your sales fall off, your next slump may be your last as a salesman. So determine not to feel sorry for yourself, no matter what happens—then stick to your determination.

Don't be like the guy of whom B. Lancaster is reputed to have said, "What I admire about him—once he's made up his mind, no power on earth can make him stick to it."

You get better inspiration from books than from bottles

Rule 16. Read inspirational books.

"What books should I read?" you ask.

Some books I recommend are: *As a Man Thinketh,* by James Lane Allen; *The Go-Getter,* by Peter B. Kyne; *A Fortune to Share,* by Vash Young; *The Message to Garcia,* by Elbert Hubbard; and *How to Live on 24 Hours a Day* by Arnold Bennett.

They were all published long ago, but old books are often the best. Maybe some of these old books are out of print, maybe some new inspirational books are better, but I doubt it. You will probably find all the books listed above in your public library and perhaps in secondhand bookstores.

My friend, Norvell J. "Brick" Brickell, sponsor for Dale Carnegie and Associates in the Memphis area, who is one of the country's top authorities on inspirational speaking, recommends these three books: *The Magic Power of Thinking Big,* by Dr. David Schwartz; *The Magic Power of Emotional Appeal,* by Roy Garn; and *Double Your Energy and Live Without Fatigue,* by Margery Wilson.

P.S. Read not only inspirational books, but also inspirational articles in magazines, and listen to inspirational speeches and sermons. They help, too.

CHAPTER 57

If you feel inferior when you aren't, you'd better do something about it now—it may be the cause of your low morale

> *The trouble with inferiority complexes is that not enough people have them.*
> —*Charlotte Observer* (N.C.)

> *Anybody who's not neurotic these days is probably underprivileged.*
> —FRANKLIN P. JONES

> *One of the most difficult tricks is to keep a balance between getting an inferiority complex and getting a swelled head.*

Now for some more rules for curing "slumpitis":

Rule 17. Cure your inferiority complex to cure your slump!

Let's start with a definition:

An inferiority complex, according to *Webster's*, is "an acute sense of personal inferiority resulting either in timidity or through over-compensation in exaggerated aggressiveness. Broadly: sense of being inferior or at a disadvantage; lack of assurance."

If you are in a slump or a period of depressed morale, it might be smart to ask yourself, "Is there any connection between my slump and my feeling of inferiority?"

Perhaps the first step is to find out if you have a genuine inferiority complex, if you really "harbor feelings of inferiority."

Your answers to the following questions will help you to determine if you have this complex—and how bad a case it is:

A. Are you constantly comparing yourself with other people—usually unfavorably?
B. Are you deeply hurt by criticism? Are you over-sensitive?
C. Are you self-conscious, that is, are you ill at ease when you are (or think you are) being observed by others? (Somebody has wisely said, "Salesmen wouldn't worry over what people think about them if they realized how seldom they do!")
D. Are you too easily embarrassed?
E. Do you worry over little breaks you have made, over minor errors or social slips? Are you actually distressed about them?
F. Do you constantly criticize yourself? Does your weakness weigh down on your mind?
G. Do you have a feeling that you can't ever be a big-time, professional salesman?
H. Do you have a feeling, right in the middle of a sale, that you can't possibly get the order and wish you had a better man there to take over the closing?

You may have a lot of other symptoms of inferiority too, but this list will enable you to make a fairly accurate diagnosis.

By the way, I can speak with some authority on an inferiority complex, because I had an acute case of it. I had all the symptoms years before I knew what an inferiority complex was. Also, I know that such complexes can be cured, because mine was—partially at least!

Maybe you need a psychiatrist—but heaven forbid!

The best way to cure an inferiority complex, if you can afford the time and money, is, I am told, to go to a psychiatrist. Be sure he is competent. A man I know once went to a psychiatrist for treatment as a neurotic, only to find that the doctor was more neurotic than the patient, and couldn't cure either one of them.

Whole books have been written about how to cure an inferiority complex. Here are a few practical suggestions from the magazine *Your Life,* from other sources, and from my own experience:

A. Look for the causes. Discover whether your feeling of inferiority is based on real inferiorities or imagined ones. (For example, my feeling that my memory was inferior was based on reality. My fear that I would never be able to stand on a platform and face an audience was imagined.) Says *Your Life*, "Too often inferiority feelings arise from superstition, and misinformation about sex, fear, mental functions, and the like." Once you know what causes your feelings of inferiority, you will be less disturbed by them.

B. Look around you and note how many other people feel inferior. Once you realize that so many others suffer from your complaint, you tend to stop taking your own feelings so seriously.

C. Stop comparing yourself with others who have had more advantages than you have. Stop expecting the impossible of yourself.

D. Stop thinking so much about what you can do for *yourself*, and think occasionally of what you can do for *others*.

E. Stop asking yourself, "I wonder how I look to other people?" Think more, instead, of how they look to you.

F. Take on interesting outside activities—activities so interesting that, when you pursue them, you can't think much about yourself.

G. Relax as much and as often as is practicable—physically and mentally.

H. Take a practical course in public speaking.

I know that this public-speaking treatment works, because I have seen it work literally thousands of times. When I taught a lot of public-speaking classes in the New York area, I noted that every class seemed to have an unusual proportion of neurotics. One day a professor of psychology in a New York university told me why. He said, "Whenever a New York City psychiatrist runs into a neurotic case he can't cure, he tells his patient, 'Take the Carnegie course in public speaking.'" My observation was that we didn't cure them all, but we did help many.

Maybe you need action—and lots of it

Rule 18. Work harder.

If there is any one great rule to overcome slumps, this is it: "Work, work, work!

Unfortunately, this simple rule is hateful to many salesmen. Just the same, it is the best answer to the cry of the stricken salesman: "How can I get out of this slump?"

So steel yourself to make more calls, see more prospects, start earlier, work longer, stick at it later. And, especially during working hours, don't hang around the office or the home.

Oh, I know it's easier to say, "I'm in a slump. What's the use? I can't sell, no matter how many calls I make." Elbert Hubbard answered you when he said, "No man fails until he no longer tries." Stick to that policy of not quitting, and your slump will not stick to you long.

"The worried person," said Dale Carnegie, "must lose himself in action lest he wither in despair."

The harder you work, the more likely you are to recover lost morale. The secret behind *staying* in a slump is to have lots of time to worry because you *are* in a slump. As George Horace Lorimer said: "If you don't have leisure, you can't be very fearful. Most of the fears of the world are imaginary, and it takes time to think them up."

Aetna-gram tells of a salesman who had drifted into a period of mental inertia. It bored him to make calls and deliver sales talks. So he prescribed for himself the remedy we have proposed to you throughout this book—more calls. He made out a list of 100 prospects and started out to see how quickly he could call on all of them. Says *Aetna-gram*, "Before he was half way through the list he was swinging into his work with the same old drive and energy that he used to have."

Don't go to a movie or to a golf course.

No salesman ever improved his morale by quitting. I believe that nobody ever golfed himself out of a selling slump. So stick in there and make calls. Jerry Delano phrased it well for T. Harry Thompson's "Scratch Pad" column in *Sales Management Magazine* when he said, "Never let down, never let up."

> *The hardest mental problem salesmen face daily comes about 4 P.M. when they have to decide whether they are tired—or lazy.*

* * *

> *It's a shame for salesmen to be idle when so little keeps them busy.*

* * *

> *Some salesmen are tired—tired of it all. The work is too hard, the hours too long. It just ain't worth it.*
>
> —A. S. GOURFAIN

CHAPTER **58**

If you are in a selling slump, try to get help from your wife, your boss, your customers, and fellow salesmen

> *If salesmen didn't ask questions, they would never learn how little sales managers know.*
>
> —WITH APOLOGIES TO RAYMOND DUNCAN

The smart salesman who suffers from low morale and is in a slump should get all the help he can. To do it, we recommend that he talk over his problem with others. This does not conflict with our advice not to talk a lot about your slump. In one case, you ask for specific help—in the other, you just talk. Some additional suggestions as to how and where to look for help are given in the rules which follow.

Rule 19. Ask your boss for help.

If you are on a small sales force, your boss will probably be the sales manager. Anyway, if he manages salesmen, no matter what his title, his main job is to keep his salesmen in production.

So, if you are in a slump and need help, you have every right to ask your boss for help—and to expect to get it.

Your boss can give you three kinds of help:

A. He can lecture you. A lazy boss will favor this method. It requires practically no effort on his part. Maybe his lecture will inspire you—more than likely, it will just bore you.
B. He can teach you, in the office, how to make a good sales talk, and can then drill you until you do it.
C. He can go out into the field and work with you.

I recommend a combination of B and C. If your boss is the over-self-confident type, he probably will want to "show you how it's done" by making some sales talks to your prospects.

That's grand for his ego, but it's poor instruction. You can't learn to sell by watching others sell, any more than you can learn to play golf by watching professionals play. You learn to play golf by standing on the practice tee and hitting ball after ball under the watchful eye of the club golf pro. You learn to sell by making sales under the watchful eye of your boss.

So beg your boss to let you try your sales talk on every prospect—then have him tell you, when you are back on the sidewalk, the one worst thing the matter with it. Then, after the next pitch, have another "sidewalk conference" on your worst fault—remember, just one fault at a time. Then when you get back to the office after a day of selling, have him summarize your faults, and drill you until you can make your talk with no errors.

Sales managers and field managers under my direction used that plan of working with salesmen in a slump for over a quarter of a century, so I know it works well. If anything will cure a salesman with sick morale, that treatment will!

Gripe if you must, but gripe tactfully

Rule 20. If you feel that you are being treated unfairly by the higher-ups in the organization, discuss the matter with your boss.

Such feelings, if not corrected, may easily cause your sales to slump.

Be sure to approach him on the right basis. Don't grumble and complain and threaten. Instead, tell your boss that you are in a slump, that your production is off and your morale is low. Tell him you need help. Then ask him if he thinks that perhaps your bad mental condition may result from the fact that . . . and go into your story.

If you approach him for help in a friendly attitude, he is almost certain to give your complaint friendly and co-operative consideration. Perhaps he can wipe out your "delusion of persecution," and build your morale back to normal or above.

Rule 21. Ask your fellow salesmen to help you.

Any salesman you ask for advice and help will surely feel flattered. Most salesmen will gladly help you.

Naturally you will use your judgment as to whose advice you will follow—and how far!

Rule 22. Challenge some salesman (preferably one who is also in a slump) to compete with you for a cash prize. Each of you should put up half the cash.

Many salesmen will sell successfully in a contest when they don't sell successfully at any other time.

Maybe a competition with another salesman will stimulate you to make more sales and to dig out of your slump. It's a good method.

Or maybe you should compete with yourself. You could pick out the six months which lie ahead, find out what you did in corresponding months last year, then set out to beat last year's mark. Or, pick out your best month and try to beat that.

"When I am in a slump!" you exclaim.

Why not? The idea is to get your mind off your slump and onto an attempt to beat somebody or to break a record.

Eugene B. Bertin summed it up neatly when he said in the *Pennsylvania School Journal*:

Tell an American he has a fever of 102, he'll probably ask, "What's the world's record, Doc?" Whether the world's headed for perdition, purgatory or paradise—the American seems bound on getting there first.

No telling who may give you good advice

Rule 23. Get some non-selling friend to listen to your sales talk and give you advice.

"Shucks," you say, "what can a man who doesn't sell tell me about what's wrong with my sales talk?" Friend, don't be too sure he can't. He can at least give you an outsider's point of view, which should be helpful.

One warning: do not tell the friend why you have asked him to listen to your talk. If you do, he will think of himself, not as a prospect, but as a critic, and most of the value of his comments will be lost.

To get real help from a non-salesman, you must, after you finish your talk, ask him such questions as:

"Did the talk make you want to buy? Why or why not?"

"Did it hold your interest all the way through, or did you feel it was too long? When did interest lag?"

"What point that I made appealed to you most—and why?"

"What part of my talk didn't you like? Why?"

"Was there any part of the talk that was not clear to you? Which part?"

If you get any worthwhile suggestions by the above method, give them a trial.

My policy has always been to listen to suggestions, advice, and criticisms from anybody. As a result, I have received a lot of promising suggestions from a lot of unpromising sources.

If you get any good advice, *act on it*. "Many receive advice," said Publilius Syrus, "only the wise profit by it." So you be wise!

Try to profit by criticism, too. Don't be one of those salesmen who welcomes criticism as a drowning man welcomes water. The way a man takes criticism is a true test of his character.

When you are criticized, keep your temper. Some salesmen "would rather be ruined by praise than saved with criticism."

Here's a suggestion. When you ask for help and get criticism, you should:

A. Insist that the criticism be specific. That is, if somebody says, "Your sales talk stinks," ask, "Exactly what's wrong with it?"

B. When your critic has told you exactly what is the matter with your talk (from his viewpoint), ask him how he suggests that you improve it. Keep prodding him with questions.

Rule 24. Ask your wife for advice and help.

I was tempted to add that this rule is as good as your wife— and no better.

However, that wouldn't be fair. Some wives are not in a position to be of much help, no matter how eager they are to give it. Family obligations, ill-health, child-bearing may keep them too busy with their own work to give much if any of their time to helping you.

However, if your wife is willing and able to give you help, she may develop into a valued assistant.

Rule 25. Compare your sales methods with those of successful salesmen, then change your methods to get them in line with those used by the leaders.

If you don't know how successful salesmen sell, ask them. They will tell you—and love doing it, if they aren't competitors.

Don't be offended if the "natural born" salesmen don't tell you how they sell. "Naturals" can't, because *they don't know how* they sell. They just *sell.*

The men who can really help you are those who had to learn how to sell by trial and error, by failure on failure. Ask them to help. They will be flattered, and in most cases will do all they can to get you out of your slump and into good production.

Kind words from satisfied customers are magic!

Rule 26. Talk to satisfied customers who are enthusiastic about your product. Thus you will acquire some of their enthusiasm and faith. This we recommend in big doses to overcome "slumpitis!"

I remember once nearly a quarter of a century ago, Dale Carnegie and I were closing up shop for the day, when, to tease Abbie Connell, Dale's secretary, a sincere and devout Catholic, I said I doubted if there would be a future life for anybody.

Abbie wasn't teased—she was shocked and incensed. Instead of laughing at us, she whirled and, in deadly earnest, delivered a sermon on life-after-death that held us speechless.

That talk of hers did more to convert me to a belief in future life than all the sermons I ever heard in all the churches I ever attended in all my life. It was vivid in my memory for months, and I think of it often to this day.

Why? Because I had interviewed a "satisfied customer" who was enthusiastic about the product.

Whether you are in a slump or out, observe this rule: *Interview satisfied customers.*

Even if your enthusiasm for your product and what it will do for prospects is way above the boiling point, you will be helped if you talk to enthusiastic customers. Besides, you will get examples you can use.

If you have never tried this plan, if you have never exposed yourself to the warming effect of a talk with a satisfied customer, take my advice and try it. I personally guarantee it. It works miracles.

_____ CHAPTER 59

If your morale is low because you are deep in debt, you should get advice from some expert on budgets and economy

Definition of success: *Making more money to meet obligations you wouldn't have if you didn't have so much money.*

Rule 27. Get out of your financial difficulties, then your slump will almost certainly depart.

If your slump is due to the fact that you are broke and steadily getting "broker," the way to get out of your slump is to get out of debt.

The normal salesman's attitude toward money was neatly summed up in *Trap* magazine in this poem:

> They call it legal tender
> That green and lovely stuff;
> It's tender when you have it,
> But when you don't it's tough.

The question in the mind of the under-financed salesman can be asked in seven short words, "How can I get out of debt?"

That question has been asked literally billions of times, starting way back before money was invented. As far as I know, nobody has yet discovered an *easy* answer. Only the hard ones really produce.

So my advice is: Try the hard way, pay your debts and get out of your slump.

I can hear most of you shriek, "Hell man, you tell me the way to get out of my slump is to cure my financial difficulties, when you know that the reason for my financial difficulties is that I am in a slump. Brother, you've got the disease and the cure mixed up. If I wasn't in a slump, I wouldn't be broke!"

There's merit to your complaint—also, there's an answer to it. Maybe at the moment what you need is not to earn more, but to spend less. Anyway, what you need is financial advice.

Let's admit that a lot of salesmen (including myself) are financial morons. Even if you aren't "one of them things," you still need financial advice if you are broke—so get it.

Here's the prescription: *Go to your sales manager or to somebody in the accounting department who knows costs and budgets, and ask him for advice.*

Then, act on his advice.

Maybe you ask, "Do you expect me to tell my financial situation to some stranger?"

Brother, if they sue you, the secret is out anyhow. Isn't it better to *whisper* it to one acquaintance rather than have the courts *shout* it to the public?

An almost certain cure for debilitated morale, due to financial worries, is to eliminate the cause of the worries.

Just the other day a salesman friend of mine was in a slump so deep you couldn't even see the top of his head. His manager found out what was wrong: the salesman was far in debt. The manager worked out a plan that relieved the pressure. Within a fortnight the salesman performed what I regard as some selling miracle. Soon he was out of debt. He still is.

Maybe all you need is a budget and a scare

Remember what Arthur Brisbane said, "There is plenty of money in this country—the difficulty is to get it."

Experience tells us that, if you give a poverty-stricken sales-man a good budget and a good fright you can often get him back into solvency.

Here are the steps you should take:

Step 1. You and your financial consultant should work out a practical plan for your refinancing. Under this plan you should (A) borrow enough money to pay your debts, (B) pay them, (C) set up a budget that includes provisions for paying back what you have borrowed, and (D) live up to it!

Note to married men: Be sure that your wife is consulted about every step of this plan.

Step 2. Borrow enough money to pay all your debts.

"Who would lend money to a guy who owes everybody?" you ask.

You will be happily surprised, I think, that once you ap-proach possible lenders with a plan and a budget that looks practicable and workable, you will find they will usually lend you a reasonable sum of money—enough to pay your debts.

You probably have some friend, relation, or customer who will finance you under these circumstances. Just remember one thing: Don't go to the loan sharks.

Step 3. Pay all outstanding bills, thus consolidating your indebtedness.

Step 4. Plan to pay off your one big bill in weekly install-ments.

"Pay it off with what?" you ask, with some show of impatience.

"With money," is the answer, "the money you make be-cause you sell more, and you sell more because your financial worries are over for the present, your morale has improved, and you can give your whole heart, mind, and strength to selling."

Step 5. Set up a spending budget for yourself and your fam-ily that is about as close to bottom as you dare get, but a good bit above starvation rations.

Step 6. Study this section of this book because it tells you how to get out of slumps and to stay out.

Step 7. Act on our advice, as presented in this section.

* * *

You will be astonished and delighted at what the adoption of a businesslike plan does to get you out of the selling dumps and back into production.

No salesman can sell much when seven-eighths of his time is devoted to his debts and only one-eighth to his prospects.

* * *

So, to summarize briefly, consult an expert on budgets, adopt a budget, live up to it, pay your debts, and don't pile up any more.

Morale goes up when worry goes down.

Rule 28. Don't buy anything more on the time-payment plan—especially don't buy anything you don't need.

Easy payments have often been the cause of uneasy sleep.

As Roger Fleming wrote in *Food Marketing in New England*:

The trouble with all this credit, and the putting off of the day of payment, is that we may get to be like the drunk who didn't like hang-overs, so solved his problem by staying drunk all the time.

Don't borrow from loan sharks—starve first!

Again I say: no matter how desperate your financial condition, don't go to a loan shark. Most of these predatory fish would bite off an arm or a leg if they could sell it for cash. Going to a loan shark to get out of debt is about like curing a leg amputated at the knee by cutting off the rest of the leg.

If your problem is that you have a multitude of small debts, your financial advisor is likely to try to get all your debts consolidated into a big one, then show you how to whittle the big one down to nothing.

It doesn't always work out pleasantly, as witness this yarn from *The Wall Street Journal*:

A businessman was telling his banker about the host of worries plaguing him, declaring, "They're beginning to smother me, dozens closing in from all sides."

"Thing for you to do," consoled the banker, "is to simplify by lumping the related ones."

"That's what I did," said the businessman, "and now I have only three problems—nagging creditors, profitless business, and the fact that I'm broke."

Just for a change—let's laugh for a couple of minutes

Below I give you some sage observations about money, debt, budgets, and the like, culled from all sorts of places, and guaranteed to interest, instruct, and maybe amuse you.

A budget is being described as a plan for pay-as-you-go if you don't go anywhere.

*   *   *

A budget is merely a mathematical confirmation of your suspicions.

—F. G. KIERNAN

*   *   *

A man has never really tested his strength until he tries to lift a mortgage.

—CAREY WILLIAMS, *Publishers Syndicate*

*   *   *

The secret of economy is to live as cheaply the first few days after pay-day as you did the few last days before.

—*Balance Sheet*

*   *   *

Poverty is not a disgrace—and that's about all that can be said in its favor.

—R. M. TUCKER

*   *   *

Salesmen's wives have a system governing expenditures. They pay when they can, and charge the rest.
                                    —FRANCES RODMAN

*   *   *

A nurse was showing a new patient to his room.
"Now," she said, "we want you to be happy while you're here so if there is anything you want that we haven't got, let me know, and I'll show you how to get along without it."

*   *   *

Twenty years ago lots of salesmen dreamed of earning the money they won't be able to get along on this year.
                                    —Grit

*   *   *

Salesmen don't really want a cheaper car. What they want is a more expensive car for less money.
                                    —Postage Stamp

*   *   *

Money talks all right. Mostly what it says is: "5-4-3-2-1-zero—and there she goes!"
                                    —Farm Journal

*   *   *

It's true that you can't buy happiness with money, but you can't buy groceries with happiness, either.
                                    —Wooden Barrel, Associated Cooperage Industries

*   *   *

An actor, down on his luck, once asked comedian W. C. Fields for a loan.
"I'd be glad to help you, my good man," Fields replied, "but my money's all tied up in currency."
                                    —EARL WILSON, HALL SYNDICATE

*   *   *

Old-timers recall when a fellow wondered where his next dollar was coming from, instead of where it had gone.
                                    —SERVICE FOR COMPANY PUBLICATIONS

*   *   *

*In the old days $10 worth of groceries would fill a
pantry to bursting. Today $10 worth of groceries won't
even burst a shopping bag. Certainly shows how much
stronger bags are now, doesn't it?*

*   *   *

*Worrying about cigarettes can be beneficial—it takes
your mind off the cost of eating.*
                    —DAN KIDNEY, SCRIPPS-HOWARD NEWSPAPERS

*   *   *

*Prosperity: that short period between the final install-
ment and the next purchase.*
                                    —HALL PULLMAN

*   *   *

*The up-to-date house has wall-to-wall carpeting, wall-
to-wall windows—and back-to-the-wall financing.*
                                    —Changing Times

*   *   *

*In the periods of prosperity, most salesmen make
more money than they earn and spend more than they
make.*
                                —Tid-Bits, LONDON

*   *   *

*Running into debt isn't so bad. It's running into
creditors that hurts.*
                                —Chicago Tribune

Now, let's wind up this list of smart sayings about money
with these gems from that great economist, Joe E. Lewis:

"Money isn't everything—it just quiets the nerves a little.

*   *   *

A lot of things are more important than money. The trouble is,
they all cost money.

*   *   *

The most valuable thing in the world is friendship, and the
richest man in the world is the one with the most money.

*   *   *

I've been rich and I've been poor and, believe me, rich is better.

CHAPTER 60

Many salesmen will read, a few will study, but it is almost impossible to get one of them to think

Let's consider now what else we can do to get back into our selling stride—and please keep on noticing that most of these anti-slump rules are valuable also for the man who is on top of a selling wave.

Rule 29. Think!

That's the shortest rule in the book. Also, alas, it is the one you are least likely to observe.

To paraphrase John Galsworthy, "A salesman, forced into a state of thought, is unhappy until he can get out of it."

Here's some advice I have given before in books, magazine articles, and lectures—and which I shall now give again because it is so important:

> *Set aside thirty minutes each day to be used as a "think period." For that period, go some place where you will not be disturbed. Write on a piece of paper your most important problem. Prop it up where you can see it. Then, for thirty minutes, think about that problem and its solution—and nothing else.*

This practice will work miracles for you. I guarantee you will find it hard work, but rewarding.

Probably the best single piece of advice in this book is: *Think!*

Rule 30. Read another good book on selling.

A good, practical how-to-sell book has worked miracles for many men.

"What book?" you ask.

Naturally I recommend my own book first, *The 5 Great Rules of Selling*.

What other books will help the man in a slump?

Well, first, Frank Bettger's *How I Raised Myself from Failure to Success in Selling*. It is, in my judgment, the best inspirational book on selling ever written—in fact, it is, I think, one of the best inspirational books of all time *in any field*.

Don't miss Charles B. Roth's *Secrets of Closing Sales*.

Another sales classic is Elmer Wheeler's *Tested Sentences That Sell*.

I recommend any book on selling by the following authors: Frank Bettger, Richard C. Borden, John M. Wilson, Edward J. Hegarty, Charles B. Roth, J. C. Aspley.

Avoid books that make wild claims as to what they will do for you. You know the kind I mean. As a general rule, the wilder the claims in a book's title, the tamer the results you will get from it.

Terence, who lived before the Christian era said, "In fine, nothing is said now that has not been said before," and Charles Dickens, at a considerably later date, wrote, "There are books of which the backs and covers are by far the best parts."

Rule 31. Read the sales bulletins put out by your organization and by the organizations whose products you sell.

Just a few years ago, I interviewed an associate sponsor in the Dale Carnegie organization to find out why he promoted so few sales course classes.

I asked him, "Do you do so-and-so?" (I have forgotten what.)

"I never heard of it," was his reply.

"Don't you get our bulletins?"

"Yes, I get them."

"Don't you *read* them?"

"No, but I *do* file them."

If you actually *file* your sales bulletins unread, dig out some back copies and *read* them. They may point to a sure route out of your slump.

Rule 32. If your formal education was not as good as that of your fellow salesmen, don't worry about it. If you do, you will generate a feeling of inferiority—and that's a sure slump-builder.

Take my own case: I attended one public school, two private schools, one college and two universities, took the Dale Carnegie course in effective speaking—and never got a diploma from anybody for anything. Maybe I'd have done better if I'd had a Ph.D., but I doubt it.

Remember, it is largely what a salesman learns after he departs from institutions of higher learning that helps him to stay out of slumps and in good production.

Rule 33. Study something every day of every year as long as you live, but study first the subjects that have a direct bearing on your product and its use. Then, after you know all there is to know about your product (or products) and its use, take up cultural subjects. They broaden your background and add to your breadth of interest.

If your only aim in life is to get rich, you can forget culture. It is amazing how little erudition some men need to get rich. For example this yarn that I picked up from the magazine *Sales Management*:

Two graduates met at their 25th reunion. One had been graduated at the head of his class. The other was low man. In fact, he Yet he seemed to have prospered.

"Joe," said the top man, "you seem to have done exceptionally well. How did you do it?"

"Well," said Joe, "after graduation I realized I was pretty dumb and I better get in some line where I didn't need to be smart like you and some of the others. So I found a product I could make for a dollar and sell for five dollars."

"Believe me, that four per cent really mounts up over the years!"

My own experience is that, if a man keeps up with current news, a few fiction books, and all sales magazines, he will have darn little time for cultural reading.

One thing about culture—if you've got it, you are constantly tempted to show it off.

Rule 34. Don't make the same old mistakes over and over.

Hugh S. Bell, in *How to Be a Winner in Selling,* said, "A great salesman has framed on his wall this statement, 'I can fail many times, but I am not a failure until I make the same almost didn't get his diploma. Mathematics was a mystery to him. mistake twice.' "

You are unlikely to make the same mistake twice if, at the end of each day, you sit down and review your day's work. Consider first the mistakes you made and why you made them. Then consider what you should have done to keep from error. Then determine that you will not make these mistakes again.

Don't stop there.

Consider, also, what smart, successful things you did— experiments that worked, techniques that moved you toward a sale. Then consider how you can repeat them, how you can make that right method a standard part of your sales talk.

To sum it up: *spot your mistakes and plan to avoid them; spot your successes and plan to repeat them.*

For example, a salesman who worked for me once was in a perpetual slump. The reason was clear to him and to me—he never stressed benefits. His talk was as factual as a dictionary, and just as dull. Still, though I urged that he use fewer facts and more benefits, he never changed. In the office he would promise to reform, but in front of a prospect he would backslide. I don't remember that we fired him—I think he just dried up and blew away.

You will deserve to share his fate if you repeatedly make the same mistake.

CHAPTER 61

Now you know how to cure your slump the question arises, "What will you do to get back into production?"

The secret of success: Get up when you fall down.
—PAUL HARVEY

You know now how to get out of your slumps, how to improve your morale, and, therefore, how to increase your sales and earnings.

If you use the rules presented in this section, you will get good results. I know about most of them first-hand because salesmen under my direction have used them, usually with success—and so have I. However, it isn't enough just to think about it—you have to *do something*.

Sophocles, who flourished from 496 to 406 B.C., remarked on this subject, "Heaven ne'er helps the man who will not act."

Neither will this book.

Don't you be the kind of guy some author had in mind when he said, "The most effective and enlightened form of education for the average salesman will continue to be a swift kick in the pants."

To put these rules into effect, and to persist until you sell the scientific way from habit will not be easy—nothing which is worth accomplishing ever is.

Your own attitude, more than anything else, will determine whether you will get out of your slump, whether you will build up your morale—or whether you will quit.

To those who think maybe they'd better quit, I recommend the following little story, which seems to have originated in the *Arkansas Baptist* magazine:

A small boy was learning to skate. His frequent mishaps awakened the pity of a bystander. "Sonny, you're getting all banged up," he said. "Why don't you stop for a while and just watch the others?"

With tears still running down his cheeks from the last downfall, he looked from his advisor to the shining steel on his feet, and answered: "Mister, I didn't get these skates to give up with; I got 'em to learn how with!"

Now that you know how to get out of a slump—*act*

Well, I have told you all I know about how to get out of a slump and back into production.

Now it's your move.

Study your situation, determine the cause of your slump, pick out the rules that seem most likely to cure you—then apply them.

"Something is wrong with me but I don't know what!"

If you are not the salesman you feel you ought to be, if you are just "wriggling by" when you ought to be up among the leaders, maybe you are a victim of the demon that defeats more salesmen in more ways than any other enemy—and I don't mean the "Demon Rum."

Maybe you don't even recognize as an enemy the "demon" I am talking about. Maybe you don't know that every day he may cost you sales and commissions, that he may help to hold you back from the recognition and status you crave and deserve.

So, let's consider now who he is—and how to defeat him.

CHAPTER 62

You will have to read this chapter to find out what it's about—and why the subject is so secret

"What you don't know don't trouble you."
—AUTHOR UNKNOWN

Before you decide that this chapter wasn't meant for you, please give yourself this "motive test":

Jot down on a sheet of paper everything you have done in the past seven days of which you are ashamed—every act that was slightly dishonest or bad-mannered or ill-tempered or untruthful. Then answer honestly about each contemptible act, "Why did I do it? What moved me to such an act? What motive prompted me? Was it the all-powerful motive of self-preservation? Or was it greed, or a desire to feel important, to have status? Or was it pride, love of family, hate?

My belief is that most such despicable acts come from one of the common motives.

What is it? Fear!

Give yourself the test—now. Remember, you are going to find what moved you to do these things you aren't proud of. Be honest with yourself in this test. Nobody need ever know what you found out.

Now ask yourself these questions:

—Why do salesmen exaggerate?
—Why do they record calls they never made?
—Why are they selfish, niggardly, stingy?
—Why do salesmen promise delivery dates they know the factory can't meet?
—Why do they quake and quiver in the face of objections?

Elsie Robinson, who suggested this test in her column in the New York *Journal-American,* answered these questions with these words: "People behave the way they do because they are *afraid.* There is only one sin—*fear.*"

Stop for a couple of seconds and ask yourself if that isn't true!

Check yourself against this list of common fears

Over half the salesmen who read this book will say, at this point, "This stuff about *fear* is not for me. Why, to make a sale I'd fight two tigers at once—barehanded."

Maybe, but I doubt it, and so did Wilson Mizner when he said, in substance, "A man who is always bragging that he isn't afraid of anything usually has his suspicions."

Everyone who has managed and trained salesmen knows that fear costs more sales than price! W. L. Barnhart, in his book *Practical Salesmanship,* said: "Fear is the chief bogey of the salesman.... Among all the failures I have seen ... fear has always been the most marked characteristic."

Maybe you are afraid and don't know it. This seems impossible, but Napoleon Hill, in *Think and Grow Rich,* says, "One may go through life burdened with fear—and never recognize its presence."

Whether or not you are willing to admit you have an occasional flutter of cowardice when you are selling, check yourself by answering the questions that follow.

Are you afraid of:

—Fire?
—Losing your savings?
—Losing your job?
—The last twenty-five days of the month?
—A penniless old age?
—Ghosts?
—Heart disease, tuberculosis, cancer, blindness?

—Thunder and lightning?

—Life, and what it can do to you?

—Heights?

—Enclosed spaces?

—Your creditors?

—Insomnia?

—Your wife?

—Your mother-in-law?

—Impossible quotas? (Remember the wise remark on the wall of a sales manager's office: "They said it couldn't be done—so I didn't try.")

I remember reading somewhere that Greta Garbo feared crowds, Joan Crawford feared the dark, Samuel Johnson was panic-stricken at the mention of death. Kaiser Wilhelm was so afraid of cats he had an officer search his room for them every night. Luther was afraid of thunder and lightning. Edgar Allan Poe was afraid of practically everything.

Elbert Hubbard summed up the deadening power of fear in these words: "Fear defeats more men than anything else in the world."

What are the fears of salesmen?

Are you just a wee bit afraid of:

—Top executives and other important (to you) personalities? (A wealthy New York dress manufacturer—I've forgotten his name, but his nickname was "Pinky"—told me that he could talk to visiting buyers of unimportant dealers but that, when buyers came from Jordan Marsh or Hudson's or Marshall Field's, he could not face them, and always let one of his assistants show the goods.)

"The better the prospect the greater the fear"

—Customers who can buy in big volume, do they frighten you? (A. B. Hamilton of Enid, Oklahoma, told me: "Every time I have a prospect that I am afraid to call on,

I know he's a good prospect. All of my best customers are people who, at one time, I was afraid of.")

—Gruff, ill-mannered buyers?

—Hostile receptionists, secretaries, and other gate-guarders?

—Direct competition?

—Indirect competition? (For example, the salesmen of mutual trust funds find that one of their toughest competitors is a new automobile. The prospect has, for example, $2,000 available. His question is: "Shall I put it in a fund or in a car?" The automobile is thus indirect competition—and often the winner.)

—What competitors will do, say, or offer? Especially do you fear that your competitors' goods are better than those you sell?

Recently, I talked with a salesman who sold for Company A. He felt that the products he offered were inferior to those sold by Company X. "Quit," I told him, "and get a job with Company X." "No use," he answered, "Because then I'd like A's products best."

Such an attitude is probably due to fear.

Let's answer the rest of the questions about fear, and let's be honest in our answers. You know quite well you are beset by troublesome fears—so why not admit it? Don't be afraid of them—they can be cured. You will learn how to cure them in this section.

Are you afraid of responsibility?

—Do you fear advancement to an executive position? ("The Stranger," the leading character in the play, *The Passing of the Third Floor Back*, said it well: "The thing that keeps men little is the fear of being big.")

Are you afraid to grow?

Joe Barstow once turned down a wonderful opportunity for advancement. When I went to work for the Central Maine

Power Company, Joe was selling the company's preferred stock. He was a fine gentleman and a well-informed securities salesman.

Joe was offered the job of sales manager. He turned down this opportunity. I don't know why, but I am almost certain it was because of fear. Maybe it was fear of taking responsibility. Anyhow, he voted to stay a salesman.

They offered the sales management job to me—I was neither salesman nor sales manager. About my only useful qualification was that I *was not afraid of the job.* That wasn't courage —it was ignorance. Soon we had five more salesmen selling successfully in Maine.

—Do you fear recessions and depressions—bad business conditions?

—Do you fear that old salesman-killer, "Your price is too high?"

—Do you fear failure? (Bette Davis, one of the screen's all-time greats, said, "The thing that makes cowards of us all is the fear of failure.")

—Do you fear speaking in public? (My friend, the late Professor Prescott Lackey, told me of a golf professional he knew, a former caddy, a man of little education, who could usually beat the best golfers when he played against them for a side bet, but who always faded out in tournaments. After this pro lost a big tournament, he said to Professor Lackey: "While I was playing, I kept wondering what I'd do at the banquet they'd throw for the winner. I don't know how I'd manage all those knives and forks they give you. And they'd call on the winner to make a speech. I don't have to worry about that now." A salesman may be as brave as a bullfighter when he faces a single prospect—then curl up like a caterpillar when he tries to sell to a board, a commission or any group of more than two or three people. My friend, Thomas H. Nelson, told me that he once heard the president of a Texas insurance company say, "I'd jump out of a third-story window for $5, but I couldn't think how much money it would take to get me on my feet to make a speech.")

—Do you fear criticism?

—Do you fear constant rejections—by a steady stream of turn-downs? (Salesmen tend to remember their defeats and to forget their victories. As Mel S. Hattwick says in his book, *The New Psychology of Selling*, "Repeated rejection is most damaging to a salesman's ego and unless he has the determination to succeed in selling and the understanding that he must face, accept and overcome frequent rejections, he will fail." And Napoleon said, "He who fears being conquered is sure of defeat.")

—Do you fear the prospect who knows more about your product than you do? (Some salesmen are in a constant panic for fear somebody will ask them a question they cannot answer. As Emerson said, "Fear always springs from ignorance.")

—Do you fear making a mistake, and hence displeasing your boss?

—Are you afraid of objections, resistance, and turn-downs? (Alfred C. Fuller, the original Fuller Brush Man, said, "The anticipation of misfortune is the curse of selling.")

—Do you fear strangers? (This fear is well illustrated in this little item which appeared in *Management Review:* "Xenophobia (the fear of strangers) is one of the toughest obstacles a salesman encounters when he attempts to open new accounts. All too often the buyer's attitude is that of the English navvy who was with a friend when someone approached. "Who is it, Alf?" the friend asked. "I don't know," said Alf. "Strynger. 'Eave a brick at 'im.'")

—Are you afraid of quitting before you have heard "no" at least seven times? ("A hero," says a Norwegian proverb, "is one who knows how to hang on a minute longer.")

You say you are not afraid of any of these common selling terrors? Then, brother, consult a psychiatrist! You're sick!

CHAPTER 63

If you are now ready to admit that you are not completely devoid of fear, let's consider how you can develop more courage

"Any physical defects?" asked the draft board doctor.
"Yes, sir," answered the hopeful inductee, "no guts."

If you are honest with yourself, you now admit—after you have read the preceding chapter and given yourself the "Motive Test"—that you are sometimes afflicted with fear.

This is progress. Before you read that chapter, I doubt if you would have admitted that you had any fears at all.

So now let's return to a more cheerful phase of the subject. *Fear can be cured, courage can be developed—and you can do it!*

Back in 421 B.C., Euripides, the great Greek playwright said, "Courage can be taught, as a child is taught to speak."

Of course you can cure cowardice

As John M. Wilson, vice president, sales, National Cash Register Company, said in his booklet "Salesmanship as an Art":

Your fears can be overcome if you deal with them properly. Fear is an emotion. Emotions come wholly from within, and have only the strength we allow them.

As a practical matter, you can never completely cure yourself of all kinds of fears—and you don't want to. The only people who never fear anything, at any time, are lunatics. As I heard a salesman say once: "I'm glad I'm a coward—it's the only normal thing about me."

Make these objectives your own:

1. Learn to fear the right things (as, for example, an avalanche) and at the right time (when you are in the path of it).
2. Learn to control and conceal your fears.
3. Learn to carry on in spite of them.

General George S. Patton, Jr., expressed it like a true soldier when he said:

If bravery is a quality which knows not fear, I have never seen a brave man. All men are frightened. The more intelligent they are, the more they are frightened. The courageous man is the man who forces himself, in spite of his fear, to carry on.

CHAPTER **64**

A *few* salesmen know *how* to cure fear, but don't be sure you are one of them until you have studied this section

"What do I do," you ask, "to build up my courage to a point where I sell more, do it more easily, and enjoy my job more?"

In the chapters which follow I shall give you some specific rules for courage-building. But first, let's consider the three basic rules to develop courage in selling situations. Here they are:

Rule 1. Know all there is to know about the product or service you sell, and know all you can about your prospect and his wants.

Of course, I have told you this before. Probably I shall again. Be sure of this: you'll never know it too well.

If a salesman is ignorant about his product and its uses, he will be afraid to talk to prospects about it. On the other hand, the salesman who can truthfully say, "This prospect can't possibly ask me a legitimate question about this product I can't answer," should be almost unafraid—and probably is.

Here's my own personal evidence on the subject:

Back in 1949, Dale Carnegie was invited to go to Detroit to discuss the use of the Dale Carnegie course as a self-improvement program for General Motors supervisors. I tagged along.

The possibilities of this order were large enough to terrify any salesman. There we were, scheduled to talk to a vice president of one of the largest corporations in the world. This sale, if consummated, might prove to be one hundred to two hundred times as large as any sale we had ever made. And anyhow, I was never any real hero when it came to big selling deals—especially to top executives.

Yet, in the face of these terrorizing facts, I was no more nervous or perturbed when we made that call than if we had been dropping in on our next door neighbors for a game of cards.

The reason I was unafraid in this challenging selling situation was that I was full of product knowledge. I could defy anyone at General Motors to ask me any reasonable question about the course that I could not answer. As it happened in this case, no selling was necessary. General Motors was sold when we got there. They agreed on the price, told us when they wanted to start, and suggested a few minor changes in the course. No word of selling passed my lips—or Dale's.

Since that day, and up to June 1962, 29,127 salaried employees of General Motors have taken the Dale Carnegie course, yet, to this day, we do not know who did the actual selling—certainly it was neither Dale nor I.

My lack of fear on this momentous occasion was due not to native heroism, but to product knowledge!

> *Rule 2.* Know and practice the rules and principles of successful selling.

> *Rule 3.* Have an eager desire to sell your product or service *because you honestly believe it will benefit the purchaser.*

"I know all these rules," you say. "You have told us about them before."

Yes, but do you *use* all of them?

Let's consider these basic rules as they apply to your fears. Let's start with *Rule 1*—Know your product.

One man who believes as I do, that fear of failure due to lack of product knowledge is at the bottom of a lot of cloudy sales situations, is Thomas F. Bartley, general sales manager, Whirlpool Corporation. In a recent letter, he said:

The majority of retail salesmen today have an overwhelming fear that the customer will walk out without buying. Salesmen ought to present features and benefits to prospects. Instead they quote price. I think this basic fear besets not only retail salesmen but many other types. I believe this fear (that the prospect will walk out rather than buy) is responsible for much of the price-cutting and lack of stability that many manufacturers are suffering from today.

Courage goes with know-how— the "pro" is rarely afraid

The average salesman doesn't read a selling book a year. That is why he is the average salesman.

As for *Rule 2* for curing fear—Know how to sell the way professionals sell—surely the more a salesman knows and observes the laws of salesmanship, the greater his courage will be in any selling situation.

The only time a salesman who uses the Five Great Rules of Selling is entitled to be afraid is when he goes into competition with another salesman who uses the Five Great Rules.

CHAPTER 65

I know why salesmen fear to admit that they are cowards, but do you know why?

For each salesman with a spark of heroism, ten have ignition trouble.

If you are ready to admit the two important points listed below, let's go on. If not, let's argue!

Here are the two points I ask you to admit:

1. Fear is at the bottom of some of your selling problems.
2. If you cure fear, you will sell more, make more money, advance faster—no matter how well you are doing now.

I beg of you, recognize the seriousness to you of the problem of fear. Here is a mental ailment that, unless you conquer it, may wreck your whole life. Don't dally with it—fight it.

Fear isn't a mental pimple—it's a mental cancer. It isn't a psychological garter snake—it's a psychological boa constrictor.

Why salesmen admit nothing and claim everything

Do you know why you and most other salesmen hate to admit that sometimes you are just a tiny bit afraid? I think I know.

It's for the same reason you will not admit that:

—Your sales talk is not perfect.

—You do not make enough calls.

—You don't know as much as you should about your product—and so on and on through an almost endless list of things you won't admit.

I don't blame you for refusing to admit anything derogatory about your selling techniques. You have a trying job. Gateguardians turn you back; prospects refuse to talk with you, or raise a lot of objections, or refuse to buy. Oh yes, and your competitors make your life miserable, your boss expects too much, your feet hurt. It's a hard life, boys!

To overcome these discouragements, to keep your spirits up, to bolster your morale, you have to tell yourself over and over that you fear nothing, that your methods are perfect, that nothing is wrong with you except your luck, your customers, and your prospects.

Maybe you tell yourself these yarns as an automatic defense. For example, take my friend, the late Tom Falvey. I heard Tom say hundreds of times, "I'm the best salesman in the world." Of course he wasn't—and he knew it. He was just a darned good salesman. He felt, however, that he couldn't afford to think of himself as anything but perfect. If anybody had accused him of being afraid, he would have been incensed. Yet, in truth, he was an awful coward—and knew it— and when not on the defensive he admitted it to his friends. He adopted the "I'm perfect" attitude to help him maintain his morale. He sold his subconscious mind.

My advice to you is: keep telling yourself that you are perfect, that you can make no selling mistake, can do no selling wrong, are fearless.

Talk that way to *your subconscious mind*—but not to *me*. In dealing with me, through this book, admit that sometimes you are afraid. Please admit, also, that you can still improve your selling techniques, that you don't "know it all." Then go to work to improve yourself.

For the moment, just admit that you are no paragon of courage, that you can sell more if you eliminate fear—then try out my suggestions for killing fear.

It is nothing unusual for a man who develops selling courage to double his income from selling. Perhaps you can—so read on.

Let's learn, in the next chapters, what you can do to cure fear. And remember what Confucius said more than five hundred years before the birth of Christ: "A serious fault is to have faults and not try to mend them."

_____ CHAPTER 66

The more you know about your fears the less horrible they seem—so analyze them

You will never do anything without courage. It is the greatest quality of the mind next to honor.

—JAMES LANE ALLEN

Basic Rule 1 to Cure Fears: Analyze them.

When I was in my mid-teens, I used to help in my father's drug store in Great Barrington, Massachusetts. Once when I was on that job, our town struggled through an epidemic of diphtheria. Back in those days a diphtheria epidemic was a visitation to be feared, even by brave men.

I was dealing each day in the store with people from homes quarantined for diphtheria, and I was afraid I would catch it. Worse than that, I was sure I would!

I had long been one of those self-induced hypochondriacs. Already I had died, mentally, over two thousand times from a variety of fatal diseases, and I was still young and healthy.

One day, in the middle of the epidemic, I announced at the midday meal, "I think I've got diphtheria." Then I went to bed. Through the afternoon I grew steadily worse. I had even given some thought to suitable dying words and to a proper funeral.

At supper time I sent for a doctor. When he came he looked me over, took my temperature and said, "You've got it."

Immediately I felt better. I now had no imaginings to deal with—just facts. In a few minutes I fell asleep. The next morning I proved the doctor a liar. I was in perfect health.

When Bovee said, "Most of our fears are imagined, the rest are discreditable," he must have had me in mind.

If I had done what I am now advising you to do—analyzed my fears—I could have saved myself a lot of worrying. As Shakespeare said, "Present fears are less than horrible imaginings."

Many salesmen suffer more when they *think* about a hard call than when they actually *make* the call, just as many people suffer more when they think about dental work than they do when they are in the dentist's chair.

This is not just guesswork. In Westport, Connecticut, Dr. Eric L. Bernstein, psychiatrist, spent many hours in the chair of a dentist, Dr. Norman Feitelson. "Give me the works," ordered Bernstein, and for the sake of science, Feitelson did. They made scientific tests of the emotional, nervous and physical reactions. And they found the *anticipation* of pain was far worse than the *realization*.

—*Coronet*

So my advice to you, my first specific rule for curing fear in selling is: Analyze your fears.

Know your fears—then murder them!

Here's how to annihilate your fears. (If you didn't make this list when I asked you to, please do it now. You will need it. Remember, list all the fears that assail you when you sell.)

Start with your most troublesome fear, then work down the list. Analyze each one. Study them as a doctor studies a patient, and with the same objective: to find out what is the matter with the patient.

To analyze any fear, ask yourself such questions as:

—Just exactly what is my fear? What are the facts in my case? Be specific.

An interesting example of a man knocked insensible by fear,

after the danger was over, came out of Charles Taylor's *History of Great Barrington*. It happened back in the days when men traveled from Albany to Boston on horseback.

A Mr. Van Rensselaer, a young gentleman from Albany, came one evening into an inn in Great Barrington, kept by a Mr. Root, just at the eastern end of the bridge across the Housatonic River. The inn-keeper, who knew him, asked him where he had crossed the river. Mr. Van Rensselaer answered, "on the bridge." Mr. Root replied that this was impossible; because it had been raised that very day, and that not a plank had been laid on it.

Mr. Van Rensselaer said it could not be true, because his horse had come over it without any difficulty or reluctance: that the night was indeed so profoundly dark as to prevent him from seeing anything distinctly; but that it was incredible, if his horse could see sufficiently well to keep his footing anywhere, that he should not discern the danger, and [that it was] impossible for him to pass over the bridge in that condition. Each went to bed dissatisfied, neither believing the story of the other.

In the morning, Mr. Van Rensselaer went at the solicitation of his host to view the bridge, and finding it a naked frame, gazed for a moment in astonishment, and fainted.

Now, go on answering questions about your own fears:

—Is my fear a genuine one or an imagined one? For example, a fear that the purchasing agent knows more about your product than you do, may be a genuine, justifiable fear. The fear that, if you push that door bell something dreadful will happen, is an imaginary one. *Note:* Very few salesmen are shot at the front door—and if they are, it's not for selling!

—Am I justified in having this fear? What are the facts? Be specific. Write down the worst that can possibly happen to you if your most terrifying apprehensions come true.

Learn not to be afraid of things that can't hurt you.

The worst is rarely as bad as you expect

Why are you afraid to make calls? What is the worst thing that can possibly happen to you when you do make a call? Ask yourself those two questions, then sit down and write the answers. You will have to admit that you will not be subjected to physical violence. Nobody will throw you out. They may insult you, but even that is unlikely.

Suppose you are afraid to tackle an ugly purchasing agent. Sit down and write out all the disagreeable, troublesome things he can possibly say to you. You will be surprised how short the list will be.

Remember that a fuzzy, formless phobia—and that's what most fears are—which you allow to run around loose in the back of your head, is a fearsome thing, a ghost, an apparition.

Catch that wraith, reduce your fear of it to writing, then put what you have written on the table in front of you. As soon as you do this, the fearsome ghost is likely to turn out a pitiable object, more afraid of you than you of it.

A little analysis will often help salesmen to wash out their fears of tough or super-important prospects. I came across a good way to build up courage for interviews with fear-breeding prospects in the *American Salesman:*

When he's about to face a particularly tough purchasing agent, a chemical salesman bolsters his own confidence by rereading an eight-point reminder he carries in his wallet:

THE MAN ACROSS THE DESK

> He doesn't know everything.
> He's mortal.
> He works for a living.
> He has a boss.
> He has a mortgage.
> He was once 11 years old.
> He needs you.
> He wants to be sold—by someone!
> WHY NOT ME?

Ask yourself:

—Is what I fear something that is really likely to happen? I was talking one day to a little country boy on a Tennessee farm. He was eating grapes in large quantities without bothering to spit out the seeds. This was back in the days when seeds were supposed to cause appendicitis. "Eating all those seeds," I asked him, "aren't you afraid of getting appendicitis?"

"Naw," was the reply, "I ain't afeered of nothin' till I gits it." This was good sound thinking!

—If the feeling of fear I have is baseless—and I know it is, why does it keep on troubling me?

If you have acted on my advice, you have listed your selling fears and have analyzed them. If you have taken these two steps painstakingly, you have made some progress.

Now let's move along to some of the other rules, which, if you observe them, will help you to cure your fears.

CHAPTER 67

To get your fears out in the open where they belong, talk them over with one you trust—your wife, I hope

Courage isn't a gift—it's an acquirement.

Basic Rule 2 to Cure Fears: Talk them over with others who are close to you, such as your wife, your instructor, your boss, your best friend.

Share your fears, get them out in the open, get used to them. A fear you talk about is never half as terrifying as one that is hidden, suppressed, and, therefore, blown up by your imagination.

The effectiveness of this "talking-them-over" method of curing fear has been proved. Scientists of the University of California made an investigation to find out, from actual experiments, which method of curing fear worked best. They found that the most effective method was to *share* your fears.

This Week magazine gave this summary of their advice, based on their findings: "Share your fears and anxieties with another person. Don't let them accumulate. Don't bottle them up. Don't try to conceal them. It's the worries you don't get off your chest that do the mental and physical damage."

The University of California experts also learned from their experiments that for best results you should talk over your fears with someone in whom you have complete confidence, preferably with someone you love. *This Week* magazine said: "Note to husbands and wives: unburden your worries to each other—and don't delay."

To sum it up: To cure your fears in selling situations, talk them over with someone in whom you have confidence—if practicable with someone you love and who loves you.

_____ CHAPTER 68

It takes guts to put this rule to use, but if you will observe it, you can forget the rest

Frightened salesmen would pay well for an easy cure for cowardice. Does anybody know one?

Basic Rule 3 to Cure Fears: Do the thing you fear to do.

You gain strength by every experience in which you really look fear in the face. You are able to say to yourself, "I lived through this horror. I can take the next thing that comes along."
—ELEANOR ROOSEVELT, *You Learn by Living*

Emerson said, "Courage comes from having done the thing before," and Publilius Syrus, at a far earlier date, said, "Valor grows by daring, fear by holding back." Both aphorisms are wasted on a salesman who is parading up and down in front of a door in an attempt to get brave enough to knock!

College professors tell me that students from the country are afraid at first to go into restaurants, but that after they have done it a few times, their fear evaporates—and their money, too!

Surgeons say that patients who have to submit to repeated operations often fear the first one, but don't fear the third one. They say, "The hardest step is the one over the threshold."

"Yes," you say, "but I'm afraid to do what I'm afraid to do." I know it—that's why I give you other rules.

Clay W. Hamlin, a famous insurance salesman, said, "We don't need the courage to face life's big tests—what we need is the courage to face life's little tests."

If you will "do the things you fear to do," you will soon cease to fear all life's tests, big and little.

_____ **CHAPTER 69**

The next rule, "act brave," is easy to say, but hard to observe

> *It is not a crabbed prospect that is a fearful thing, but fear of a crabbed prospect.*

Rule 4 to Cure Fears: Act brave.

To apply this rule you must take two steps: (1) picture in your mind how you would act if you were brave; and (2) then act that way.

This is a rule for overcoming cowardice that you can start to work on today.

It is easy to apply—and it works. It is based on the principle that, if you act as though you have a quality, you tend to develop it. That is, if you want to become animated, act animated; if you want to become cheerful, act cheerful; if you want to become courageous, act courageous.

Let's assume you are afraid, as many men are, to talk to some prospect with a poisonous disposition and a biting tongue. To get over this particular fear: (1) Picture in your mind how you would talk to him if you had no fear. Picture yourself walking into his office with your shoulders back and your head high. Picture yourself looking him in the eye, speaking in good firm tones. (2) Do it—just that way! You may not feel like holding your head up, you may not feel like looking the prospect in the eye, but force yourself to do it. Act brave and note how rapidly you will *feel* brave.

Men have made basic changes in their personalities by using this rule—and so will you, if you will give it a conscientious trial.

This method of curing fear by acting brave is no new discovery. Aristotle, who was acting as advisor to a lot of young men back in the fourth century B.C., once said, "Men acquire a particular quality by acting in a particular way."

It helps if you just act brave

Somewhat more recently, William James (1842–1910) said, in substance, "Action and feeling go together. You can act as you want to and this tends to make you feel as you want to. Thus the . . . path to cheerfulness . . . is to sit up cheerfully, look around cheerfully and act and speak as if cheerfulness were already there . . ."

Equally, the path to courage in selling is to walk in bravely, look around bravely, and act and speak as if bravery were already there.

If you wrestle with your fear, you pin your attention on fear; if you act as if you were brave, you pin attention on courage.

A good example was "Moose" McCormick, one of the greatest pinch-hitters in all baseball history. My friend, the late Grantland Rice, in writing about the "Moose," quoted him as follows:

The percentage was against me every time I went to bat in a pinch. . . . Look at the book. The good hitter is a fellow who hits

.300 or better. That means the odds were 10 to 3 at least, against me. But that never seemed to occur to the pitchers. When I walked up there, all I thought of was that the Giants needed a hit or a run or two. And I'd look out at the pitcher, and rub my hands and say: "Well, here I am again."

A bit of advice: Don't say, "Well, here I am again" to prospects, but *think* it.

McCormick acted brave and, therefore, he tended to become brave.

It even helps to "talk brave." My friend, Jack Small, told me of an insurance salesman who called on a notoriously crusty, truculent prospect. Here is the dialogue that ensued:

Salesman: "I want to talk to you about life insurance."
Prospect: (In a roar) "What the hell do I want with life insurance?"
Salesman: (Growling right back at him) "How the hell do I know?"
Prospect: (Laughing) "Young man, you talk my language. Tell me about insurance."

That salesman will probably never again fear a boorish prospect. He talked brave and, as a result, became brave.

This rule works in prize fighting, too

Failure to act brave may have cost Jim Jeffries his famous comeback fight with Jack Johnson. When the first bell rang in this battle, instead of heading right for Johnson, Jim sidled off to one side of the ring, as if he wanted to reach a neutral corner. Johnson watched him with amazement—and with understanding. He knew then that Jim was afraid of him. From there on, it was an easy fight for Johnson.

"Tex" Rickard, the prize-fight impresario, expressed the opinion in a *Saturday Evening Post* article that "if Jeffries had gone straight at Johnson and tossed a few punches he might have won the fight. . . . Johnson was afraid of Jeffries—a bold front by Jeffries would have stimulated the fear. Instead, Johnson saw Jeffries instinctively shirk the clash ... and the fight was his."

Jeffries, by failing to act brave, lost his chance to become brave.

As Dr. John Dollard said, "One single bold act may change your whole life."

So act as though you were brave, and you will tend to become brave.

Many salesmen who suffer from cowardice have found it helps them not only to *act* brave, but also to *talk* brave. For example, there was this salesman, whose story appeared in the *American Salesman:*

A salesman, who had done a million dollars worth of business last year, received a telegram of congratulations from the sales manager of his company. "What about $2 million next year?" the telegram asked. Shortly the salesman's reply came back to the home office: "I didn't plan to stop at $2 million, but I'll follow orders. What do you suggest I do after July?"

—MORTIMER R. FEINBERG

Emerson said, "Do the thing you fear to do and the death of fear is certain." If that weren't true, the death of a lot of salesmen would be certain!

Remember, also, something else Emerson said: "He has not learned the lesson of life who does not every day surmount a fear."

So, screw up your courage, do the things you fear to do, and thus cure yourself of fear. And remember—to cure doorbell-itis, punch doorbells!

CHAPTER 70

Affirmation will cure cowardice—if you don't use faith talks now, you ought to start to do it today

Rule 5 to Cure Fears: Use affirmation, autosuggestion, faith talks.

To become brave, forget fear and learn courage. This is how to do it: (1) empty your mind of fear; and (2) affirm (tell yourself) you are brave.

"That's silly," you say. "I'm not brave and I know it. What good will it do me to tell myself something I know isn't so?"

It is a comforting and gladsome fact, as I have pointed out elsewhere in this book, that your subconscious mind will believe what you tell it—even when, in your conscious mind, you don't believe it yourself.

So, if you keep on telling yourself you are brave, your subconscious mind will finally believe it. By and by, you will become brave—or at least braver than you were. Then you tell yourself no lie when you say, "I'm not afraid."

Start today to use anti-fear faith talks

"Specifically how do I go about affirming that I am brave?" you ask. "What is the schedule?"

It's quite simple. First, write out your own anti-fear faith talk.

If I were selling today and needed to bolster my courage, I might use a faith talk that went something like this: "I'm not afraid of anything or anybody—I'm brave. Hot doorbells can't burn me, tough prospects can't scare me, sour objections can't throw me. I'm brave now and I will stay brave." Probably most of the time I would use, as a shorter version, the sentence, "I'm brave now, and I'm going to stay brave."

This particular anti-fear faith talk usually works for me, but maybe it wouldn't work for you. So write your own. Make it fit your situation. Do it right now.

Now you have an anti-fear talk and you are ready to use it. You remember, however, that before you begin to use your faith talk, you need to pump negative thoughts out of your mind.

Here, in substance, are Norman Vincent Peale's suggestions for this unloading process:

Drain the mind daily. Do it just before you go to sleep at night. Use your imagination—see in your mind all fear thoughts flowing out of your head as water flows out of a hand bowl. Then repeat to yourself these words, "I am now emptying my mind of all fear." As you repeat these words, see in your mind's eye these thoughts flowing out—then go to sleep.

Each morning, as soon as you are awake, give yourself your faith talk. Use it again and again throughout the day. Repeat it before every hard call and after every turn-down.

As you repeat your faith talk, picture yourself making a sale, or bring to mind in detail some great success you have had in selling. As Paul Speicher says in *The Gift of Courage:*

Be brave once—then just repeat

Hang on the walls of your mind the memory of your successes. Take counsel of your strength, not your weakness. Think of the good jobs you have done. . . . Think of the big moments of your life!

This same thought was well expressed by James T. Mangan in *Specialty Salesman.* He said: "If you have been brave once, you can be brave always. It's a simple matter of recalling one of the thousands of brave deeds you have done: dwell on it boldly and even immodestly for a few moments."

Don't say your faith talk over without *feeling*—don't sound like a defective Victrola record. Say it with animation, with force, with purpose. Otherwise, it may not penetrate to your subconscious mind.

Lots of people who have tried autosuggestion will tell you it doesn't work. And I'll tell you why I think it doesn't—for them. They do not give it a chance—they quit too soon.

Napoleon Hill said it well: "The price of ability to influence your subconscious mind is everlasting persistence."

My friend, Mrs. Ethel Knight Pollard, a great salesman and a great sales manager when she was in the business world, recommends that salesmen, to build up their morale and their faith in themselves, go mentally through each step of some successful interview or a closed sale. Do it every night or every morning—one sale each day. Go through it in detail: what you said, what he said, what objections he brought up and how you answered them.

If you didn't have a successful sale yesterday, go back to the last good one you had. Don't hesitate to go mentally through the same successful sale again and again.

The value of this exercise comes from reminding yourself that you have been brave and successful.

Ben Sweetland, in an article for the magazine, *Specialty Salesman*, said, in substance: "The poor salesman sees himself as a poor salesman. The good salesman sees himself as a big producer."

The more clearly you see this picture of your successful self, the more often you show this moving picture to your subconscious mind, the better results you will have.

To sum it up: As you *tell* yourself, "I shall sell the next prospect," have in your mind a picture of yourself getting the signed order. See yourself make the sale and walk out with the order.

Do it and watch sales increase.

Rule 6 to Cure Fears: Remember your successes—forget your failures.

You have a right to be wrong. Learn from your mistakes. The perpetuation of an error is far more destructive than making that error.

—DR. LESTER L. COLEMAN, AUTHOR OF *Freedom from Fear*

Think of your successes—forget your failures

I wish every frightened salesman—yes, and every unsuccessful salesman, too—might have read an article in *The Reader's Digest* by Arthur Gordon entitled "Where Success Comes From."

I am reproducing part of it here, with much gratitude and appreciation to the author and to *Reader's Digest*:

A single-barreled, 20-gauge shotgun, given to me for Christmas, had made me the proudest 13-year-old in Georgia. On my first hunt, moreover, by a lucky freak, I had managed to hit the only bird I got a shot at . . .

The second hunt was a different story. My companion was an elderly judge, a friend of my father's. . . . We found plenty of birds, and the judge knocked down one or two on every covey rise. I, on the other hand, didn't touch a feather . . .

Then old Doc, the pointer, spotted a quail in a clump of palmetto. He froze, his long tail rigid. Something in me froze, too, because I knew I was facing one more disgrace.

This time, however, instead of motioning me forward, the judge placed his gun carefully on the ground. "Let's set a minute," he suggested companionably. . . . Then, slowly, he said, "Your dad was telling me you hit the first quail you shot at the other day."

"Yes sir," I said miserably. "Just luck, I guess."

"Maybe," said the judge, "But that doesn't matter. Do you remember exactly how it happened? . . ."

I nodded, because it was true. I could summon up every detail . . .

"Well, now," the judge said easily, "you just sit here and relive that shot a couple of times. Then go over there and kick up that bird. . . . Just think about that one good shot you made the other day—and sort of keep out of your own way . . ."

Out flashed the quail. Up went the gun, smoothly and surely. . . . Seconds later, Doc was at my knee, offering the bird.

I was all for pressing on, but the judge unloaded his gun. "That's all for today, son," he said. "You've been focusing on failure all afternoon. I want to leave you looking at the image of success."

. . . And tension, which nine times out of ten is based on the memory of past failures, can be reduced or even eliminated by the memory of past successes.

At first I applied this image-of-success technique only to athletics. Later I began to see that a similar principle operated for many of the successful career people whom I met through my work . . .

One such man, a corporation president, reminisced to me about his first job. "I started my sales career," he said, "by selling pots and pans from door to door. The first day I made only one sale in 40 attempts. But I never forgot the face of that woman who finally bought something . . . how it changed from suspicion and hostility to gradual interest and final acceptance. For years I used to recall her face as a kind of talisman when the going was rough." To this man, that housewife's face was a mirror which reflected the image of himself as a successful salesman.*

The British magazine *Tid-Bits* summed it up nicely with: "Always forget the past. No man ever backed into prosperity."

There you have the six Rules to Cure Fears that block your way to sales success. You have ample evidence that these rules will work for you as they have for tens of thousands of other salesmen.

Start today to use them. Start now, this moment! Do this and feel your fears fall away.

_____ CHAPTER 71

I've told you what to do to cure fear—now I tell you a few things you shouldn't do

> *Courage isn't lack of fear. It's standing your ground in spite of it.*

Here are some "don'ts" for men whose courage needs bolstering.

* Copyright 1960 by *The Reader's Digest* Association, Inc.

1. Don't expect to become brave in a minute. You took a long time to become the coward you are, so be willing to take a lot of time to get rid of your fears.

2. Don't delay—start now. As Dan Bennett said, "Some people never put off a hard task *until tomorrow*. They put it off for good."

3. Don't expect ever to rid yourself completely of fear.

4. Don't depend on Dutch courage. The Scots have a saying, "There is no medicine for fear"—especially no "medicine" that comes out of a bottle. Alcoholic courage has many weaknesses: you can't time anything alcoholic—you don't know when it may explode; you can't gauge the force of the explosion; "Dutch courage" gets on your breath.

5. Don't fear your prospects. Quintus Ennius said wisely, "Whom they fear they hate."

6. Don't ever quit your fight against fear. The fear habit is almost as treacherous as the narcotic habit. So persevere in your fight. Remember the definition of perseverance given by a Negro minister who had his troubles. "Perseverance," he said, "means firstly to take hold; secondly to hold on; and thirdly and lastly to never leave go." So, to put it in the vernacular, "Don't never leave go!"

7. Don't take the battle too lightly—remember, fear is a fierce foe. Anybody who says fear is easy to whip just hasn't tried. As Uncle Eben said in the *Washington Star*: "When I hears a man tellin' 'bout how easy he can drive a mule, I knows right off he ain't no reg'lar mule-driver."

8. Don't use reverse affirmation. Don't use negative suggestion. As the Dutch philosopher, Spinoza said, "So long as a man imagines that he cannot do this or that—so long is it impossible to him that he should do it."

> *Courage is a priceless jewel which you can give your-self, but which no one else can give you.*
> —PAUL SPEICHER IN *The Gift of Courage*

_____ CHAPTER 72

What some great men, from Confucius to Norman Vincent Peale, have said in aphorisms about fear and courage

Leadership requires courage. It cannot be based on timidity.
> —STANLEY L. MC MICHAEL, *Selling Real Estate*

*   *   *

Bottled-up fears are as dangerous as bottled-up volcanoes.

*   *   *

Samuel Butler said that life was one long process of getting tired. With some salesmen it is one long process of getting scared.

*   *   *

The one thing that's worse than a quitter is a man who's afraid to begin.

*   *   *

Fear is the great destroyer. Give fear command of your life and you will be powerless to achieve anything worth while.
> —CLAUDE M. BRISTOL

*   *   *

A famous psychologist asserts that "fear is the most disintegrating enemy of human personality."
> —NORMAN VINCENT PEALE

*   *   *

A salesman who says he is not interested in curing his fear makes about as much sense as a man in the middle of a desert who isn't interested in a flowing artesian well.

*   *   *

It is good to fear the worst; the best will favor itself.

—DRAXE

*　*　*

The fear inspired by a superior being is a mystery which cannot be reasoned away.

—BERNARD SHAW, *Saint Joan*

*　*　*

Fear kills more than disease.

—GEORGE HERBERT, *Jacula Prudentum*

*　*　*

As a man grows older it is harder and harder to frighten him.

—JOHN PAUL RICHTER

*　*　*

It is not the size of the dog in the fight
But the size of the fight in the dog.

—TOM BARRETT

*　*　*

Tough selling is tough because we fear it.

*　*　*

A good place to find good prospects is where other salesmen fear to go.

*　*　*

To make a hard call harder, put it off.

—WITH APOLOGIES TO OLIN MILLER

*　*　*

Fears cannot always be believed. Most of them are liars.

—FRED PIERCE CORSON

*　*　*

Bravery never goes out of fashion.

—THACKERAY

*　*　*

Get the better of bad fortune by proving you can stand worse.

—FINNISH PROVERB

*　*　*

Our greatest glory is not in never failing, but in rising every time we fall.

—CONFUCIUS

*   *   *

If you have courage, you have twice the chance to win that you would otherwise have.

*   *   *

Unless a man shows courage, he has no security for preserving any other virtue.

—JAMES M. BARRIE

Think over that Barrie quotation. If a man lacks courage, what certainty has he that when fear overtakes him he will not lie, steal, forge, murder? Fear and greed—if we could kill them off, what a wonderful world we would have!

PART THREE

Four perplexing problems
that plague most salesmen

Problem 11. *Many salesmen don't know what the market-ing concept is and what to do about it.*

Problem 12. *How to sell to buying committees.*

Problem 13. *How to sell yourself to yourself.*

Problem 14. *Many salesmen do not know the difference between "primary objective" and "dominant buying motive," or how to use either one of them.*

The new "marketing" concept may affect you or it may not, but you'd better know about it

If you read business magazines—and you ought to—you have read a lot about the "marketing" concept.

It is not, in my judgment, quite as new, different, or wonderful as some writers on sales subjects would have us believe.

However, it is new and in some ways revolutionary. So, if you work for a company which goes in for "modern marketing," you should learn all about it. If your company has not adopted it, you should learn about it so you will know what other salesmen are talking about when they discuss it.

"Marketing" is modern—maybe

If you work for a company that has adopted the "marketing" concept, you may find yourself in a more responsible job

What is "marketing" as the word is now used?

I own a copy of the newest and largest American dictionary. But new as it is, and big as it is, I find no mention in it of the word "marketing" to mean what some writers and speakers now say it means. That's how new it is!

The new idea of "marketing" is that it takes in the whole process of making the right products and moving them from the manufacturer to the ultimate consumer.

Selling is merely a step in this "marketing" process.

"Marketing," as we now use the word in its new meaning, calls for a new kind of salesman. To quote from an article headed, "The Salesman Isn't Dead—He's Different," by Carl Rieser, in *Fortune:* "The new era salesman is involved with the whole distribution pipeline, beginning with the tailoring of the products to the customer's desire and extending through their promotion and advertising to final delivery to the ultimate consumer."

Some of those who write about the new "marketing" predict that the conventional salesman will soon be as obsolete as the acetylene automobile lamp. They don't always bother to point out that these dire predictions do not apply to all kinds of salesmen, but only to one small group of salesmen.

My advice to salesmen in general is: don't be alarmed. Barring a nuclear war, salesmen will be around for quite a spell. The "marketing" concept will for a long time directly affect only a relatively small number of the salesmen of America.

259

"Marketing" affects some salesmen,
but by no means all of them

One of the new features of "marketing" which will adversely affect some salesmen is the use of the IBM and
similar machines for electronic data processing. These machines make possible automatic ordering and automatic inventory control. When machines take over the job of ordering,
less need will exist for the "reorder salesmen."

Ed Mooney, manager, packaged goods merchandising, *Life*
magazine, writes me:

As automation expands and improves, it is certain that fewer and
fewer salesmen will be needed for reorder calls.

An increasing number of volume buyers—both chain and wholesale—are handling reorders of merchandise on an electronic basis.
I've been told, for example, that 2,000 buying offices were due to
install IBM-type equipment this year alone, for the purpose of re-
ordering goods.

Very simply, then, the X-Chain buyer of soup will merely check
his warehouse inventory and pipeline stocks via IBM and issue an
order to his supplier which will bring his soup inventory up to the
desired level. The buyer doesn't have to interview the soup salesman. His needs are at his fingertips.

As for the writers who talk about the "downgrading of salesmen," they ignore most varieties of salesmen. I wonder what
percentage of the 4,638,985 men and women rated by the
recent United States census as workers in the sales field will be
directly and materially affected by "marketing?" No retail
salesmen surely, no insurance salesmen, no investment security
salesmen, or appliance salesmen, or door-to-door salesmen.
More than four million salesmen will not, I believe, be
affected, adversely or otherwise, by the new "marketing"
concept.

So let's not be disturbed for now by the "passing of the
salesman."

The relatively few salesmen who do have to face the changed situation brought about by what is referred to as the "marketing" concept, must, however, change with the times.

Says *Fortune* magazine:

The old-time drummer has been replaced by a new kind of salesman. He doesn't sell the product; he sells service....

The trend is away from the "sales engineer".... His successor is a man capable of absorbing stacks of information churned out by the marketing department, and of applying it to his customers' problems.

Since few salesmen are affected by the "marketing" concept, and so little is known about it by so few, I do not feel justified in giving it more space.

My advice (this is written in the spring of 1964) is, if you are likely to be affected by "marketing," watch it closely to see just what changes you must make in your manner of selling in order to stay even with progress. Maybe you are one of the salesmen mentioned in the *Fortune* article who can "absorb stacks of information ... and apply it to your customers' problems." If so, you are in line for a more responsible job.

Another great change in the field of selling has been wrought by the use of buying committees. Let's consider them in subsequent chapters.

Did you ever sell to a committee?

_____ CHAPTER 74

Buying in the billions is done yearly by committees, so it behooves salesmen to learn to sell to committees

Part and parcel with self-service is the hardheaded, two-fisted buying committee. An increasing share of the marketer's output will be bought through such committees.
—Sales Management Magazine

When buying committees took over the purchasing for chains and supers, they wrought almost as big a change for salesmen who sell to those giant organizations as the advent of moderate-priced automobiles did for salesmen of harnesses and buggies.

The buying committee is not a new institution. Forty-odd years ago, when I managed an organization that sold investment securities, our salesmen ran into them once in a while. Even then, some banks had buying committees which considered new bond issues.

Two experts on selling to chains give us information about buying committees

Two men who are experts on the subject of selling to chains and super markets were kind enough to give me some information about the present condition and probable future trend of selling to buying committees. They are Ed Mooney, manager of package goods merchandise for *Life* magazine, and Robert S. Larkin, director of chain store sales for Philip Morris, Inc. I am going to give you the substance of some letters they wrote me about the buying committee situation and how it affects salesmen.

First, the letter from Bob Larkin:

The buying committee represents an interesting search for an answer to one of the biggest business problems (How to buy efficiently). It should not, however, be regarded as the complete and final solution.

Some companies have tried buying committees and discarded them. Some companies have been accused of using the buying committee as a shield. It certainly gives the buyer a potent device (or objection), since the company's "no" can always be ascribed to buying committee action—whether or not the item or plan has ever seen the light of day before the full committee. Some chains, on the other hand, make full use of the buying committee.

Safeway's division in Washington, D.C., has experimented with the tape recorder. Salesmen are given two minutes to make their pitch on tape. The tapes are later played before the buying committee.

If you sell to chains, you generally deal with committees

Mr. Mooney's letter was in answer to a series of questions I asked him and reads, in part, as follows:

Let me merely comment on the questions you proposed in your letter of February 14th, keeping in mind that these comments deal only with the retail grocery business:

1. Figuring that some 800 chains and 1500 wholesale grocery headquarters purchase the major share of grocery products from suppliers, I would estimate that perhaps 2000 of these 2300 offices use the buying committee system.
2. It is a rare thing when a salesman is allowed to appear before a committee. I don't think we would be far off in guessing that only one or two per cent of these buying committees allow the salesmen to give their pitch to them in person.
3. In those very rare cases where the salesman is permitted to go into the committee meeting, I think that his sales story would be of sufficient importance to give him 10 or 15 minutes.
4. I believe that the head buyer or director of purchases would be the man to authorize a salesman's appearance before the buying committee.

"Life Merchandising" is working at this time very closely with buying committees. I won't bore you with the details, but will send a discussion of the advent of the buying committee and some of the complexities that exist in food distribution.

Here is the result of the work of one committee at one meeting:

New items approved------------------------------ 31
Items held over for future discussion---------- 6
Items not approved------------------------------ 141

(*Note:* What follows is from the discussion mentioned in Mr. Mooney's letter. Most figures in the letter and the discussion are estimates.)

Buying committees become tremendously important to some salesmen

Food retailing is the largest single industry in the country. In 1960, for example, retail food store sales approximated 58 billion dollars.

Roughly, there are 260,000 grocery stores in the United States. Of these 260,000 stores, 33,000 (or 12.7% of the total) are supermarkets. The rest are superettes, semi-self-service stores, or just plain "mom 'n' pops."

Chains, voluntaries and co-ops observe the same general buying procedures. In essence, one successful sale at headquarters gets a broad store distribution for a product.

Thus, taking the Los Angeles market for example, when the Safeway chain purchases a new item, it will invariably be shipped to all 197 Safeway stores in the area.

The average chain considers one hundred new items a week

Manufacturers are coming out with new items every day. Added to these new items are the many existing products whose manufacturers are attempting to broaden distribution. In 1960, the average chain or wholesaler was offered 100 new items a week—

5000 during the year! Of the 100 items offered, each week, some
85, on an average, were rejected, 15 accepted, and 10 items already
in stock were dropped to make room for the 15 new ones.

With the avalanche of new products since World War II,
chains and wholesalers set up "buying committees," whose purpose
it was to evaluate the new items being presented and make a group
decision. That would seem to be an ideal solution to the problem,
except that, buying committee members, being extremely busy with
many other duties, could devote only a minimum of time—a
minute or two—to each item considered.

Let's look at the buying committee procedure in sequence. Let's
say that Pillsbury has developed a new cake-mix item—has spent a
great deal of money in research and development, has formulated
a costly advertising budget, built inventories and fired up the sales
department! The salesman calls on chain headquarters, presents
the item to the cake-mix buyer in a brief few minutes. He cannot
get the decision from the buyer, but must wait for the decision of
the committee; *nor can he pitch his product to the committee*, but
must rely on the buyer to be his spokesman in the committee meeting. It is apparent that Pillsbury's tremendous investment is hang-
ing by a very slim thread!

Bond salesmen who sell to banks have had long experience
with buying committees. Almost all banks of any considerable
size have a committee which decides whether or not to purchase new issues. Banks seem to have no standard practice with
respect to allowing bond salesmen to present issues to buying
committees. A few do, most don't.

As Vernon Schwaegerle, executive vice president of the
Financial Public Relations Association, wrote, "Whether to
allow salesmen to appear before the Investment Committee
or a member of it, or not at all, is a decision reserved by
individual banks."

These bank buying committees resemble those in the
grocery business, in that they rarely allow a salesman to appear
before the whole committee. The salesman either makes his
pitch to one member of the committee, or, in many cases, is
required to submit his talk in writing.

Is this the end of the conventional salesman in the chain and grocery fields?

E. B. Weiss, vice president, merchandising, Doyle Dane Bernbach, Inc., in a series of ten articles in *Sales Management* magazine "The Revolution in Personal Selling," painted a gloomy picture of the fate of the traditional salesman in the chain store and grocery field where, as we know, most of the buying is done by committees which have little or no time to listen to conventional pitches.

As Mr. Weiss points out, in most cases in the grocery field, the salesman must tell his story to a buyer, who will pass it on to the committee. (As most salesmen have learned, the sales pitch given to one man and passed on by him to a second is usually incomplete, and is frequently garbled.)

Probably the salesman was limited to five to fifteen minutes with the buyer and had small chance to get his whole story clearly into the buyer's head.

What is the way out?

Naturally, the salesman who is no longer allowed to sell in the conventional way will look around for other ways.

With some help from articles by Joan and Leslie Rich, and by Mr. Weiss, I have worked out suggestions for salesmen who are not allowed to appear before buying committees which may enable them to sell, in spite of such a formidable obstacle:

1. Pay a lot of attention to filling out the forms on which your product must, in many cases, be presented to buying committees. You should try to get permission to add matter not called for in the form.
2. Try to train the buyer to be enough of a salesman to sell your product to the buying committee. (That's a forlorn hope, at best!)
3. Put into the hands of the buyer the pitch you want him to make to the committee.

4. Supply the buyer with the results of marketing tests of your product.
5. Supply information about your product to the research division of the company you are trying to sell.
6. Be sure, if you do get the chance to appear before a buying committee, that you have a strong presentation prepared.
7. Have a slide film or picture film which is brief enough to be acceptable, and interesting enough to hold the attention of a committee which perhaps has already heard pitches for about fifty or a hundred other products.
8. Send personal letters to buying committee members.
9. Get a top executive of your company to make a sales pitch to a top member of the prospect's organization.

Robert S. Larkin, who is mentioned earlier in this discussion of selling to chains and supers, wrote:

I could give a lot of emphasis to Item 9. What filters down from the top is becoming more and more important. In other words, the salesman of today is shooting for bigger stakes. Why should you expect him to write train-load orders when he has been trained to write orders for cases?

10. Fit yourself for this new form of selling by knowing all there is to know about your product and about competing products.

Salesmen in the field of supers and chains are advised to buy and read Mr. Weiss's book, *The Vanishing Salesman*, published by the McGraw-Hill Book Company.

Some further rules were worked up from a talk made by James Cooke, president of Allied Supermarkets, Inc., before the New York Sales Executives Club. Here they are:

Talk in terms of "categories"

11. Point out that the selling and marketing activities of your company are not strictly self-seeking and that they

coincide with the distributor's interests. As Mr. Cooke said, "You will never get the other guy's vote unless you can demonstrate that your self-interest coincides with his."

12. When you talk with a prospect, talk not in terms of your own individual product, but instead of the whole category in which your product falls. Mr. Cooke points out that a retailer may sell 5,000 different items with an average net profit, after taxes, of about a nickel an item. Mr. Cooke said:

It isn't likely that a retailer would be expertly informed on so many products. Nor will he get very excited about his 5¢ net profit per store on the total sale of an item. However, the distributor and manufacturer begin to approach common ground when they talk of the category in which the item is found. First of all, the problem becomes manageable for the retailer on the basis of categories because there are about 50 of these compared with 5,000 items.

Secondly, the *net profit per category* becomes substantial—something in the neighborhood of $10 per week per store—not a five-cent piece. The grocery manufacturer who approaches a retailer with a survey of an entire category, makes suggestions for better space allocation and position based on fairness and a sound study of movement, presents honest recommendations on product eliminations, helps with the necessary rearrangement, and generally assists the retailer in merchandising the total category, will find himself getting a warm reception, a willing ear and cordial cooperation.

13. Keep your promotional plans simple.
14. When you present a new product, make a recommendation, also, for the elimination of another product that has outlived its usefulness.
15. Become a professional specialist. Mr. Cooke commented:

Salesmen and missionaries could be the most valuable personnel if they were well-informed professional specialists in all the operational and merchandising aspects of their products and of the categories in which they fall . . .

The *real* salesman sends the buyer into the committee meeting absolutely convinced that the new product in question is a must for the committee to authorize.

The *real* salesman sells committee members in advance on his product's merits.

The *real* salesman doesn't ask the committee to waste its time on trivia. When one of his products is presented, the committee knows that he and his company mean business.

In a nutshell, then, in my opinion, the way to get around the buying committee is to meet it head on. Let the weak sisters complain about the big, bad ogre. The smart salesman, the reputable salesman will get the order, or at least a darn good hearing. And he'll be listened to on future calls.

Some further suggestions that may help salesmen to make sales to buying committees I took from an article, "How to Reach the Off-bounds Buying Committees," by Joan and Leslie Rich in the *American Salesman* (April 1963). The substance of some of their suggestions is embodied in the following rules:

16. When you are asked to fill out a form to present your product to a buying committee, be sure you fill it out completely, clearly, and honestly.

As Donald E. Stout, district manager of the Campbell Sales Company, said, "The trick is to find out what the store is most interested in—traffic, profit margin, etc., then concentrate on that."

17. Try to get the buyer to fill out the form while you are there.
18. After you have convinced the buyer of the worth of the product you are pushing, drill him on what you want him to say to the committee. (You'd better be on friendly terms with the buyer if you expect him to let you drill him on anything! I'd rather drill a rattlesnake than some buyers I have known.)
19. Supply samples of the new product.
20. If your product is something that can be effectively

demonstrated, try to get the buyer to sit in on a demonstration.

21. It is usually safe to call on committee members or to take them out to lunch, provided you handle everything through the buyer.

This section tells you how to use a miracle sales stimulator that can revolutionize your sales career

Most of you know about affirmation—or faith talks, positive thinking, and autosuggestion. I wonder how many of you who know about these miracle-workers use them consciously and consistently in your selling?

Salesmen who fail to use affirmation every day are costing themselves money.

Unless you are a confirmed user of positive thinking, read this section—and profit by it.

CHAPTER 75

A single twenty-two-word sentence converted an apparently hopeless failure into a sparkling success

Once you give up expecting that tomorrow will be a better day, the chances are it won't be.
—BURTON HILLIS IN *Better Homes & Gardens*

I started this book with the amazing story of Johnny Post.

You will recall that affirmation—a pep talk he delivered to himself—converted him from a pitiful failure to a gratifying success.

What miraculously changed this man?

The miracle-worker was a twenty-two word faith talk repeated over and over. To put it a bit more scientifically, this marvel was performed by affirmation.

It will work for you, too

From the Johnny Post example anybody could work out the rule that follows: *To sell successfully, tell yourself you will sell successfully.*

This rule works. Don't argue with me about it—I *know.*

Oh yes, some salesmen will tell you, "I tried it and it's no good." Usually if you ask these "failure boys" about their experience, you will find they did not give affirmation a fair trial. The man who tries it a couple of minutes a couple of times can't hope for success—much less miracles!

I admit, also, that some people are more "suggestible" than others and that the most suggestible seem to benefit most from autosuggestion. I doubt, however, if many salesmen are so "unsuggestible" that they cannot make more sales if they give themselves sincere, enthusiastic, and repeated faith talks.

Evidence that affirmation really increases sales was given by Ben Sweetland in *Specialty Salesman*. He wrote: "In one of my books I describe an experiment I once conducted with a group of salesmen. I urged them ... for a period of a month, at least ... to repeat to themselves frequently from morning 'till night, 'I am a great salesman.' Results were fabulous."

—————————————————————————————————— CHAPTER 76

"Tell cowards they are brave and you induce them to become brave," said Napoleon, who was an authority

Blaise Pascal, French scientist and philosopher (1623–1662), said: "Man is so made that by continually telling him he is a fool, he believes it, and by continually telling it to himself, he makes himself believe it. For man holds an inward talk with himself alone, which it behooves him to regulate well."

"Behavior can be changed," wrote Matthew N. Chappel, "by two mental processes—one process is learning and the other is forgetting."

So, if you wish to become brave, forget fear and learn courage. That is: (1) empty your mind of fear; and then (2) affirm (tell yourself) you are brave.

The magic of this method for building self-confidence was well expressed in an article in *Specialty Salesman* magazine. It said, in part:

The world belongs to the man who shouts loud and clear, "I can do anything! I don't care how impossible it is, I can do it." More important, the self-confident man is he who makes this wholesome boast, not out loud, but *inside* himself. He's constantly repeating to his inner self, for his ears alone, the thrilling gospel, "I can do anything!"

As many salesmen know already, the practical way for a salesman to use affirmation on himself is to give himself both pep talks and faith talks.

Just to be sure we all know what we are talking about, let's have a few definitions:

To Affirm—To declare to be true, to assert (*Thorndike-Barnhart Dictionary*).

Affirmation—An assertion, a statement made positively, a protestation, a suggestion to the subconscious mind.

Pep Talk—A brief, inspirational statement made to yourself by yourself to stir you for a brief period into greater animation, greater exertion, greater excitement, and greater belief in your ability to do what you are about to attempt.

Faith Talk—(For our purpose) a form of affirmation designed to create in a person a belief in himself and his ability to perform successfully whatever he attempts. It is to be used over long periods—perhaps a lifetime.

The pep talk is the talk you give yourself just before an important sale or in some selling emergency. It should be brief. It will be effective, normally, for only a short time. A pep talk effectively delivered to yourself will enable you to greet your prospect with excitement and to open your sales talk with real enthusiasm. This enthusiasm will be the kind that telegraphs to your prospect this message: "I really believe I can do for you something you want done—I can benefit and serve you."

The faith talk, on the other hand, is a serious "inward talk" you give yourself daily—or more often—over months or even years. It is usually longer than the pep talk, and more serious in wording and in purpose. It is designed to build up over the years your faith in yourself, to keep you always full of belief that you will succeed. The smart salesman will give himself a faith talk every night of his business life.

To make your pep talks and faith talks more effective, use the suggestions you will find in the following chapter.

_____ CHAPTER **77**

If you don't know all you should about how to use these "talks," this chapter will be of real help

You'll never get astigmatism by looking on the bright side.

Now let's consider how we can best use pep talks and faith talks to increase our sales, our income, and our happiness.

I like the jingle that Charles Churchill wrote on the subject:

The surest way to health,
    say what they will,
Is never to suppose we
    shall be ill.
Most of those evils we
    poor mortals know
From doctors and
    imagination flow.

Suggestion 1. (Perhaps the most important suggestion of all) Be persistent.

Napoleon Hill said it well: "The price of ability to influence your subconscious mind is everlasting persistence."

Suggestion 2. Think positively.

An amazing testimonial to the effectiveness of positive thinking came in an article written by Alex Haley, "Phyllis Diller, The Unlikeliest Star," published in the *Saturday Evening Post* and reproduced with their permission.

What positive thinking did for Phyllis Diller

The tension inside Phyllis exploded early one Sunday evening. Neither she nor Sherwood (her husband) can remember what trivial incident made her scream at him, slam out of the house and walk, she thinks, for miles. Passing a strange church, she turned back. "Something forced me," she says. As she slid down in the last pew she heard the minister reading, "Whatsoever things are true ... whatsoever things are pure ... think on these things."

"The words seemed to be addressed directly to me, as if God Himself were giving me a message," Phyllis says. "I went home from the church and I stayed home having skull-and-soul sessions with myself and reading self-help books. Before, I had always scoffed at claims that anyone could change his life for the better by positive thinking. But considering the shape we were in, I was willing to try anything.

"I didn't change my life overnight, but at least I glimpsed what I had to do. I had to stop wallowing in negative thoughts about what a hard time we were having. I knew I had to think and work in positive ways with the good things I had."

It was astonishing to hear the outlandish funny woman credit "positive thinking" and her family's cooperation for making her a comedienne . . .

Phyllis has had her share of failures. "Honey, I've been smashed!" After one night, the Fontainebleau Hotel in Miami fired her. She flubbed a Hollywood screen test and once, after three rehearsals, the *Steve Allen Show* dropped her.

Phyllis never once considered giving up. "I've had fear thoughts —I'm only human. But every fear thought and I battled it out eyeball to eyeball, and I won."

Don't get faith talks and positive thinking confused.

In faith talks you *talk* to yourself; in positive thinking, you *think* to yourself.

Maybe you say, "I can't control my thinking."

That's true, you can't—not completely. But you can control it to some extent, even at the time you start to practice positive thinking, and the more you drill yourself at thought control, naturally the more command you will have over your thoughts.

So do your best to:

1. Wash negative thoughts from your mind. When you are selling, direct your attention away from yourself—your worries and doubts—and think just one thing: "I shall sell my next prospect."

2. Force yourself to think thoughts of success, courage, and happiness. You will be surprised how you can control your thoughts if you practice positive thinking.

Is it worth the bother? I know of few drills that will do more to increase your success and improve your character than the drill of replacing negative thoughts with positive thoughts.

Suggestion 3. It is not enough merely to *tell* yourself that you will succeed—you must actually *see* yourself succeeding.

Maxwell Maltz, M.D., in the condensation of his book which appeared in *The Reader's Digest*, tells of an experiment which was made on basketball players. Two groups of basketball players were given a twenty-day drill in throwing the ball into the basket. Each group worked for twenty minutes a day. One group worked with a real ball and a real basket. The other group merely *imagined* that they were sinking throws.

As might have been expected, the men who worked with real balls and real baskets improved materially—24 per cent, in fact.

But now for the miracle: the players who *imagined* that they were throwing the ball into the basket improved almost as much.

With respect to this experiment, Dr. Maltz said, "Such mental rehearsals or dry runs have been used to advantage . . . by salesmen preparing to face a difficult prospect."

See yourself a success

To get the best results from faith talks, not only tell yourself that you are going to make the sale—actually *see yourself making it.*

"Your automatic mechanism," says Dr. Maltz, "cannot tell the difference between an actual experience and one which is vividly imagined." The doctor goes on to point out that, if we picture ourselves as successful, success becomes real to us and rewards us with success-type responses and emotions. "To accomplish this," says the doctor, "the goal must be seen so clearly that it becomes real to your brain and nervous system."

Neglect these two rules
at your peril!

CHAPTER **78**

You are not ready to make your pitch until you know what your prospect wants and why he wants it

My friend, the late James A. Peoples, who was in Vanderbilt University at the same time I was, and who lived at Gatlinburg, Tennessee, gave me this example of the danger any salesman faces when he does not know the prospect's *primary objective.*

A group of land speculators came to Thad D. Smith, attorney of Gatlinburg, and told him that they wanted to buy a tract of land owned by Squire Maples. They then asked Mr. Smith for his advice as to how they should go about buying it.

Thad told them to go home, get a first-class salesman and have him report to Mr. Smith.

In due course, not a salesman, but a sales*woman* arrived and said she had come to buy Squire Maples' land for her clients.

Thad warned her that, because she was a woman, and because the Squire felt the way he did about women in business, it would be difficult if not impossible for her to buy the land from the Squire but suggested a procedure that he felt would succeed if anything would. Here, in substance, is what Mr. Smith said to the sales gal:

"The Squire owns a car but cannot drive it. He loves to ride around. So you take him for a ride every day. Always end the ride at the property. Then tackle the Squire to give you a price."

The lady followed instructions for four or five days and each day, at the end of the ride, asked the Squire to put a price on the tract.

Each time the Squire answered, "I'll think about it."

By that time the sales gal felt sure her present technique was not what she needed. So she said at the end of the next ride, "Squire, you have again and again promised to give me a price on that land, and you have failed to do it. Now I am going to make you an offer."

"That's agreeable to me," replied the Squire.

"We will give you one hundred thousand dollars for that tract."

At that remark, the Squire suffered a slight heart attack and fell out of the car!

The sales gal finally got him back in the car and drove him home. The saleswoman then packed up and returned to Florida.

A few days later Thad saw the Squire on the street and asked, "Why did you turn down that woman's offer for your land?"

"Why," answered the Squire, "*What would I do with a hundred thousand dollars!*"

You may demur and say, "That proves nothing. The saleswoman wasn't trying to *sell*, she was trying to *buy*."

Brother, know this: when you try to buy from somebody who does not want to sell, you have, not a buying problem, but a selling problem.

If the saleswoman had found out what the Squire's primary interest was, she might, for instance, have worked up a trade to take the Squire's land in return for a vastly larger tract of less valuable land—and thus have gained her objective.

What she should have learned before she tackled the Squire was that the oldtimers up in the Great Smoky Mountains of Tennessee don't measure their wealth in money. They don't need much cash for their simple living. They measure their wealth in land.

The moral: always make it part of your pre-approach to learn the prospect's primary interest.

CHAPTER 79

"Dominant buying motives" and "primary interests" are worthy of much attention

Two favorite subjects for argument among salesmen are these:

1. What is "high pressure," and when does legitimate sales effort go over the line?

Let's not try to define "high pressure." Better lexicographers than you and I have run head-on into this problem, and bounced back. I merely mention it as I ramble along in the hope that, if you discover an adequate definition, you will send it to me. My address is simply: Montrose, Alabama.

The other question is intensely practical:

2. What is the difference between a "primary interest" and a "dominant buying motive," and how do you use them?

Let's decide first just exactly how you define those two phrases.

The generally accepted definitions are: The "primary interest" is *what the prospect wants;* the "dominant buying motive" is *why he wants it."*

I suspect that "why he wants it" hardly covers the "dominant buying motive." "The motive that makes him want it," or "that which motivates him to want it," comes nearer, I think.

We all understand, I'm sure, what the phrase "primary interest" means. "Primary" means "first in importance."

As to the word "interest" the definition is not so simple. Probably the phrase would be clearer if we added the word "self" and made the phrase "primary self-interest."

The prospect's primary self-interest is not always easy to learn. When I managed a force of men who sold investment securities, they often found it impossible to learn a prospect's chief interest.

How do you locate this "interest?" Ask questions. That is half the answer. The other half—and the one that salesmen neglect so often—is *listen!*

Incidentally, if somebody asked me for a list of salesmen's worst failings, I would place near the top "Salesmen don't ask enough questions, and when they ask questions, they don't really *listen* to the answers."

Too often a salesman, after he asks his prospect a question, is so busy formulating his next remark that he forgets to listen. So here is the rule again: *Ask lots of questions—then listen for the answers.*

Sometimes it pays to ask your prospect straight-out what his primary self-interest is in connection with your proposition. Sometimes he will tell you, which saves time and eliminates guessing.

Now comes the question, "What will motivate this man to buy?"

To find out what moves a man to buy, you ask questions, of course.

Before you do, be sure you understand what a motive is. For our purposes, a motive is "something within a person . . . that moves (or drives or incites) him to do anything." (I made up that definition. I had to combine definitions from two dictionaries to arrive at it, but I think it meets our needs.)

I never knew any two authorities who agreed on a list of buying motives. For your purposes, all you need to know is that the common motives are self-preservation, fear, greed, anger, love of family, and pride. You want to find out which of these buying motives will have the most influence in determining the prospect's attitude toward your product. So, in most cases you ask him point blank what his motive is.

For example, if you ask a very rich man why he always buys tax exempt bonds and no other kind, presumably he will tell you. His answer might be either "to gain income," or it might be "to hold down income tax payments."

If you sold insurance, you might not find it so easy to guess a prospect's buying motives. However, by asking some questions—and listening to the answers—you would ordinarily be able to tell.

Once you get this information, use it!

You are just not ready to start a serious sales talk until you know both the prospect's objective and his motive.

For example, if you offered a piece of property to a prospect who was interested only in "gain," your sales talk would be quite different from the one you would give to a man whose primary interest was to own a suitable home for the family he loved.

The above facts ought to be enough to convince you that you should never get into your sales talk until you have these two vital pieces of information about your prospect: (1) his main interest, and (2) his main buying motive. You need this information for at least four of the steps of the selling process —sometimes for all five.

Admittedly, interests and motives are not important to all salesmen. Door-to-door salesmen would be one exception; those who sell to jobbers are another.

Often, retailers have different objectives. One might buy your line to gain prestige, another to meet the competition of a neighboring store which offers something similar, another to bring a higher class of prospects to his store. So, if you sell retailers anything, except a routine item, you should know what their main purpose in business is—so ask them.

To sum up: If you are a professional salesman—or aspire to be one—be sure (when it is practical) to ask your prospect enough questions, and to listen hard enough to the answers, so that, before you start your sales talk, you will know his primary interest and the motive that makes him want it.

And once again, listen, listen!

When I used to go out with salesmen to try to help them learn how to sell, I would ask, before we left the office, "Do you always listen to your prospects when they talk?"

Always, with great positiveness, the salesman would answer, "Yes, I always listen when the prospect talks."

After I had listened all day to salesmen as they made sales talks, I came to this conclusion: *Salesmen never listen!*

Of course that conclusion is not too exact, but it is near enough, I hope, to make you ask yourself, "Am I one of those salesmen who thinks he always listens, but rarely does?"

If you are honest—and observing—you will probably admit that you are just that kind of salesman.

If you seriously intend to reform, you must consider that you deal with an established bad habit. So observe this rule: *Remind yourself constantly.*

If you carry a portfolio or a briefcase, tape the word "Listen" in very small type, on the front of the case. Then prop the case up where you can see the warning. Or tape it on your pack of cigarettes. Or use the old device: tie a string around your finger.

Then, as you go from prospect to prospect, tell yourself over and over, "I will listen, I will listen."

Stay with it until you have cured yourself of the "non-listening" fault. Then watch sales successes multiply.

Is there a "magic formula" for sales success?
Some writers think so.

CHAPTER 80

You can get some real sales help from these magic formulas for sales success by best American writers on salesmanship

If two heads are better than one, think how good eighteen heads must be!

Since the beginning of sales history, when enterprising aboriginal salesmen peddled war clubs and stone hatchets from cave to cave, each salesman has been looking for the "magic formula of selling."

He didn't know that there was any magic about it. He was merely looking for the one best way to sell—the way that would bring him the best results for the least effort.

Whether he called it a "magic formula," or "the one best way to sell," he was talking about a subject that is of interest to every salesman. Give any salesman the "invincible recipe for successful selling"—and time—and he will be a rich man.

Let's stop talking foolishness and get down to something practical. We know that no magic sales formula exists now, or ever will. But is there anything close to it? Can the vital rules of selling be boiled down into a sentence, or, at most, a few brief sentences?

Every enterprising salesman—and that's the kind who will read this book—would like to see, in summary form, the recipes for sales success that have been worked out by the best writers on the subject of salesmanship. So, to find them, I dug through the 158 books on salesmanship in my library.

I am giving you on this and the following pages a summary of what I found; some of the "magic formulas" for sales success by some of the best writers on the subject of salesmanship.

Read them carefully. They represent the distilled brains and experience of some of the world's best salesmen—all directed toward telling you, in a few words, what you have to do to sell successfully.

Here are the "magic formulas":

The most important secret of salesmanship is to find out what people want and help them get it.
—FRANK BETTGER, *How I Raised Myself from Failure to Success in Selling*

*   *   *

Present the advantages of an offer in a way which makes a direct appeal.
—JOHN ALFORD STEVENSON, *Constructive Salesmanship*

*   *   *

"Tell a story you really believe to enough people day in and out."
—QUOTED BY W. L. HALBERSTADT

*   *   *

In this business of selling, the thing of least importance is the sales talk. The thing of real importance is the personality, character and inner life of the man who presents that sales talk.
—W. L. HALBERSTADT, *Successful Selling in Two Steps*

*   *   *

You must have the interest of your customer at heart, know everything possible about the prospect, have faith in what you are selling, believe in your ability to sell, know the right method of presenting your product.
—ARTHUR DUNN (SLIGHTLY ABBREVIATED),
Successful Selling and Advertising

*   *   *

Get the customer to sell himself.
Make it a friendly situation. Help the customer feel

*important. Inspire trust. Make it easy for the customer
to decide.*

—DONALD & ELEANOR C. LAIRD,
Practical Sales Psychology

*   *   *

*Get your company's ideas of its goods and service
into the mind of the prospect by means of vivid images
so that his desire to buy will impel him to favorable
action.*

—NELG RIVOLO, The Art of Selling

*   *   *

*Stand in the customer's shoes. Sell others the way you
like others to sell you.*

—W. E. SAWYER AND A. C. BUSSE,
Sell As Customers Like It

*   *   *

*Attract favorable prospect attention, rouse a felt need,
and establish a solution for it, which the prospect will
feel is of more value to her than the money she has to
pay for it.*

—GERALD E. STEDHAM, For Salesmen Only

*   *   *

*The salesman must find a need for his product, and
then convince the prospect that it will pay him or his
company to own the new product.*

—L. R. ADDINGTON, VICE PRESIDENT, ART METAL
CONSTRUCTION COMPANY

*   *   *

*If a man believes in his product and loves it, so will
all the world.*

—ART LEWYT

*   *   *

*To sell either a product or a political idea success-
fully, a man must be able to continue fighting enthusi-
astically and honestly in the face of any defeat.*

—JIM FARLEY

*   *   *

Wear out the soles of your shoes instead of the seat of your trousers. Hard work alone will accomplish remarkable results. But hard work with method and system will perform seeming miracles.

—W. C. HOLMAN

*   *   *

Be eager to learn more about salesmanship. Never stop trying. Never become disheartened. Always ask for the order. Work hard. Be determined in spite of rebuffs. Be absolutely and sincerely friendly. Think straight. Keep fit. Cover more ground and see more prospects. Stick close to your fundamentals. Show what you are selling (demonstrate). Have confidence in yourself and your ability to sell. Believe in yourself and the power of good salesmanship.

—CHARLES B. ROTH,
My Lifetime Treasury of Selling Secrets

The following preachment on the secret of selling success was taken from the writings of my friend George Mather:

For Rule 1, "Go to work," there is no short cut and no substitute. Rule 1 stops most men flat, but it is still Rule 1.

This business of selling leaves time for practically nothing but work. "When do you play and have fun?" You don't.

You will, of course, catch hell from your wife. Remember her? She is the woman who wants this and that, and both of them cost money! She is the woman who wants you to take her there and here when you should be following Rule 1. Your very first, and one of your very biggest selling jobs is to sell *her* on helping *you* to be a better salesman—fail on that one and you can throw the book into the ash can.

Rule 1 is mighty hard to follow, but the next one is harder . . . it gets most of those that Rule 1 missed so there are very few really good salesmen.

Rule 2. "You will just have to *think*."

To avoid this punishing labor of thinking, a man will go hungry and shabby, and sleep on a hard bed under a leaky roof.

Nobody can ever guess how many millions of useless miles are covered each year by salesmen willing to drive, but who absolutely refuse to think.

Rule 3. "You'll have to quit saying, 'It won't work.'"

Rule 4. "Know your products."

Rule 5. "You must know your words."

Words are the things that make sales.

The words you say and the way you say those words determines your earnings as a salesman.

Don't be afraid to use a canned sales talk. You can't possibly think up a new story for every prospect, and ninety per cent of the stuff you use is canned. Anybody who wants one can have a *good* canned talk on any product, but few there be who want a good talk badly enough to get one. Feeble and ineffectual words hold most men in the low priced group.

There they are . . . just five simple rules that you can read in a minute or two.

Possibly the smartest thing you can do is to say, "They won't work," and toss this book in the fire. After all, plenty of salesmen do seem to wander through life getting nowhere and to be very happy and contented as they drift.

These rules are not offered as a guide to happiness, but as an unfailing guide to success in selling. They may never make you great, but they can't fail to make you better than you are.

> *Prove to your prospect that he needs something and that you've got the best thing that he can use to fill his need. Then make him want it enough so that he decides to go ahead with it right now.*
> —JACK LACY, IN A TALK BEFORE
> THE NEW YORK SALES EXECUTIVES CLUB

The Magic Formula for Sales Success is:

1. *Know that the prospect needs your product and can profit greatly by owning it.*
2. *Be certain that your product is the best one to satisfy the prospect's wants and needs.*
3. *Love your work.*
4. *Expect to sell successfully.*
5. *Appeal to the prospect's self-interest.*

6. *Forget yourself and think only of the prospect and his needs and wants.*
> —SUMMARIZED FROM THE BOOKLET,
> "THE MAGIC FORMULA OF SALES SUCCESS,"
> BY W. L. BARNHART (*Printers' Ink,*
> MAY 2, 1952).

All the thinking and all the talking of all the salesmen and all the sales managers of all time have enabled them to come up with only four basic rules to increase sales. Here they are:

1. Make more calls.
2. Make better calls (a better sales talk).
3. Make your calls on better prospects.
4. Get in a better state of mind (positive attitudes, not negative).

The first of these rules, "Make more calls," is largely in your hands (and feet). Up to your limits in time and endurance, you can "make more calls."

As to the third of these rules, "Call on better prospects," sometimes the salesman has something to say about it, sometimes he doesn't.

Now to go back to Rule 2, "Make better calls," which means "better sales talks." That is largely in the hands of the salesman himself. Any normal salesman can make "better calls" if he is willing to work at it. His sales manager will tell him how, his sales trainer will show him how, sales courses will instruct him how. So will this book.

As to your mental attitude, the fourth rule, that also is largely within your power to control. Use affirmation—and keep on using it.

This, in four brief rules—nineteen words—is my own "secret of selling success."

... *And Now to Say Good-bye*

So this is the end of my book.

I hope that you and a lot of other salesmen will buy it—not

only because I get a royalty, but also because I know that the rules presented here work and will help you to solve your sales problems and to sell more.

Most of the rules I have given you here are rules that salesmen under my direction have used successfully for more than four decades. I know from actual experience that they work. They will produce more sales for your company and more income for you.

Please remember this: Don't try to make a perfect salesman of yourself all at once. You can't do it ker-splash! As I have told you before, you have to start on one rule. It should be the one that will solve your greatest selling problem. Learn to observe that one rule. Make it part of your sales life. Then tackle your next worst problem.

Stick to this policy: Whip your enemies one at a time.

As you solve your sales problems, watch your sales methods improve and your sales increase. This improvement may be slow, but it is inevitable.

And now reluctantly I bid good-bye to you.

May God be with you till we meet again.

With good wishes to you and to all salesmen,
your sincere friend and well-wisher,

Percy H. Whiting

Index

Affirmation, 70–72, 192, 246–250, 270–273
Ambition, 7
Animation, 98–100, 180
Appearance and clothing, 4, 193, 196
Automation, effect on selling, 260–261

Brainstorming, 44–48
Buying committees, 262–270

Calls, 19–24, 27, 73, 238–240, 288
Carnegie, Dale, 54, 74, 88–89, 143, 180, 204, 210
 course in public speaking, 15, 54, 57, 90, 203, 232
Chain stores, buying committees, 262–270
Closing the sale, 98, 124–131
Communications, 77–104
Courage, developing, 75, 230–254
Creative selling, 31–49

Demonstrations, 139–140

Education of salesmen, 220–221
English, using correct, 80–82, 103–104
Enthusiasm, 7, 180
Examples, used in answering objections, 60–61

Faith talks, 72, 246–250, 270, 274–277
Fears, 83–84, 224–254
Financial difficulties, handling, 211–219
Franklin, Benjamin, 43, 71, 189

Goals, 15–17, 73
Group sales talks, 82–104

Habits, 17, 67–68
Hard work, to overcome slumps, 164–165, 204–205
High pressure selling, 279
Humor in selling, 48–49, 215–217

Ideas that sell, 36–39, 41–48
Imagination, 32–34, 41, 68–69, 96

Inferiority complex, 201–205, 220
Inspirational speakers and books, 75–76, 200, 218–219

Letters that sell, 78–79

Magic formula for sales success, 282–288
"Marketing" concept, 259–261
Mistakes, avoiding, 221
 learning from, 248–250
Morale, regaining lost, 71
Motivation, 15–17, 66–76
Motives, buying, 21, 279–282

New York Sales Executives Club survey, 5–7

Objections, 21, 50–65, 183
Organization in selling, 6–30

Pep talks, 4, 271–277
Perseverance, 43, 66
Persistence, 274
Positive thinking, 270, 274–276
Presentations (see Sales talks)
Problem solving, assembling facts, 37–41, 46–47
Product knowledge, 91–94, 115–120, 231–233
Products, belief in, 122–123
Prospects, 50–65, 84–85, 114–115, 120–131, 231–233
 convincing, 122–123
Public speaking, 80–94, 99–104

Record-keeping, 14–15, 24–26
Relaxation, need for, 23–24

Sales bulletins, 219–220
Sales talks, 288
 asking questions, 162–164
 "canned," 137–140, 146–147
 committing to memory, 143–144, 157–159
 delivering, 151–152
 developing, 132–134
 group (see Group sales talks)
 improving, 174–177, 194–200

290

Sales talks, openers, 138–140
    preparation, 143–145, 147–150
    rules for, 95–100
    standardized, 132–134, 141–147
    testing, 158–159, 208–210
Sales training, 181
Salesmen, belief in product, 182, 186–190
    motivation, 66–76
    qualifications, 178–179
    quitting too soon, 124–131
    self-confidence, 4, 272–274
Self-confidence, developing, 4, 272–274
Self-motivation, 66–76, 276–277
Self-organization, 6–30
Selling, magic formula, 282–288
    magic rules, 190–221
    organizing, 6–30

Slumps, selling, 165–190
    anti-slump rules, 190–222
    cures, 179–183, 190–222

Testimonials, 153–154
"Tickler" or follow-up file, 25–26
Time, selling, 7, 9–10
    scheduling, 13, 15–17, 19–24
    spent with prospects, 12–14, 27–29
    suggestions for saving, 27–28
    wasting, 11, 27–29

Will power, 69–70
Work, habits, 7, 9
    organizing, 17–18
    to overcome selling slumps, 204–205

About the Author

Percy H. Whiting has been a newspaper reporter, sports editor, advertising writer, sales manager, and head of his own investment securities firm. In 1935 he took the Dale Carnegie Course in Effective Speaking. The next year he was made director of a Dale Carnegie speech class. Shortly thereafter he joined the Dale Carnegie organization full time—and remained with it for 25 years. Mr. Whiting was managing director of the organization and, later, Vice President in charge of the Dale Carnegie Sales Course, which he wrote.

The Five Great Problems of Salesmen and How to Solve Them was written to complement Mr. Whiting's *The Five Great Rules of Selling,* one of the most popular books on salesmanship ever written.